D1565695

THE FIAT STANDARD

THE FIAT STANDARD

*The Debt Slavery Alternative
to Human Civilization*

Saifedean Ammous

THE FIAT STANDARD
The Debt Slavery Alternative to Human Civilization

ISBN   978-1-5445-2647-8   *Hardocver*

         978-1-5445-2645-4   *Paperback*

         978-1-5445-2646-1   *Ebook*

To my mother, sister, brother, and grandparents

Contents

PART II: FIAT LIFE

About the Author

Saifedean Ammous is a world-renowned economist and author of *The Bitcoin Standard: The Decentralized Alternative to Central Banking*, the definitive and best-selling book on bitcoin, translated to 25 languages. He is also the author of the forthcoming textbook *Principles of Economics*. Saifedean teaches courses on the economics of bitcoin, and economics in the Austrian school tradition, on his online learning platform *Saifedean.com*, and also hosts *The Bitcoin Standard Podcast*.

Supporters

The author dedicates this book to the following readers who supported the self-publication of this book by preordering signed copies. Your support and interest are the reason that I write!

60e75d5207d67cef0b16cea187be29f3c97b80cec30420427187892f-4f004a4c, A. Milenkovic, A.W. Steinly, Aaron Dewey Olsen, Abdullah Moai, AceRich2020, Adam Miller, @Adelgary, Afsheen Bigdeli, Ágúst Ragnar Pétursson, Akihiko Murai, Alberto Toussaint, Alex Bowe, Alex Chizhik, Alex Gladstein, Alex Toussaint, Alexander Tarnok, Ali Meer, Alistair Milne, Amber D. Scott, Amelia Alvarez, Amine Rahmouni, Andrés M. Tomás, Andrew K Sloan, Andrew Masters, Andrew P Hickman, Andrew W. Cleveland III, M.D., Andrewstotle, Andy Goldstein, Andy Holmes, Angelina Franklin, Anonymous, Antoni Taczanowski, Antonio Caccese, Armand Tuzel, Arvin Sahakian, Arxnovum Investments, Askar Kazhygul, Avtarkaur Sachamahithinant, Chaivit Sachamahithinant, Sujitra Sachamahithinant, AZHODL.com, Baron Bloe, Bartosz Granowski, Basem Jassin, Ben Davenport, Benoit Fontaine, Bert de Groot, Bill Daniels, Bill Sousa, @BitcoinIsThePin, bitcoin-schweiz.ch GmbH, bitcoinsverige.org, BklynFrank, Braiins & Slush Pool, Brandon Nabors, Bret Leon Lusskin Jr., Brett Bondi, Brian Lockhart,

Brian Bilnoski, Brian Fisher, Brian L. McMichael, Britt Kelly, Browning Hi-Power 9mm, Bryan Boot, Bryan Hennecken, Bryan S. Wilson D.O., C&H, C4R3Bear, Carlos Octavio Chida Suárez, Cedric Youngelman, Chad Welch, Chafic Chahine, Charles Ruizhongtai Qi, Chiefmonkey, Chris Rye, Chris Vallé, Christian Cora, Christof Mathys, Christophe Masiero, Christopher Chang, Christopher S. Widger, CJ Wilson, Central Valley Bitcoiners, Clancy and Joe Rodgers, Clayton Maguire, Colin Heyes, Conscious Money Creators, Craig McGarrah III, Craig S Smith, D. Akira Ulmer, Dan Carman, Dan J, Dan Skeen, Daniel Carson, Daniel G. Ostermayer, Daniel Marulanda, Daniel Oon, Darin Feinstein, Darin Wilmert, Dave Burns, David Adriani, David B. Heller, David Barry, David Bryson, David Carre, David and Shauna Jeffries, David Love, David McFadzean, David Strimaitis, Decrypted LLC, Dennis Eibel, Dennis Kohler, Derek Sheeler, Derek Waltchack, Dick Trickle, Dicka, Dmitriy Molla, Doug Devine, Doug Hemingway, Michael Milmeister & the Stormrake team @stormrake.com, Dr. And Mrs. Douglas M. Moeckel, Dr. Paul Essey, Dustin Dettmer, Dylan Hedges, Dylan Wettasinghe, Ed Becker, Edgar R Tapia Gonzalez, ElCapitan, Eliah van Dijk and Anaïs van Dijk, Elias Andalaft—co-founder Webempresario.com, Elio S. Fattorini, Emmanuel Azih Jr., Eric Dosal, Érick Zazueta Ávila, Eugen Zimbelmann, Evangeline and Jacob, Fabian, Fabian Bürger, Fadi Mantash, Felix L., Filip Karađorđević and Danica Karađorđević, Filipe Neves, Frank Acklin, Frank T. Young, Frederick D'Mello, G Charles Harrison, Gabe C., Gabriele "gurgamezcla" Gussoni, Gaël Giusti, Gareth Hayes, Gary Lau, @gauchoeddy, Gerard N, Gerd Lüdtke, Gert Kleemann, Gina Jaramillo, Giuseppe Bueti, Glenn T., Gordon S Greer, Greg and Joy Morin, Gregory Zajaczkowski, Hadi, Harvinder Singh Sawhney, Hashim Elmegreisi, Hendel Bouchelaghem, Henry Gonzalez, Herman Vissia, Housam Majid Jarrar, Hugh Fowler, Hunter Hastings, Imre Michalsky, Isabella V. Fernando, Isaias De Leon, Isandi, J Dixon, J Flow, J. Kevin Coffin, J. Woods, J.M.B., Jack Heitger, Jacob Boyer, Jacob Cherian, Jakob Kucharczyk, James DelGuercio, James Harris, James Ian Thompson, James Machado, James McCoy, James Sutherland, James Swinhoe, James Viggiano, Jan W.F. van Dort—Master in digital currencies, Janajri Family, Coinbits Team, Jarod M. Bona, Jasper de Trafford, Javier Gil, Jay Chin, Jeff and Beth

Ross, Jeff Aurand, Jeff Bennett, Jeff Packard, Jeff Smith, Jeffrey S. Van Harte, Jeffrey Poppenhagen, Jeffrey Williams of ILA Local 1654., Jeremiah Albright, Jeremiah James, Jeremy Cooper and #TeamCooperOhana, Jeremy Showalter, Jerrold Randall, Jerry Aguirre, Jez San, Jimmy Weaver, @JMFM_89, Joachim B., Joe Rubio, Johan M. Bergman, John Brier, John Brown, John Connor, John Dixon, John Jolly, John Mcmillan, John Silvestro, Johnathan Ly, MD, Johnny, Johnny Walsh, Jon Tan Ling Peng, Jonas Konstandin, Jordan Friedman, Joris Kemperman, Joseph Anthony Debono, Joshua D A Vincent, Justin Won-Jun Kim, @k9ert, Kami Niles, Kapitein Geweldig, Kenny G, Kenny Mayerhofer, Kenton Ralph Toews, Kevin McKernan, Kevin Sang, Kevin Wesley Avent, Kim van Nie, Kota Kojima, Kristian Kolding, Kristian Wiborg, Kyle and Rachel Ford, Lapo Pietro, Roberto Masiero, Laura Ann Feathers, Leeron Galimidi, Lennart Zahn, Leon Lawrence Stubbs, Les DeFelice, Lexbury, Liam Birch, Lincoln Liu, Lisa Cheng, Lloyedkoh, Loay Malahmeh, Locky McWilliam, Louferlou, Louis B, Lowina Blackman, Luis C. Alonso, Luis Rivera, Lynley Pillay, Maciej Kazimieruk, Manu Beuselinck, Marco Bühler, Marco Giangiulio, Marius Reeder, Mark Ioli, Mark Moss, Mark Mulvey, Mark Rodney Gardner, Mark Simonson, Mark W Roen, Markus Lindgren, Marquie Mosley, Marquita Robinson-Garcia and DVINITI Skin Care, Marshall Long, Martin Brochhaus, Martin Roberto Richmond CFA, Mathew O'Keefe, Matija Grlj, Matt "yabapmatt" Rosen, Matt Maiuri, Matt Moran, Matt Sellitto, Maurice and Jeanne Schutte, Max, Max Guimarães, Maxon LaForge, Mazhar Memon, Michael Atwood, Michael Baker, Michael Byrne, Michael Fink, Michael Goldstein, Michael Harris, Michael Jonsson, Michal Duska and Roman Filipoiu, Milan Radojicic, Mina Eklad, Mischa Zed, Mitchel Edwards, Mitchell Kennedy, Mohammad Nauman, Money Phlow pty ltd, Mr. W. B., Nader S Dahdaleh, Nadir Seha Islam, Sibel Karakurum, Nazir Cihangir Islam, Nathan Mahaffey, Nathan Olmstead, Neal Nagely, Nicholas Sheahan and Martina Marcinska, Nick Karadza, Nick Ligerakis, Nicolás Ahumada, Nicolas Cage, Noor Elhuda El Bawab, Olly Stedall @saltedlolly, Omar Ruiz Geronimo, Omar Sabek, Omran Kaskar, Paige Webley, Pan Dermatis, panaccoman, @panicbuyingbtc, Panties for Bitcoin, Pantiesforbitcoin.com, Paolo Illing, Pattaravut Maleehuan, Paul I.

Sung, Paul John Gaston, Paul Rylands, Paul Trentham, Pedro Brannum, Pei-Hsun Kao, Per Treborg, Perry Hester, Pete Cochran, Peter & Carren Egyed, Peter Francis Fenwick, Petr Žalud, Philip Guncill, Phillip Byrne, Pierre Alessandro Gmeiner, Pieter N., Pieter Voogt, PtAd, pij, pijankengur, Piotr Krzak, Piriya Sambandaraksa, Raj Shreyas Padliya, Rajan Sohal, Rauderce O., Rami Korhonen, Raven de la Cruz, Ravi Sohal, Red Pill Songs, Reina Bitcoin, Richard and Gigi, Richard Wiig, Richard Yu, Rick Pauw, Rickie Chang, Rijk Plasman, Rits Plasman, Rob (SATJ) Clark, Robert Alan Koonce, Robert B. Ferraro, Robert Del Riego, Robert Mearns, Robert Schulman, Roberto Costa Ramalhete, Roberto De Leon, Robin Thirtle, Rodolfo Novak (NVK), Rodrigo Gualberto, Roman Engelbrecht, Roman Filipoiu, Rory Orr, Rosa Jara, Rosie Featherby, Ruben Waterman, Ruslan Kuvaev, Russ, Rustin Watt, Ryan Anthony Williams, Ryan Blair, Ryan C Wilhoit, Ryan Cole, Ryan Jordan, Ryan Niles, Ryan Rinaldo, Ryan W. Slot, Sachin & Manavi Sharma, Samuel Claussen, Samuel Rufinatscha, San Family, Sanjay Srivatsa, Satoshi's Domains, Scott C. Morgan @BtcVires, Scott S. Manhart, DDS, MS, Scott Schneider, Seb Walker, Sebastian Liu, SensibleYapper, Sergio Ruocco, Shakti Chauhan, Shao-Hsuan Kao, Shaun Thomson, Sheldon Friesen, Shire HODL, Shone Anstey at LQwD Fintech, Shone Sadler, Siim Männart, Simon Ree, Simona Macellari, Stacy, Stefano D'Amiano, Stephan Livera, Stephen Cole, Stephen Saunders, Steve and Paige Crozier, Subhan Tariq Esq., Tammy Fuller, Tarek, Tariq Al Muhtassib, Tarun K Chattoraj, The Goodspeed Family, The Stormrake team @stormrake.com, The Yingling Family, Thomas Hartland Mackie, Thomas Jaeger, Thomas Jenichen, Thomas Shelton, Tim Y., Tinoosh Zand, M.D., Tipton Cole, Tom G., Tom Karadza, Torstein Habbestad, Tyler W. Thornton, U.C.J., Esq., Mrs. Vicky Essey, Victor Goico, Vijay Boyapati, Vince Oscar Benitez, Vincent en Daan, Vinicius Kenji Hashimoto, Wallet of Satoshi, Wayne Keith (@SatoshiPrime_io), Wesley Brockman, William J. Blehm, William Johnston, wiz, Yorba, Zac Woods, Zach Herbert, Zachary Hollinshead, Zafer Özkavlak, Zane Pocock, Zsurka Zoltán András

Foreword

by Ross Stevens

Founder and Executive Chairman, NYDIG

Immediately upon its publication, Saifedean Ammous's *The Bitcoin Standard* became an instant classic—required reading for anyone seriously interested in understanding the importance and power of bitcoin. First taking the reader on a captivating journey through the history of money, *The Bitcoin Standard* then proceeds to comprehensively lay out the first principles of bitcoin's comparative appeal. Indeed, amidst a selection of outstanding bitcoin literature, *The Bitcoin Standard* sits atop the "if you only read one book about bitcoin, read this book" mantle from the bitcoin community.

Almost four years later, *The Bitcoin Standard* has aged well. Bitcoin is relevant to the lives of over one hundred million people worldwide today, strongly confirming the validity of Saifedean's central insights. Given that bitcoin, unlike fiat, is voluntarily adopted by its users in every instance, it's appropriate to be astonished that, despite bitcoin's short life, it has become a significant global monetary institution, providing a nonstate and non-bank means of wealth storage, as well as an apolitical and neutral transactional medium.

Overall bitcoin adoption figures are compelling, but per capita penetration rates tell an even more interesting story. Bitcoin's greatest per capita penetration is in sub-Saharan Africa, Latin America, Eastern Europe, and Southeast Asia. That citizens of these neighborhoods are among the most fervent early adopters makes sense. Whether the symptoms are advanced inflationary episodes or suffocating capital controls, citizens in the highest per capita adoption countries are attracted to bitcoin due to the failure of their local institutions, spanning weaknesses in government integrity, property rights, and monetary freedom.

Perhaps as intuitively as explicitly, the attraction hinges on bitcoin's free-market, predetermined issuance model, which ensures that the privileged elite cannot emerge with sole access to the monetary spigot. Bitcoin's proof of work—whereby bitcoin miners surrender electricity and computational resources to acquire new tokens—establishes a real-world cost for the resource, requiring miners to "buy in" should they want to occupy the position of the mint.

This is where Saifedean brilliantly turns things upside down in The Fiat Standard. His penetrating insight is to explain the operation of fiat by analogy to the operation of bitcoin. In this context, we can think of fiat as a digital currency, like an altcoin, defining its qualities and characteristics and its strengths and weaknesses. Saifedean analogizes fiat mining as credit creation and fiat miners as any institutions with fractional reserve requirements. Like bitcoin miners, fiat miners are incentivized to maximize token issuance for themselves. However, unlike bitcoin miners, fiat miners are not constrained by the difficulty adjustment. Thus, fiat mining has no mechanism for controlling issuance, which powerfully explains the accelerating explosion in fiat tokens, country after country, decade after decade. Saifedean's framework further demonstrates that observed fiat collapses, like poorly designed bridges, represent nothing more than the inevitable, and inexorable, result of poor engineering.

Far from a one-sided attack on fiat, The Fiat Standard clearly illustrates and explains the advantages that made fiat's global adoption possible. Whereas The Bitcoin Standard's analytical framework centered around assessing salability across time, and how it explains the monetary rise of gold and bitcoin, in *The Fiat Standard*, Saifedean uses the framework of salability across space to explain the rise of fiat and how it replaced gold. This framework further forms the basis for assessing bitcoin's rise in a fiat world, its security model, and chances of continued success.

Leveraging Saifedean's language of "fiat tokens," we also gain clarity on why modern central and commercial banking—combined—cause, not cure, severe economic downdrafts. By giving in to the populist clamor for ever more abundant, freely issued fiat tokens, fiat mining cripples the role of the wisest regulator, the market, by removing the most important mechanism for efficient, economy-wide allocation of capital: relative prices of sound (i.e., strictly limited) monetary tokens. Lacking restraint in fiat token issuance, sovereign defaults in 2020 were the highest they've been in more than twenty years, and the ratio of sovereign credit downgrades to upgrades was at an all-time high of ten to one.

With the flaws in fiat's engineering infrastructure firmly established, Saifedean then takes us on a wide and unexpected journey, a tour de force that demonstrates the implications of these flaws in various areas of our day-to-day life, spanning architecture, family, food, science, and energy, among others. This controversial section will leave certain readers angry, strongly disagreeing, or worse. However, many open-minded readers will emerge with a cannot-unsee collection of thought-provoking questions and insights regarding fiat's perniciousness. Saifedean's framing of fiat as a fundamental explanation represents an important and original contribution to the discussion of why a monetary system governed by rulers leads to vast inequities, imbalances, and unintended consequences.

I will spoil no surprises here. However, as a preview of what's to come, recall that while bitcoin requires its appropriately expensive proof-of-work process to create new tokens, fiat mining's process obliterates the concept of opportunity cost in creating its tokens. This contrast explains the mad dashes for, and desperate clinging to, power among fiat token creators—and therefore the utter lack of surprise that this crowd feels most threatened by bitcoin. Seeing no opportunity cost to minting fiat tokens with abandon, many fiat miners act like they are getting something for nothing. Consider the wide-ranging societal implications of that perceived, of course not actual, reality.

Saifedean ends on a note of optimism mixed with practicality, exploring how fiat and bitcoin can coexist, including bitcoin potentially driving a gradual reduction in fiat debt via voluntary fiat liquidation. Accelerating bitcoin adoption, coupled with fiat's continued decline in real terms, can generate a glide path for humanity's step-by-step, voluntary transformation to sound money. Thus, the rise of bitcoin need not cause a catastrophic collapse of fiat, and a strong case can be made for bitcoin as a form of fiat-denominated wealth insurance, strengthening the case for a corresponding nonzero bitcoin allocation for everyone.

However, bitcoin is also a form of life insurance, though not in the traditional sense of a big payout if you die. Rather, bitcoin provides a big payout while you live, in the form—pricelessly—of personal sovereignty, freedom, and dignity. In a world replete with monetary unfairness, injustice, the institutionalization of moral hazard, and the State's increasing domestication of our individuality, bitcoin's incorruptible fairness, justice, truth, and beauty represent a beacon for all optimists who seek personal improvement and peace.

Perhaps just in time, each global citizen now has a choice. You can stay on the fiat standard, in which some people get to produce unlimited new units of money for free, most likely not you. Or opt in to the bitcoin standard, in which no one gets to do that, including you. With the option, now, of a monetary system governed by rules, not rulers, we can each be grateful for the opportunity, and personal responsibility, of making that choice.

PART I

Fiat Money

Chapter 1

Introduction

This year marks the fiftieth anniversary of the U.S. government closing the gold-exchange window and putting the world on a fiat monetary system. The vast majority of people alive today have never used anything but fiat money. This cannot be written off as an unexplained fluke, and economists should be able to explain how this system functions and survives, despite its many obvious flaws. Fiat's longevity makes it unreasonable to keep dismissing it as an irredeemable fraud on the brink of collapse, as many of its detractors have done for decades. There are, after all, plenty of markets around the world that are massively distorted by government interventions, but they nonetheless continue to survive. It is no endorsement of these interventions to attempt to explain how they persist.

In his 1929 book *The Thing*, G. K. Chesterton tells the story of a man who finds a fence that appears to serve no purpose and decides to remove it. Another man counters, "If you don't see the use of it, I certainly won't let you

3

clear it away. Go away and think. Then, when you can come back and tell me that you do see the use of it, I may allow you to destroy it."[1] Fifty years after taking its final form, and more than a century after its genesis, with a new competitor threatening to potentially remove it, an assessment of the uses of the fiat system is now both possible and necessary.

While fiat has not won acceptance on the free market, and though its failings and limitations are many, there is no denying that many fiat systems have worked for large parts of the last century and facilitated an unfathomably large number of trades all around the world. Its continued operation makes understanding it useful, particularly as we still live in a world that runs on fiat. Just because you may be done with fiat does not mean that fiat is done with you! Understanding how the fiat standard works, and how it frequently fails, is essential knowledge for being able to navigate it.

It is also not appropriate to judge fiat systems based on the marketing material of their promoters and beneficiaries in government-financed academia and the popular press. While the global fiat system has so far avoided the complete collapse its detractors predicted, that cannot vindicate its promoters' advertising of it as a free-lunch-maker with no opportunity cost or consequence. More than sixty episodes of hyperinflation have taken place in countries using fiat monetary systems in the past century.[2] Moreover, avoiding regular catastrophic collapse is hardly enough to make a case for it as a positive technological, economic, and social development.

Beyond the relentless propaganda of its enthusiasts and the rabid venom of its detractors, this book attempts to offer something new: an exploration of the fiat monetary system as a technology, from an engineering and functional perspective, outlining its purposes and common failure modes, and deriving the wider economic, political, and social implications of its use. Adopting this approach to writing *The Bitcoin Standard* contributed to making it the bestselling book on bitcoin to date, helping hundreds of thousands

---

1   Chesterton, G.K. *The Thing: Why I Am a Catholic.* New York: Dodd, Mead, & Co., 1929. Print.
2   Hanke, Steve. "Lebanon Hyperinflates." Cato Institute. 23 Jul. 2020. Web.

of readers across more than twenty-five languages understand the significance and implications of bitcoin.

Perhaps counterintuitively, I believe that by first understanding the operation of bitcoin, you can then better understand the equivalent operations in fiat. It is easier to explain an abacus to a computer user than it is to explain a computer to an abacus user. A more advanced technology performs its functions more productively and efficiently, allowing a clear exposition of the mechanisms of the simpler technology and exposing its weaknesses. My aim is to explain the operation and engineering structure of the fiat monetary system and how it operates in reality, away from the romanticism of governments and banks that have benefited from this system for a century.

The first seven chapters of *The Bitcoin Standard* explained the history and function of money and its importance to the economic order. With that foundation laid, the final three chapters introduced bitcoin, explained its operation, and elaborated on how its operation relates to the economic questions discussed in the earlier chapters. My motivation as an author was to allow readers to understand how bitcoin operates and its monetary significance without requiring them to have a previous background in economics or digital currencies. Had bitcoin not been invented, the first seven chapters of *The Bitcoin Standard* could have served as an introduction to explaining the operation of the fiat monetary system. This book picks up where chapter 7 of *The Bitcoin Standard* left off. The first six chapters of this book are modeled on the last three chapters of *The Bitcoin Standard*, except applied to fiat money.

How does the fiat system actually function, in an operational sense? The success of bitcoin in operating as a bare-bones and standalone free-market monetary system helps elucidate the properties and functions necessary to make a monetary system work. Bitcoin was designed by a software engineer who boiled a monetary system down to its essentials. These choices were then validated by a free market of millions of people around the world who continue to use this system and currently entrust it to hold around $800 billion of their wealth. The fiat monetary system, by contrast, has never been put on a free market for its users to pass the only judgment that matters.

The all-too-frequent systemic collapses of the fiat monetary system are arguably the true market judgment emerging after suppression by governments. With bitcoin showing us how an advanced monetary system can function entirely independently of government control, we can see clearly the properties required for a monetary system to operate on the free market, and in the process, we can better understand fiat's modes of operation and all-too-frequent modes of failure.

To begin, it is important to understand that the fiat system was not a carefully, consciously, or deliberately designed financial operating system like bitcoin; rather, it evolved through a complex process of compromise between political constraints and expedience in managing government default. The next chapter illustrates this by examining newly released historical documents on just how the fiat standard was born and how it replaced the gold standard, beginning in England in the early twentieth century and completing the transition in 1971 across the Atlantic. This is not a history book, however, and it will not attempt a full historical account of the development of the fiat standard over the past century, in the same way *The Bitcoin Standard* did not delve too deeply into the study of the historical development of the bitcoin software. The focus of the first part of the book will be on the operation and function of the fiat monetary system, by making an analogy to the operation of the bitcoin network, in what might be called a comparative study of the economics of different monetary engineering systems.

Chapter 3 examines the network topography and underlying technology behind the fiat standard. Contrary to what the name suggests, modern fiat money is not conjured out of thin air through government fiat. Government does not just print currency and hand it out to a society that accepts it as money. Modern fiat money is far more sophisticated and convoluted in its operation. The fundamental engineering feature of the fiat system is that it treats future promises of money as if they were as good as present money because the government guarantees these promises. Government coercion can maintain such a system for a very long time, even if it would not survive free-market competition.

Chapter 4 examines how the fiat network's native tokens come into existence. As fiat money is credit, credit creation in a fiat currency results in the creation of new money, which means that lending is fiat's antiquated and haphazard version of mining. Fiat miners are the financial institutions capable of generating fiat-based debt with guarantees from the government and/or central banks. Unlike with bitcoin's difficulty adjustment, fiat has no precise or engineered mechanisms for controlling issuance. Credit money, instead, causes constant cycles of expansion and contraction in the money supply, with devastating consequences.

Chapter 5 then analyzes balances on the fiat network, exploring how many, if not most, users have negative account balances—a unique feature of the fiat network. The ability to mine fiat by issuing debt means individuals, corporations, and governments all face a strong incentive to get into debt. The monetization and universalization of debt is also a war on savings, and one which governments have persecuted stealthily and quite successfully against their citizens over the last century.

Based on this analysis, Chapter 6 concludes the first section of the book by discussing the uses of fiat and the problems it solves. The two obvious uses of fiat are that it allows for government to easily finance itself, and it allows banks to engage in maturity-mismatching and fractional reserve banking while largely protecting themselves from the inevitable downside. But the third use of fiat is the one that has been the most important to its survival: salability across space.

I must confess, attempting to think of the fiat monetary system in engineering terms and trying to understand the problem it solves has given me an appreciation of its usefulness and a gentler assessment of the motives and circumstances that led to its emergence. Understanding the problem this fiat system solves makes a move from the gold standard to the fiat standard appear less outlandish and insane than it had appeared to me while writing *The Bitcoin Standard*, as a hard money believer who could see nothing good or reasonable about the move to an easier money.

Seeing that the analytical framework of *The Bitcoin Standard* was built around the concept of salability across time, and the ability of money to hold its value into the future, and the implications of that to society, the fiat standard initially appears as a deliberate, nefarious conspiracy to destroy human civilization. But writing this book and thinking very hard about the operational reality of fiat has brought into sharper focus the property of salability across space, and, in the process, has made the rationale for the emergence of the fiat standard clearer and more comprehensible. For all its many failings, there is no escaping the conclusion that the fiat standard was indeed a solution to a real and debilitating problem with the gold standard, namely its low spatial salability.

Fiat's low temporal salability remained a problem, but a tolerable one, because of its advantages in transferring value across space. More importantly, fiat allowed governments worldwide tremendous leeway to bribe their current citizens at the expense of their future citizens by creating the easy fiat tokens that operate their payment networks. Fiat was convenient for users, but it was more convenient for the government officials who controlled the only full nodes. As we take stock of a whole century of operation for this monetary system, a sober and nuanced assessment can appreciate the significance of this solution for facilitating global trade, while also understanding how it has allowed the inflation that has benefited governments at the expense of their citizens, present and future. Fiat may have been a huge step backward in terms of its salability across time, but it was a substantial leap forward in terms of salability across space.

Having laid out the mechanics for the operation of fiat in the first section, the book's second section, Fiat Life, examines the economic, societal, and political implications of a society utilizing such a form of money with uncertain and usually poor intertemporal salability. Fiat increasingly divorces economic reward from economic productivity, and instead bases it on political allegiance. This attempted suspension of the concept of opportunity cost makes fiat a revolt against the natural order of the world, in which humans, and all other animals, have to struggle against scarcity every day of their lives. Nature provides humans with rewards only when their toil is successful, and similarly, markets only reward humans when they can produce something that others subjectively value. After a century of economic value being assigned at gunpoint, these indisputable realities of life are unknown to, or denied by, huge swaths of the world's population who look to their governments for their salvation and sustenance.

The suspension of the normal workings of scarcity through government dictate has enormous implications on individual time preference and decision-making, with important consequences to many facets of life. In the second section of the book, we explore the impacts of fiat on family, food, education, science, health, fuels, and international governance and geopolitics. This section focuses on analyzing the implications of two causal economic mechanisms of fiat money: the utilization of debt as money and the ability of government to grant this debt at no cost. Part 2 concludes with a cost-benefit analysis of the fiat monetary system.

While the title of the book refers to fiat, this is still a book about bitcoin, and the first two sections build up the analytical foundation for the third part of the book, which examines the all-too-important question with which *The Bitcoin Standard* leaves the reader: what will the relationship between fiat and bitcoin be in the coming years? Chapter 13 examines the specific properties of bitcoin that make it a potential solution to the problems of fiat.

While *The Bitcoin Standard* focused on bitcoin's intertemporal salability, *The Fiat Standard* examines how bitcoin's salability across space is the mechanism that makes it a more serious threat to fiat than gold and other physical monies with low spatial salability. Bitcoin's high salability across space allows us to monetize this hard asset itself, and not credit claims on it, as was the case with the gold standard. At its most basic, bitcoin increases humanity's capacity for long-distance international settlement by around 500,000 transactions a day and completes that settlement in a few hours. This is an enormous upgrade over gold's capacity, making international settlement a far more open market and much harder to monopolize. This also helps us understand bitcoin's value proposition as not just harder money than gold, but also money that is far easier to transport. Bitcoin effectively combines gold's salability across time with fiat's salability across space in one apolitical, immutable, open-source package.

By being a hard asset, bitcoin is also debt free, and its creation does not incentivize debt issuance. By offering finality of settlement every ten minutes, bitcoin also makes the use of credit money very difficult. At each block interval, the ownership of all bitcoins is confirmed by tens of thousands of nodes all over the world. There can be no authority whose fiat can make good a broken promise to deliver a bitcoin by a certain block time. Financial institutions that engage in fractional reserve banking in a bitcoin economy will always be under the threat of a bank run as long as no institution exists that can conjure present bitcoin at significantly lower than the market rate, as governments can do with their fiat.

Chapter 14 discusses bitcoin scaling in detail and argues that it will likely happen through second-layer solutions, which will be optimized for speed, high volume, and low cost, and involve trade-offs in security and liquidity. Chapter 15 builds on this analysis to discuss what banking would look like under a bitcoin standard, while Chapter 16 studies bitcoin's consumption of electric power, how it is related to bitcoin's security, and how it can impact the market for energy worldwide. Chapter 17 then performs a cost-benefit analysis to upgrading from fiat to bitcoin.

The final chapter tackles the questions: How can bitcoin rise in the world of fiat, and what are the implications for these two monetary standards coexisting? Various threats to bitcoin are assessed from the economic perspective, and the economic incentive for bitcoin's continued survival is presented. Will bitcoin's rise necessitate a hyperinflationary collapse of fiat? Or will it be more like an orderly software upgrade? How will credit market dynamics and the rise of central bank digital currencies affect this relationship?

Chapter 2

The Never-Ending Bank Holiday

On August 6, 1915, His Majesty's Government issued this appeal:

> In view of the importance of strengthening the gold reserves of the country for exchange purposes, the Treasury have instructed the Post Office and all public departments charged with the duty of making cash payments to use notes instead of gold coins whenever possible. The public generally are earnestly requested, in the national interest, to co-operate with the Treasury in this policy by (1) paying in gold to the Post Office and to the Banks; (2) asking for payment of cheques in notes rather than in gold; (3) using notes rather than gold for payment of wages and cash disbursements generally.[3]

---

3   Osborne, John. "Gold and Silver." *The Bank of England 1914–21 (Unpublished War History)*. Vol. 2. Bank of England Archive, 1926, p.148. Web. https://www.bankofengland.co.uk/-/media/boe/files/archive/ww/boe-1914-1921-vol2-chapter5a.pdf.

With this obscure and largely forgotten announcement, the Bank of England effectively began the global monetary system's move away from a gold standard, in which all government and bank obligations were redeemable in physical gold. At the time, gold coins and bars were still widely used worldwide, but they were of limited use for international trade, which necessitated resorting to the clearance mechanisms of international banks. Chief among all banks at the time, the Bank of England's network spanned the globe, and its pound sterling had, for centuries, acquired the reputation of being as good as gold.

Instead of the predictable and reliable stability naturally provided by gold, the new global monetary standard was built around government rules, hence its name. The Latin word *fiat* means "let it be done," and in English, the term has been adopted to mean a formal decree, authorization, or rule. It is an apt term for the current monetary standard, as what distinguishes it most is that it substitutes government dictates for the judgment of the market. Value on fiat's base layer is not based on a freely traded physical commodity but is instead dictated by authority, which can control its issuance, supply, clearance, and settlement, and even confiscate it at any time it sees fit.

With the move to fiat, peaceful exchange on the market no longer determined the value and choice of money. Instead, it was the victors of world wars and the gyrations of international geopolitics that would dictate the choice and value of the medium that constitutes one half of every market transaction. While the 1915 Bank of England announcement, and others like it at the time, were assumed to be temporary emergency measures necessary to fight the Great War, today, more than a century later, the Bank of England is yet to resume the promised redemption of its notes in gold. Temporary arrangements restricting note convertibility into gold turned into the permanent financial infrastructure of the fiat system that took off over the next century. Never again would the world's predominant monetary systems be based on currencies fully redeemable in gold.

The above decree might be considered the equivalent of Satoshi Nakamoto's email to the cryptography mailing list announcing bitcoin.[4] However,

---

4   Nakamoto, Satoshi. "Bitcoin P2P E-Cash Paper." *The Cryptography Mailing List*....

unlike Nakamoto, His Majesty's Government provided no software, white paper, nor any kind of technical specification as to how such a monetary system could be made practical and workable. Unlike the cold precision of Satoshi's impersonal and dispassionate tone, His Majesty's Government relied on an appeal to authority and the emotional manipulation of its subjects' sense of patriotism. Whereas Satoshi was able to launch the bitcoin network in operational form a few months after its initial announcement, it took two world wars, dozens of monetary conferences, multiple financial crises, and three generations of governments, bankers, and economists to ultimately bring about a fully operable implementation of the fiat standard in 1971.

The Bank of England's troubles started at the dawn of the Great War. On July 31, 1914, large crowds stood outside the doors of its Threadneedle Street headquarters looking to convert their bank balances and banknotes into gold coins before the August bank holiday. The Austro-Hungarian Empire had just declared war against Serbia following the assassination of Archduke Franz Ferdinand and a month of escalating tensions across Europe. All over the continent, investors rushed to convert financial instruments into gold, as they worried governments would devalue currencies to finance war. That fateful July, English newspapers referred to the coming war as the August bank holiday war, expecting it to be a swift victory for the British military. Yet the lines of depositors outside the world's most important financial institution foretold a different story: the bank holiday that would never end.

Had the Bank of England maintained full cover for its notes and bank accounts in gold, as they would have had to under a strict gold standard, war would not have posed a liquidity problem. All depositors could have had their banknotes and bank accounts redeemed in full in physical gold, and there would have been no need to queue outside the bank. However, the Bank of England had become accustomed to not backing all its notes with gold. Depositors had good reason to hold money in the form of

---

...31 Oct. 2008. Web. https://archive.is/20121228025845/http://article.gmane.org/gmane.comp.encryption.general/12588.

banknotes and bank accounts rather than in physical gold. Compared to gold, banknotes were easier to carry and convert into either smaller or larger denominations, and an account at an English bank allowed the depositor to make payments by checkbook anywhere in the world far faster than sending physical gold. Global capital sought the bank's superior safety and clearance mechanisms, which provided the bank a solid cushion to diverge from a strict 100% gold standard.

At the time, the Bank of England was the center of the financial universe, and its pound sterling was recognized worldwide for being as good as gold. The creditworthiness of the British government, its powerful military, and its unrivaled global payments settlement network had given it the supreme position in the global financial order, with around half of global foreign exchange reserves held in sterling.

In the prewar period, the bank had also offered its own currency as a reserve for the central banks of its colonies, under what was known as the gold-exchange standard. Since the colonies used the bank to settle their international payments, they were expected to hold on to significant amounts of these reserves and not seek redemption in gold. This allowed the bank a certain inflationary margin, to the point that by 1913, the ratio of official reserves to liabilities to foreign monetary authorities was only 31%.[5] The bank had exported its inflation to the colonies, financing its operations but placing itself in a precarious liquidity position. So long as most colonies, depositors, and paper holders did not ask to convert their bank accounts and notes to gold, liquidity would not be a problem.

For a generation of bankers reared on the peace and prosperity of the Victorian Era and the gold standard, there was little reason to worry about a liquidity crisis. There was also very little reason to worry about a world war, but both the war and the liquidity crisis materialized in the summer of 1914. While the Great War triggered the bank's liquidity troubles, the deeper causes were self-inflicted, and typical of the fiat century, government monopoly over the payments network encouraged abuse of the currency.

---

5   Officer, Lawrence. "Gold Standard." *EH.Net Encyclopedia.* 26 Mar. 2008, Web.

As trouble brewed on the continent, many foreign depositors sought to withdraw their assets from Britain, and many Englishmen preferred to hold gold over the bank's paper. In the last six working days of July, the bank paid out £12.3 million in gold coins from its £26.5 million total reserves.[6] The previously unthinkable prospect of the bank of England defaulting on its promise to redeem its notes and accounts in gold suddenly appeared plausible. A devaluation of the pound at that stage would have allowed the bank sufficient reserves to back the currency but would have been unspeakably unpopular with the British public, permanently undermining their faith in the bank.

In November 1914, the British government issued the first war bond, aiming to raise £350 million from private investors at an interest rate of 4.1% and a maturity of ten years. Surprisingly, the bond issue was undersubscribed, and the British public purchased less than a third of the targeted sum. To avoid publicizing this failure, the Bank of England granted funds to its chief cashier and his deputy to purchase the bonds under their own names. The *Financial Times*, ever the bank's faithful mouthpiece, published an article proclaiming the loan was oversubscribed. John Maynard Keynes worked at the Treasury at the time, and in a secret memo to the bank, he praised them for what he called their "masterly manipulation." Keynes's fondness for surreptitious monetary arrangements would go on to inspire thousands of economic textbooks published worldwide. The Bank of England had set the tone for a century of central bank and government collusion behind the public's back. The Financial Times would only issue a correction 103 years later,[7] when this matter was finally uncovered after some sleuthing in the bank's archives by some enterprising staff members and published on the bank's blog.[8]

---

6   "Gold, Banknotes and Money Supply in the First World War." *NatWest Group Remembers*. Web. 3 Oct. 2021.

7   McClean, Paul. "A Correction 103 Years Late: How the BoE Covered Up Failed War Bond Sale." *Financial Times*. 8 Aug. 2017. Web.

8   Anson, Michael, et al. "Your Country Needs Funds: The Extraordinary Story of Britain's Early Efforts to Finance the First World War." *Bank Underground*. 8 Aug. 2017. Web.

The Bank of England decided to continue on the gold standard; however, its dwindling stockpiles meant it had to figure out some way to stem the tide of redemptions. Its solution was to declare an unofficial war on gold. The fascinating details of this war can be found in *The Bank of England 1914–21 (Unpublished War History)*, an obscure but highly detailed study commissioned by Bank Governor Montagu Norman, authored by his personal secretary John Osborne, and completed in 1926. This study remained unpublished until the bank uploaded it to its website in September 2019.[9]

With the public not keen on lending for war, and the bank holding large amounts of government debt instead, the bank needed to shore up its liquidity with more gold. The Treasury issued the appeal quoted at the beginning of this chapter, asking the public to pay the post office and banks in gold, take payment in notes rather than in gold, and use notes for paying wages and cash disbursements. After this appeal, the Bank of England and the Treasury instructed banks to collect coins and hold them in reserve to be at the disposal of the Treasury throughout the war.

"In 1915, the sum of £20,823,000 was collected from the Bankers of the United Kingdom and, in order to furnish the Treasury with further credit, was exported to United States," Osborne wrote. He added in a footnote, "The Bank kept £2,423,000 sovereigns because their stock was seriously depleted." He continued, "In November 1915 it became necessary for the Government to appoint a Committee—London Exchange Committee—to advise on the subject of the Foreign Exchanges. In order to assist the Committee in their operations it was arranged that Bankers should cease to issue gold to their customers, whose requirements could of course be satisfied by Currency Notes." The custom of committees determining monetary arrangements would become very common in the fiat century.

Osborne continues:

---

9   Osborne, John. "Gold and Silver." *The Bank of England 1914–21 (Unpublished War History)*. Vol. 2. Bank of England Archive, 1926. Web. https://www.bankofengland.co.uk/-/media/boe/files/archive/ww/boe-1914-1921-vol2-chapter5a.pdf.

During the following year it became evident that as a result of the appeal referred to and the action of the Bankers the public were becoming more accustomed to the use of paper money and more reconciled to the absence of gold.

In order to meet an obligation of the London Exchange Committee in connection with the loan of $50,000,000 made to them by a group of United States Bankers in November 1915, the Clearing Bankers in June 1917 paid to the account of the Treasury the sum of £10,000,000 in gold coin, which was "set aside" on behalf of the Federal Reserve Bank of New York.

A further appeal to the Banks was made in a letter dated the 25th July 1917 from the Chancellor of the Exchequer. Bankers were asked to hold their stocks of gold coin at the disposal of the Government, in view of the existing state or the American exchange. The Chancellor urged the Banks, in the interests of general credit, to hand over their gold by private arrangement and so obviate the necessity for a compulsory order which could be issued under the Defence of the Realm Regulations. As a result of this appeal Bankers throughout the country agreed to hold 90% of their gold at the disposal of the Treasury.

On the 1st April 1919 the export of gold coin was prohibited by Order in Council end on the same date, at a meeting of Bankers, it was agreed that all gold coin and bullion then held and thereafter acquired by them (excepting only such gold as might be imported by the Banks themselves) should be held at the absolute disposal of the Treasury, and that delivery of it should be made to the Bank of England and when required. Furthermore, they agreed that all gold already earmarked for foreign account should, if released, be paid in to the Bank of England at once. Details of all holdings of gold were to be furnished to the Bank once a month and the Bankers agreed to discourage by every means in their power withdrawals of gold from the Bank of England.

It was realised that it was absolutely essential both to Bankers generally and to the whole country that the available supplies of gold should be ready at hand, if necessary, for use centrally to meet any threatening developments in foreign exchanges, and particularly in the American exchange. At the end of the year the Treasury requested the Bank to collect the entire stocks of gold coin held by Bankers throughout the Kingdom.[10]

The bank would periodically purchase gold coins from banks using banknotes. In December 1919, the Treasury requested the bank collect all the gold coins held by bankers in the United Kingdom. Private bankers surrendered £41,793,000 of gold coins by June of 1920, practically all of their gold holdings, in exchange for paper notes. The entire operation cost £5,516, at a rate of a little over £1 per £10,000 collected. The discipline of proof-of-work mining was conspicuously absent at fiat's genesis and throughout its century. Most of the gold was shipped to the United States in exchange for credit to fight the war.

From the beginning of August 1914 to the end of August 1921, the bank's net gain totaled £62,411,000 of gold. The British government confiscated 14,684,941 ounces of gold, or around 455.2 metric tons. Today, that gold would be worth around £20 billion, roughly 300 times what it was worth in 1914. At the time of writing in 2021, the Bank of England's gold reserves stand at only 310.3 metric tons of gold.

The war, which caused this demand for gold, necessitated suspending most aviation, relieving the bank from shipping gold to its foreign depositors. In April 1919, as the war ended and aviation resumed, the export of gold coins was prohibited. Economic historian Lawrence Officer summarized this period:

> With the outbreak of war, a run on sterling led Britain to impose extreme exchange control—a postponement of both domestic and international payments—that made the international gold standard non-operational. Convertibility was not legally suspended; but moral suasion, legalistic

---

10 Osborne, John. "Gold and Silver." *The Bank of England 1914–21 (Unpublished War History)*. Vol. 2. Bank of England Archive, 1926, p.149–51. Web. https://www.bankofengland.co.uk/-/media/boe/files/archive/ww/boe-1914-1921-vol2-chapter5a.pdf.

action, and regulation had the same effect. Gold exports were restricted by extralegal means (and by Trading with the Enemy legislation), with the Bank of England commandeering all gold imports and applying moral suasion to bankers and bullion brokers.[11]

With less gold in the hands of the people and more notes, the bank had succeeded in protecting the official gold-to-sterling exchange rate of £4.25 per troy ounce of gold, the same price set in 1717 by Master of the Royal Mint, Sir Isaac Newton. The Bank of England's reliable record in redeeming its notes at this rate for two centuries, interrupted only by the Napoleonic Wars, was a matter of national pride and global renown. It not only gave sterling its legendary reputation of being as good as gold, but also turned the phrase "gold standard" into the proverbial benchmark and paradigm for excellence, predictability, and reliability—a phrase that was never threatened with replacement by a century of the fiat standard.

By using the war to suspend redeemability abroad and discourage it at home, the bank had successfully used its fiat, regulations, and monopoly control over the most important financial infrastructure in the world to finance the war effort without officially coming off the gold standard, announcing a suspension of gold redemption, or devaluing the pound. Thus was born a new science of government-sponsored financial alchemy. By controlling banks and confiscating gold, central banks could create money by fiat. By making the pound as good as gold, the new paper alchemists succeeded where Newton and the old alchemists failed. Gold could be produced at will after all. The printing press and the checking account were the alchemists' long-sought philosopher's stone.

In the immediate aftermath of the war, there seemed to be no downside to the world's central bank and its currency diverging from the sound gold anchor. Over time, the costs of these monetary shenanigans became apparent, as governments would increasingly abuse these schemes, ultimately making them a permanent feature of the fiat century—surreptitiously

---

11 Officer, Lawrence. "Gold Standard." *EH.Net Encyclopedia.* 26 Mar. 2008, Web.

trading long-term prosperity for the illusion of short-term stability. The economic consequences of the inflation would weigh on the British economy for decades.

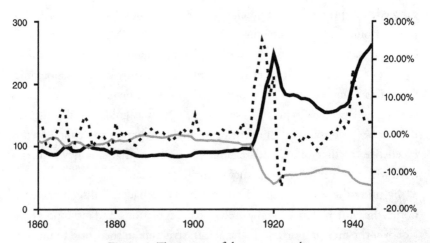

■■ Price index (1974=1000), left axis   ━━ Value of pound (1974=10), left axis
■ ■ ■ Change in price on year before, right axis

Figure 1. The impact of the war on sterling.

Source: Twigger, Robert. "Inflation: The Value of the Pound 1750–1998." *House of Commons Library Research Paper 99/20.* U.K. Parliament (23 Feb. 1999), pp. 9–22. Web.

By maintaining the pound sterling at the prewar gold rate, the Bank of England sowed the seeds of several problems that became common in later implementations of the fiat standard. The bank maintained the nominal exchange rate between notes and gold, but in reality, the prices of normal goods and services increased sharply. According to recent research by the Economic Policy and Statistics Section of the House of Commons Library, the annual change in prices from 1915–1920 were 12.5%, 18.1%, 25.2%, 22%, and 10.1%, a cumulative five-year rise of 124%. Price increases made life difficult for the average Englishman, spurring the rise of organized labor and popular demands for price and wage controls. Inevitably, rationing and shortages followed, as well as mass unemployment. The war's end brought millions of military servicemen home, but the price and wage controls made it very difficult for the British economy to accommodate their return to the workforce. Revaluing the pound to accommodate the inflation would have meant devaluing the population's savings; however, prices of goods and labor would have readjusted on the market. By foregoing this revaluation, maintaining an overvalued exchange rate, and discouraging the redemption of paper into gold, the bank delayed the necessary economic adjustment and prolonged the dislocations brought about by inflation and price and wage controls. Pressure grew on the government to spend to support the unemployed and the poor. However, further spending and expansionary monetary policy caused even more price increases and put greater pressure on sterling in international markets. A populist clamor grew for the bank to bring gold coins back into circulation and return to the prewar gold standard.

Britain's problems were not just domestic. While all European countries effectively went off the gold standard in 1914, the U.S. had only done so in 1917, attracting large quantities of gold fleeing Europe. With the credit it provided to the Bank of England, the U.S. Federal Reserve also secured a large part of the British supply of gold. As goes gold, so goes power. The Bank of England was learning to readjust to a new global economic reality in which the United States and its Federal Reserve played a supremely important role. The alchemy of the U.K.'s fiat standard continued to become more expensive as the U.S. took on its global leadership role and sterling continued to face troubles throughout the coming century, losing three-quarters of its value against the U.S. dollar, and more than 90% of its value against gold.

All major European economies engaged in large-scale inflation to finance the war, after which their currencies were devalued against gold and were no longer redeemable at the prewar rate. At this point, the prudent step would have been to acknowledge that the fiat standard had served its purpose as a temporary war-financing measure and return to the gold standard. Governments had repeatedly promised this, and Europe's citizens had expected it. However, returning to the gold standard at the prewar parity would have meant an inevitable end to the inflationary boom started by the credit expansion that financed the war and, subsequently, a painful recession. The U.S. chose this path, resulting in a sharp but quick recession in 1920, after which the U.S. economy began one of its longest expansions in history. U.S. gold redemption resumed in 1922 after a five-year suspension. Britain, on the other hand, tried to square the impossible circle of maintaining the Treasury's high spending, the union's high wage requirements, the gold peg at its prewar rate, and sterling's role as a global reserve currency. Having experienced the sweet taste of paper alchemy, the Bank of England thought it could manage its way out of overt default on its gold redemption obligations through financial and political engineering.

Rather than formalize the reality of inflation and devalue the pound to get back on the gold standard, the Bank of England and the Treasury chose to kick the can down the road and across the pond, where it would continue to be kicked into the next century. So began the habit of obtaining short-term relief at the expense of long-term solvency and stability.

As economist Murray Rothbard described it:

In short, Britain insisted on returning to gold at a valuation that was 10–20 percent higher than the going exchange rate, which reflected the results of war and postwar inflation. This meant that British prices would have had to decline by about 10 to 20 percent in order to remain competitive with foreign countries, and to maintain her all-important export business. But no such decline occurred, primarily because unions did not permit wage rates to be lowered. Real-wage rates rose, and chronic large-scale unemployment struck Great Britain. Credit was not allowed to contract, as was needed to bring about deflation, as unemployment would have grown even more menacing—an unemployment caused partly by the postwar establishment of government unemployment insurance (which permitted trade unions to hold out against any wage cuts). As a result, Great Britain tended to lose gold. Instead of repealing unemployment insurance, contracting credit, and/or going back to gold at a more realistic parity, Great Britain inflated her money supply to offset the loss of gold and turned to the United States for help. For if the United States government were to inflate American money, Great Britain would no longer lose gold to the United States. In short, the American public was nominated to suffer the burdens of inflation and subsequent collapse in order to maintain the British government and the British trade union movement in the style to which they insisted on becoming accustomed.[12]

As Benjamin Strong, chairman of the New York Fed, writes in a letter quoted by Rothbard:

> The burden of this readjustment must fall more largely upon us than upon them [Great Britain]. It will be difficult politically and socially for the British Government and the Bank of England to face a price liquidation in England...in face of the fact that their trade is poor and they have over a million unemployed people receiving government aid.[13]

Britain sought to ease the pressure on its pound by convincing the U.S. to engage in expansionary monetary policy under the pretext of providing global liquidity. By devaluing the dollar next to gold, the U.S. stopped the drain of gold from Britain to the U.S. and thus reduced the pressure on the pound. To further protect the pound, the Bank of England dumped some of its pound reserves on other countries that needed to use its clearance and settlement mechanisms. Britain and the U.S. arranged the Genoa Conference in 1922 to try to reestablish a global monetary order around their currencies and gold. The conference recommendations included the line, "Gold is the only common standard which all European countries could at present agree to adopt."[14]

However, returning to the gold standard was very difficult when the Bank of England, still the center of the financial universe, had yet to resume the redemption of its notes into gold. Instead, the U.S. and the U.K. attempted to introduce a gold-exchange standard, modeled on the monetary

12   Rothbard, Murray. *America's Great Depression*. 5th ed. Auburn, AL: Ludwig von Mises Institute, 2000, p. 143.
13   Rothbard, Murray. *America's Great Depression*, p. 146.
14   Kemmerer, Edwin Walter. *Gold and the Gold Standard: The Story of Gold Money, Past, Present and Future*. New York: McGraw-Hill, 1944, pp. 163–64. Print.

arrangements that had prevailed in some Asian countries before the war, the abuse of which caused the Bank of England to have a gold shortage at the eve of the war. In essence, global central banks would deposit gold at the Bank of England and U.S. Federal Reserve and use their international settlement network to add salability across space to their gold. This gave the Bank of England and the Federal Reserve significant leeway to go off the gold standard, because other countries' reliance on these institutions' financial infrastructure for international trade settlement meant they would rarely attempt to take physical custody of the gold.

As American inflation devalued the U.S. dollar, the U.S. provided loans to Britain, and international central banks acquired large amounts of sterling reserves, it became feasible for the Bank of England to restore some form of gold redemption in 1925. It was not a return to the gold standard, but the introduction of a variation of it: the gold bullion standard. Under this standard, the Bank of England only offered redemption of standard 400-ounce "good delivery" gold bars. Banknotes were no longer redeemable in gold, and the Royal Mint denied the public the ability to purchase its gold. The bank had effectively gone off the gold standard for the majority of the population, and the value of the pound was less tethered to its supposed gold backing than before the war.

While people could no longer redeem their banknotes for gold, they could sell their gold abroad for more than they would have received from the Bank of England. Perversely, by devaluing gold, the bank had subsidized the precious metal's exit from British shores, as gold always goes where it is valued most. More inflation in the U.S. was needed to prevent more gold from leaving Britain, as detailed in Rothbard's *America's Great Depression*.

That inflation set in motion the familiar business cycle. As inflation subsided in late 1928, the stock market crashed in late 1929, and the boom of the 1920s gave way to the bust of the 1930s. This pattern of bubbles and collapses, the endless cycles of boom and bust, became a regular feature of the fiat standard worldwide, to the point that modern economic textbooks began to treat this phenomenon as if it is an inherent part of a normal market economy, something as normal and inevitable as the seasons.

The depression and the inflation to counter it made the pressure on the pound unbearable. The last pretense of maintaining the prewar gold parity was finally dropped in 1931 as the Bank of England devalued the pound by 25%. One wonders just how different history would have been had it performed this devaluation in 1920, allowing the return to solid gold footing and full gold redemption with stricter limits on inflation.

During the crisis of the 1930s, the U.S. government engaged in fiscal and monetary expansionism to ward off the collapse of its banking system and economy. These policies would not have been sustainable had the dollar continued to be redeemable for gold at $20.67 per troy ounce. In 1934, President Franklin D. Roosevelt ordered the confiscation of Americans' gold, buying it from the public at $35.00, effectively devaluing the dollar by 43%. Less than two decades after Britain had set the fiat standard by taking hard money from the hands of its citizens and giving them fiat tokens, the U.S. followed suit. Both events were sovereign defaults, though history books rarely call them that.

This was the fiat standard protocol installation, and the whole world copied it: run unsustainable deficits, default by confiscating and restricting the movement of gold, suspend redemption, increase the supply of paper notes, and if you can, try to get other countries to hold your currency as reserve. The U.S. did it best.

The suspension of gold redemption and endless amounts of government-held fiat combined to extend the Great Depression while also giving rise to a bureaucratic monster that lived endlessly off inflation. The flow of gold from Europe to the U.S. continued through the 1930s and 1940s. After the Second World War, the U.S. was in a monetary league of its own, with gold reserves that dwarfed other nations and the world's most important international payments network. The new monetary reality was enshrined into the architecture of the nascent global financial system in 1946 with the signing of the Bretton Woods Agreement. That agreement returned the world to a gold-exchange standard similar to the one Britain had deployed to its colonies; the same system Britain abused to leave itself in the precarious liquidity position that started this entire sordid history.

The new global monetary system was built around the U.S. dollar, which only other central banks could redeem for gold. The U.S. federal government still prohibited Americans from owning gold, and most other countries imposed restrictions on the metal's ownership and trade. With all its extra gold, and its ability to export dollars to the rest of the world, there was very little restraint on the capacity of the U.S. government to spend in the postwar years. The military-industrial complex President Dwight D. Eisenhower warned of in his farewell address secured itself a continuous trickle of global war with which to harvest profits from the fiat spigot. FDR's New Deal welfare programs grew in the 1950s and metastasized in the 1960s under Lyndon B. Johnson's so-called Great Society—a permanent welfare state that needed to be financed by fiat. The world still bought dollars because they needed them, and there was no reason for Americans to suspect a liquidity problem. But just like England in 1914, the late 1960s placed the U.S. in a gold crunch, as European central banks moved to redeem their increasingly devaluing hoard of U.S. dollars for hard gold.

On August 15, 1971, President Nixon delivered the 'Nixon shock,' a series of government edicts aimed at containing rising inflation and unemployment. Nixon said the following in a nationally televised broadcast:

> The third indispensable element in building the new prosperity is closely related to creating new jobs and halting inflation. We must protect the position of the American dollar as a pillar of monetary stability around the world.
>
> In the past seven years, there has been an average of one international monetary crisis every year. Now who gains from these crises? Not the workingman; not the investor; not the real producers of wealth. The gainers are the international money speculators. Because they thrive on crises, they help to create them.
>
> In recent weeks, the speculators have been waging an all-out war on the American dollar. The strength of a nation's currency is based on the strength of that nation's economy—and the American economy is by far the strongest in the world. Accordingly, I have directed the Secretary of

the Treasury to take the action necessary to defend the dollar against the speculators.

I have directed Secretary Connally to suspend temporarily the convertibility of the dollar into gold or other reserve assets, except in amounts and conditions determined to be in the interest of monetary stability and in the best interests of the United States.

Now, what is this action—which is very technical—what does it mean for you?

Let me lay to rest the bugaboo of what is called devaluation.

If you want to buy a foreign car or take a trip abroad, market conditions may cause your dollar to buy slightly less. But if you are among the overwhelming majority of Americans who buy American-made products in America, your dollar will be worth just as much tomorrow as it is today.

The effect of this action, in other words, will be to stabilize the dollar.

Now, this action will not win us any friends among the international money traders. But our primary concern is with the American workers, and with fair competition around the world.[15]

Nixon's prognostications and guarantees were off the mark; prices skyrocketed over the coming decades. Instead of stabilizing, the dollar collapsed in value, and the new system of international partial barter, unhinged from its golden anchor, would turn money trading into a lucrative career and a gigantic industry. Even though the U.S. Treasury suspended gold redemption, it committed to maintaining the dollar peg to gold at a certain level. But that sound money mirage only lasted until 1973. It was at that point that the cost of living began to climb, and fast.

In summation, the Bank of England effectively went off the gold standard in 1914 and only returned in 1925 on a gold bullion standard, which it abandoned in 1931. The U.S. abandoned the gold standard in 1917 but restored it in 1922 and abandoned it again in 1934. Britain and the U.S. adopted a

---

15   Nixon, Richard. "Address to the Nation Outlining a New Economic Policy: 'The Challenge of Peace.'" *The American Presidency Project*. 15 Aug. 1971. Web.

gold-exchange standard in 1922 and abandoned it in 1971 to go on a fiat dollar standard. Since 1914, both currencies have lost more than 95% of their value relative to gold. The fiat standard installation process has been a long one, but it has had these hallmarks: gold confiscation, price increases, price controls, central planning, inflationary credit expansion, booms and busts, and the aspiration to export inflation by trying to dump fractionally backed currency on foreign regimes.

The fiat standard was not the design of an engineer. It was instead the central banks' desperate solution to their looming insolvency, the inevitable geopolitical outcome of a sixty-year-long marriage of politics and money. The history of fiat is the history of government-run financial institutions managing defaults. It was not a technology consciously designed to provide sound money or payment transfers. Central banks the world over would closely follow the prototype set by Britain and the U.S., as they too would default on gold and force the use of their fiat.

The process of implementing this standard, which started in 1914, had been practically completed by 1971. A century after its genesis and a half century after it took on its final operational form, it is now possible to pass judgment on this monetary standard.

Chapter 3

Fiat Technology

etween 1914 and 1971, the global monetary system gradually and haphazardly moved from the gold standard to the fiat standard. Governments effectively took over the banking sector everywhere, or depending on who you ask, the banking sector took over governments. Details of who wore the pants in this relationship are of no concern to this book, which focuses on its bastard spawn. Like *The Bitcoin Standard*, this book is focused on exploring the characteristics of its subject monetary system as demonstrated in practice, eschewing a detailed historical account of its development.

Fiat can be defined as a compulsory implementation of debt-based, centralized ledger technology monopolizing financial and monetary services worldwide. The fiat standard was born out of the need for governments to manage their de facto default on their gold obligations. It was not designed to optimize the user experience of currency, transactions, and banking. With this in mind, this chapter takes a closer look under the hood of the monetary technology powering most of the world's trade today. Contrary to what the name suggests, modern fiat money is not conjured out of thin air through government fiat. Governments do not just print currencies and hand them out to societies that accept them as good money. Modern fiat money is far more sophisticated and convoluted in its operation. The fundamental engineering feature of the fiat system is that it treats future promises of payment of money as if they were as good as present money, so long as they are issued by the government, or an entity guaranteed a lending license by the government.

In the bitcoin network, only coins that have already been mined can settle transactions. In a gold-based economy, only existing gold coins or bars can be used to settle transactions and extinguish debt. In both cases it is possible for a seller or lender to hand over their present goods in exchange for a promise of future bitcoin or gold, but they take on risk personally, and if the buyer or lender fails to provide the coins on time, they are lost to the lender, who would learn a valuable lesson about being more careful with lending. With fiat, government credit allows nonexistent tokens from the future to be brought to life to settle transactions in the present when a loan is made, allowing the borrower and lender to have a larger amount of fiat tokens between them than when they started, thus devaluing the rest of the network's tokens. The fiat network creates more tokens every time a government-licensed entity makes a loan in the local fiat token.

Having been born out of government default, the essential characteristic of the fiat standard is that it uses government decree as the token of value on its monetary and payment network. Since the government can decree value on the network, it effectively makes its own credit money. As the government backs the entire banking system, this makes all credit issued by the banking system effectively the government's credit, and so part of the money supply. In other words, the U.S. Congress and Federal Reserve are not the only institutions capable of conjuring money from thin air; any lending organization also has the capacity to increase the money supply through lending.

Blurring the line between money and credit makes measuring the money supply practically impossible. In a payment system like gold or bitcoin, only mature money (or money of full maturity, meaning money that does not have a future period of maturity at which it acquires its full liquid value) can be used to settle payments and debts. Under a fiat system, money that has not matured, and will only do so in the future, can be accepted as payment, so long as it is guaranteed by a commercial entity with a lending license.

Unlike with a pure gold standard or with bitcoin, the supply is not a set objective number of units being traded between network members. The units are ephemeral, constantly being created and destroyed. Their quantity is dependent on a subjective choice of which imperfect definition of money one uses. This makes it virtually impossible to obtain an objective, agreed-upon measure of the supply of money, or to audit the supply, as is the case with bitcoin.

When a client takes out a $1 million loan to buy a house, the lending bank does not take a preexisting mature $1 million present in its cash reserves, or from a depositor's balance at the bank. It will simply issue the loan and create the dollars that are used to pay the seller of the house. These dollars did not exist before the loan was issued. Their existence is predicated on the borrower fulfilling their end of the bargain and making regular payments in the future.

No present goods are used in the home purchase; no saver had to set the tokens aside to give to the borrower to pay the house seller. The present good of the house is handed to the borrower without them having to offer a present good in exchange, and the house seller does not grant the credit to the borrower nor take on the risk of default. The bank grants the credit, and the credit risk is ultimately borne by the central bank guaranteeing the bank, the loan, and the currency. Had the house seller granted the credit, they would be taking on the risk of default and giving up their present good willingly, affecting no other parties. But by utilizing the fiat standard, the house seller receives their payment in full up front, and the buyer receives the house in full up front. Both parties walk away with present goods they can use in full, even though only one of these goods existed before the transaction took place. The new fiat tokens created to allow this transaction place the risk of the buyer defaulting on all holders of the currency.

All three parties involved in the house transaction are happy, but could such a system survive in a free market? It appears favorable to the buyer, who can buy a home without having to pay the full price up front. It appears favorable to the seller because it finances more potential buyers and bids up the price of their home. It also appears favorable to the bank, which can mine new fiat tokens at roughly zero marginal cost every time a new lender wants to buy a house. However, the transaction only works by externalizing the risk to society at large, protecting the buyer, seller, and bank from default by having the government's currency holders effectively absorb the risk premium through the inflation of the money supply. The sacrifice of the present good that allows both to spend can only come at the expense of the currency being devalued.

Should a fiat system coexist with a hard money system in a free market, one would expect the rational investor to prefer to hold their wealth in the harder money, which cannot be debased to finance credit. However, even without the rational self-interest of the investor, inflation causes a currency to lose value over time next to the harder currency. This means that it is inevitable, in the long term, that most economic value will accrue to the harder currency. But by monopolizing the payment networks necessary for the modern division of labor, governments can make currency holders take that risk for significant periods.

To create an analogy with bitcoin's operation, we could say that the fiat network creates or destroys a number of new tokens with each block, equal to the amount of lending that has taken place minus the amount of credit repaid and defaulted on. Rather than a set new number of coins to be added with each block, as with bitcoin's protocol, the number of fiat tokens added in each fiat time period is the net result of debt creation, which can vary widely and can be positive or negative.

Network Topography

The fiat network comprises around 190 central bank members of the International Monetary Fund (IMF), as well as tens of thousands of private banks, with many physical branches. At the time of writing, the fiat network has achieved almost universal adoption, and almost everyone on earth is either dealing with a fiat node or handling fiat paper notes issued by these nodes. Joining the fiat network is not voluntary; it can be best likened to mandatory malware. With the exception of a few primitive and isolated tribes yet to have fiat enforced upon them, every human on earth is assigned to a regional node where they must pay their taxes in their local "fiatcoin." Failure to pay with the local fiatcoin can result in physical arrest, imprisonment, and even murder. These are powerful incentives for adoption that both bitcoin and gold lack.

The fiat network is based on a layered settlement system for payment clearance. Individual banks handle transfers between their clients on their own balance sheets. National central banks oversee clearance and settlement between banks in their jurisdictions. Central banks, and a few hundred international correspondence banks, oversee clearance across international borders on the SWIFT payments network. The fiat network utilizes a highly efficient centralized ledger technology with only one full node required to validate and decide the full record of transactions and balances. That entity is the United States Federal Reserve, under the influence and supervision of the United States government. "The Fed," as it is known to fiat enthusiasts, is the focal and central point of the fiat network. It is the only entity that can invalidate any transaction and confiscate any balance from any other fiat node. The Fed rules unilaterally over the SWIFT payments network and can prevent entire nations from joining it and settling trades with other nations.

The fiat network's base layer operates using a native token of debt denominated in U.S. dollars. While fiat enthusiasts portray the network as having a variety of tokens, each belonging to a different country or region, the reality is that every currency but the U.S. dollar is merely a second-layer token, a derivative of the dollar. The value of non-U.S. fiat money depends on its backing in the U.S. dollar and can best be approximated as the value of the dollar with a discount equivalent to the country risk. For a variety of historical, monetary, fiscal, and geopolitical reasons, these tokens have not appreciated significantly against the U.S. dollar over the long term. For all practical intents and purposes, national central banks managing their currencies can either maintain their exchange rates with the dollar or devalue them faster than the dollar.

Financial institutions mine the network's native token—fiatcoin— through the arcane, centralized, manual, risky, and haphazard process of lending. A complex web of government rules and regulations determines how an institution can obtain the lending license that allows it to issue loans. These rules and regulations are typically promulgated by central governments, central banks, the Bank for International Settlements, or the IMF. Unlike with bitcoin, there is no easily verifiable proof-of-work protocol and no algorithmic adjustment to ensure the fiatcoin supply remains within known and clearly auditable parameters.

As a centrally planned system, the fiat standard does not allow for the emergence of a free market in capital and money where supply and demand determine the interest rate, i.e., the price of capital. Lending ultimately determines the money supply, and lending levels are in turn shaped by the interest rate and Federal Reserve policy. The Federal Reserve's full fiat node holds periodic meetings for its central planning committee to decide the optimal interest rate to charge other nodes. The rate these unelected bureaucrats set is known as the federal funds rate, and all other interest rates are derived from this and rise as they get further away from the central node. The closer the borrower is to the Federal Reserve System, the lower the interest rate they can secure and the more likely they are to benefit from inflation of the money supply.

While a small percentage of fiatcoin is printed into paper bearer instruments with local insignia, the vast majority is digital, stored on the central node's ledger or the ledgers of the peripheral nodes. The digital fiat network offers limited possibility for final settlement, as all balances are tentative at all times, and partial nodes, or the full node itself, can revoke or confiscate any balance on any ledger at any time. Withdrawing fiat in paper notes is one way to increase the finality of settlement. But that is not final either because the notes can always be revoked by the central bank and can easily be devalued by local fiat nodes, or the Fed's full node.

The Underlying Technology

The core functionality of the fiat standard lies in the functions of the network's nodes. Under the fiat protocol, each central bank has four important functions:

1. A monopoly on providing the domestic fiatcoin and determining its supply and price
2. A monopoly on clearing international payments
3. A monopoly authority over licensing and regulating domestic banks, holding their reserves, and clearing payments between them
4. Lending to its respective national government by buying its bonds

To perform these functions, each central bank has a cash balance, commonly referred to as the international cash reserve account. This is the base-layer fiat token and has the highest spatial salability, as it can perform international settlement between central banks. In what is arguably the most catastrophic monetary engineering decision in all human history, this cash balance is used to perform four simultaneous functions. And the intermingling of these functions is the root of all financial and monetary crises of the past century. They comprise:

1. Backing the local currency
2. Settling international trade
3. Backing all bank deposits
4. Buying government bonds to finance government spending

Each of these tasks is discussed in more detail in the following sections, before the implications of their comingling are examined.

1. Backing the Local Currency

No form of money has ever emerged purely through government fiat. Statist economists like to speak of the state's ability to decree what money is, but the existence of central bank reserves illustrates the limits of that view. No government can decree its own debt or its own paper as money without holding other assets it cannot print in reserve, using them to make a market in its paper and debt obligations. Even if a government were to force its people to accept its paper at an artificial value, it could not force foreigners to do so. If its citizens want to trade with the rest of the world, the government must create a market in its currency that is denominated in other currencies. Unless the government accepts foreign currencies in exchange for its own, its own currency would devalue very quickly, as happens to any fiat currency when its central bank stops offering dollars at the market price. Everyone will prepare to hold harder currencies with more salability across space.

Even through the century of fiat and supposed gold demonetization, central banks have massively increased their gold holdings, and they continue to add to them at an increasing pace. The fiat standard's main reserve currencies are used to settle trade between central banks. However, central banks evidently do not believe they have demonetized gold and do not trust their currencies' ability to hold value into the future, so they continue to include increasing quantities of gold in their reserves. All fiat currencies that exist today are issued by central banks that hold gold in reserve or by central banks that hold currencies in their reserves issued by central banks that hold gold. This not only illustrates the absurdity of the state theory of money, but it also illustrates the fundamentally unworkable nature of political money on an international level. If every government could issue its own money, how and at what value would they trade with one another?

All central banks back their currencies with international reserve currencies they cannot print. For most countries, this is the U.S. dollar, and for the U.S., it is gold. At the end of the third fiscal quarter of 2020, the dollar constituted around 51% of global reserves, the euro 18.3%, gold 13.7%, the Japanese yen 5.2%, the British pound 4.1%, and the Chinese yuan 1.9%. Other currencies had smaller shares. The dollar has the lion's share of the foreign exchange market, taking part in 88.3% of all the foreign exchange market's daily trades.[16]

The dollar is the base-layer token of the global fiat network, and national currencies are derivatives of it. There are 180 national currencies in the world today. Other than the dollar and euro, national currencies are mainly used domestically in the secondary national fiat banking layers.

---

16   "Triennial Central Bank Survey: Foreign Exchange Turnover in April 2019." *Bank for International Settlements*. 16 Sep. 2019, p. 10. Web.

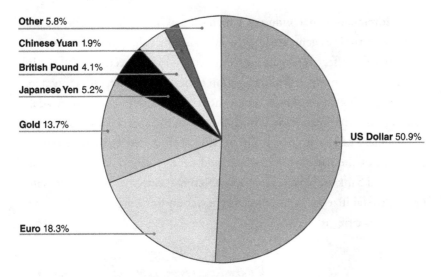

Figure 2. World Central Bank Reserves, 2020.
Source: "Currency Composition of Official Foreign Exchange Reserves
(COFER)." *International Monetary Fund.* 30 Sep. 2021. Web.

2. *The International Cash Account*

Central bank reserves also settle the central bank's international current
account (which includes international trade transactions) and its international capital account (which settles international movements of capital).
All international payments to and from a country have to go through its
central bank, allowing it a strong degree of control over all of its international trade and investment activities. Central bank reserves increase when
foreign investment inflows or exports increase, but they fall when foreign
investment outflows or imports increase. As individuals seek to transact with
one another internationally, they must resort to a system of partial barter, as
Hans-Hermann Hoppe termed it,[17] wherein they need to buy a foreign currency before buying the foreign good. This has led to the enormous growth

---

17   Hoppe, Hans-Hermann. *Democracy: The God That Failed.* Rutgers, NJ: Transaction
      Publishers, 2001, pp. 16. Print.

of the foreign exchange industry, which only exists to profit from the arbitrage opportunities generated by the ever-shifting values of national currencies. This also effectively makes governments and their central banks third parties in every international transaction their citizens have with foreigners.

By also using national reserves for the settlement of international trade, a country's international trade is held hostage to the central bank's successful management of its currency. If the creation of debt were to increase quickly, the value of the national currency would decline against other currencies. The central bank would have to start depleting its international reserves if it needed to stabilize the value of its currency, compromising its ability to settle trade for its citizens.

3. Bank Reserves

Central bank reserves ultimately back the banking system's reserves. Central banks were intended to be the entities in which commercial banks would hold part of their reserves in order to settle with each other without having to move physical cash between their headquarters. Under a fractional reserve banking system, the central bank also uses its reserves to provide liquidity to individual banks facing liquidity problems. This means that the inevitable credit contractions that follow the banking system's credit-fueled booms are remedied by central banks using their reserves to support illiquid financial institutions, in effect increasing the money supply. Given that central banks make markets in their domestic currencies relative to foreign currencies, if credit expansion were to increase the supply of a domestic currency and a central bank's foreign reserves were to remain unchanged, the domestic currency would be expected to depreciate against foreign currencies.

4. Buying Government Bonds

The modern central bank and government song-and-dance routine adopted the world over involves the central bank using its reserves to purchase government bonds, thus financing the government. Central banks are the main market makers in government bonds, and the extent of a central bank's purchase of government bonds is an important determinant of its national currency's value. As governments ultimately control central banks, despite their constant protestations to the contrary, they can lean on them to purchase their bonds to allow for more government spending. When a central bank buys larger quantities of its government's bonds, the value of its currency declines, since it funds these purchases by inflating the money supply. As monetary continence has continued to erode, central banks no longer just buy government bonds; they also engage in monetizing all kinds of assets from stocks to bonds to defaulted debt to housing, and much more.

The intermingling of these four functions in the hands of one monopoly entity protected from market competition is ultimately the root cause of most economic crises globally. It is easy to see how these four functions can conflict with one another, and how a monopolist will have the perverse incentive to protect their own interests at the expense of the long-term value of their currency and, thus, the wealth of their citizens.

Maintaining the value of a currency is arguably best served by using hard assets as reserves, gold in particular. However, the second function, settling payments abroad, is only doable with the U.S. dollar and a handful of other national currencies used for international settlements. The first conflict central banks face is between choosing a monetary standard for future needs or present needs. This dilemma would not, of course, exist in a globally homogeneous monetary system, such as a true gold standard, since gold would offer salability across time and space.

Not only are governments likely to pressure their central banks to buy their bonds, but they are also likely to lean on their central banks to engage in expansionary monetary policy to "stimulate" their economies. This has a similar effect of inflating a country's money supply and lowering the value of its currency against other currencies. By engaging in inflationary monetary policy, governments endanger their foreign reserves. Individuals start looking to sell the local currency for harder currencies, which creates more selling pressure on the local currency against other currencies. This forces the local central bank to sell some of its international reserves to attempt to stabilize

the exchange rate. These individuals will also seek to send their newly purchased international currencies abroad to be invested in other countries. This
could lead the government to impose capital controls to stop that flow in
order to maintain its foreign reserves.

Similarly, as these individuals expect the value of their national currency
to decline, they are also more likely to purchase durable goods rather than
hold on to cash balances. This can mean increasing imports of expensive
foreign goods, which also depletes the central bank's foreign reserves. The
government is then likely to retaliate with trade barriers, tariffs, and subsidies. Trade barriers are intended to discourage the local population from
converting their local currency to international currency and sending it
abroad. Tariffs are intended to reduce the flow of reserve currency abroad
and to force importers to hand over reserve currency to the government as
they import. And export subsidies are intended to encourage local exporters
to increase their inflows of foreign reserves. This context helps us to understand how the collapse of the fiat system in 1929 ultimately gave rise to the
protectionism of the 1930s, worsening the economic depression and fueling
hostile nationalism.

The last two points are extremely important for the developing world
because they have enormous implications for the three drivers of economic growth and transformation: capital accumulation, trade, and
technological advancement. As governments restrict the ability of individuals to accumulate or move capital and goods, it becomes ever harder for
individuals to accumulate capital, trade, specialize, and import advanced
technologies. The global monetary system built around government-controlled central banks effectively puts local capital markets and all imports
and exports under governmental control. They can dictate what can enter
and exit their countries through their control of national banking sectors.
The fact that governments can always squeeze imports, exports, and capital
markets for foreign exchange revenue makes them very attractive borrowers for international lending institutions. Countries' entire private economies can now be used as collateral for governments to borrow from the
global capital markets.

At its essence, the fiat standard destroys savings and the ability to plan for the future in order to operate a payments network. As a thought experiment, imagine what would happen to a country that adopted a fiat standard before accumulating significant industrial capital. This is the position the developing world finds itself in today, as will be discussed in more detail in Chapter 11.

Chapter 4

Fiat Mining

Chapter 4 of *The Bitcoin Standard* discussed fiat money from a quantitative perspective. It looked at its supply growth over the previous decades compared with those of commodities and bitcoin. As a measure of the salability of fiat money across time, its supply growth in the second half of the twentieth century was found to be far higher, on average, than those of gold and silver. However, *The Bitcoin Standard* did not delve too deeply into the operational details of the fiat monetary system, how it produces new monetary units, and how they are destroyed. This chapter will begin by explaining the dynamics of fiat money creation through the process of lending, and how this process results in erratic and unpredictable money supply growth. We will then examine how this supply translates to price increases and what their long-term implications are.

Lending as Mining

While a small percentage of a country's currency exists in the form of physical cash, the majority exists in digital form, created whenever a financial institution backed by the central bank lends. New money is not created when currency bills are printed, but rather whenever new debt is issued. Bill printing just turns some of the already existing money supply from digital to physical form.

Anyone who finds a way to get other people into debt profits not only from a positive interest rate return, but also by bringing new money into existence. Getting others into debt is the fiat standard's version of gold prospecting. Rai stones were used as currency in Micronesia until Captain O'Keefe imported superior foreign technology to flood the market with new supplies. The monetary role of seashells was destroyed when modern industrial boating inflated their supply. Copper, silver, and gold miners constantly try to increase their supply, but gold's indestructibility and scarcity combine to restrain its supply from growing too quickly. Bitcoin miners try to mine as much bitcoin as possible, but they are successfully constrained by the difficulty adjustment and a network of thousands of nodes worldwide enforcing Nakamoto's consensus parameters. On the other hand, politicians and bankers diligently find new excuses for extending credit in government money. Various political, constitutional, and intellectual safeguards against inflation have only sporadically, temporarily, and unreliably succeeded in controlling the debt creation underwritten by central banks. The most effective restraint against credit growth spiraling out of control in the fiat system has been the inevitable deflationary recessions it precipitates, and the concomitant collapses in the money supply.

Since lending is effectively the mining of new fiat tokens, there is a strong economic incentive to issue debt. Financial institutions stand to profit from creating new money, and a lending license is highly sought after. Politicians and bureaucrats also face strong incentives to encourage lending, as increased lending leads to increased investment and spending. According to the simplistic Keynesian economic model, which dominates the highest levels of politics and academia, increasing these factors in the short term is always the first solution to any economic problem. The short-term economic boom from credit expansion is all that a politician cares about, as the long-term consequences will likely be left for their successors to deal with. Moreover, these long-term consequences can always be blamed on convenient current scapegoats rather than obscure past credit policy decisions.

In 1912, Ludwig von Mises published *The Theory of Money and Credit*, a foundational text in economics. He summarized its central conclusion: "The expansion of credit cannot form a substitute for capital."[18] Since 1912, the fiat standard has provided object lessons for economists to point to in support of Mises's contention. Capital consists of economic goods that can be used to produce other economic goods. Money can be traded for capital goods, but it cannot substitute for or supplement them. The stock of capital that exists in any society at any point in time can only be increased by deferring the consumption of existing resources. It cannot be increased by producing more claims on it.

Instead of accumulating capital from savers and lending it to borrowers, fiat banking just creates new claims on existing capital and hands them out to borrowers. There is little incentive for people to save, and there is no longer any real capital scarcity for those who are politically well connected. There is also no capital for those who are not well connected. Government fiat allows this form of banking to survive when it would not do so in a free market.

All that can be achieved from credit expansion is an increase in the perception of wealth in the minds of entrepreneurs, whose ability to acquire financing drives them to think they can secure the capital resources they need. However, since more credit is being produced without savers deferring consumption, the capitalists are in fact beginning a bidding war for fewer capital resources. As the bidding war escalates, the profitability of many of the capitalists' projects evaporates, and their projects declare bankruptcy, defaulting on the credit they received from the banks.

Central banks have a pervasive influence over all banks allowed to operate in their respective countries. As such, the fiat standard leaves all of a society's wealth and its monetary and financial system vulnerable to the central bank's reckless monetary central planning and the shenanigans of individual

---

18   von Mises, Ludwig. *The Theory of Money and Credit*. 2nd ed. Irvington-on-Hudson, NY: Foundation for Economic Education, 1971, p. 22. Print.

financial institutions. One bank engaging in fraud and facing a bank run will not only cause repercussions for its own clients but also for other banks and their clients. Even perfectly solvent and profitable businesses would no longer be able to operate in a banking collapse because their financial counterparties would be compromised by liquidity crises. The fact that everyone is forced to use the same inflationary monetary asset leaves everyone vulnerable to its failure and makes the financial system as strong as its weakest link.

As these defaults pile up at the bust stage of the business cycle, the money supply begins to contract, threatening the financial system's solvency. Should the liquidation of insolvent businesses continue, many of the banks that lent to them would necessarily go bankrupt. However, since banks have a monopoly on vital economic functions, their collapse is a catastrophe that politicians and the public want to avoid, leading to a clamor for the central bank and government to step in and inject liquidity into the financial system.

The reflationary logic is seemingly compelling. People's livelihoods would be destroyed through no fault of their own, just because their financial institutions and counterparties in the financial system became insolvent. If the central bank already allocated reserves for the banks, and they can extend credit without causing a perceptible decline in the value of their currency, it would be cruel to just let these businesses and livelihoods go to ruin. Since the central bank can create liquidity at will by fiat, then relieving the liquidity crunch would prevent the destruction of many livelihoods. After all, the monetary policy of the monopolist central banks ultimately causes the recession stage of the business cycle, and none of these businesses have a choice in whether to opt into it. Opposing deflation and supporting reflation is also a surefire career-maker in politics and academia because it naturally finds large supportive constituencies among citizens and businesses.

A significant number of fiat economists have built entire careers and appointments at the Federal Reserve from supporting this position, which is exceptionally popular with governments, banks, and central banks. Milton Friedman's *A Monetary History of the United States* was an elaborate labor of statistical huffing and puffing whose only piece of actionable advice was not to allow the money supply to contract during banking crises.[19] His central conclusion was that the Great Depression was caused by the Federal Reserve not reflating the monetary system after the 1929 stock market crash. There is no mention of the causes of the crash in the expansionary monetary policy of the 1920s or in the highly unstable nature of fractional reserve banking built on top of an elastic currency not redeemable for gold. Former U.S. Federal Reserve Chair Ben Bernanke wrote his dissertation on this episode as well, sharing Friedman's conclusion.

After one hundred years of the fiat standard, a consensus has developed between academics and policymakers on the importance of preventing monetary contraction at all costs. However, without considering how credit inflation itself sets the scene for a deflationary credit collapse, this consensus is built on conceptual quicksand. The treatment is predicated on having to ignore the possibility of prevention and having to ignore the long-term impact of reflation, which is the fueling of future bubbles. And so, the fiat credit money system trudges along from one cycle to another, with inflationary bubbles and deflationary collapses following each other like the seasons. Each cycle misallocates much of society's capital stock into unprofitable ventures that must be liquidated, with many lives upended in their wake. The business cycle shows how the fiat standard has a deflation as well as an inflation problem.

While these deflationary episodes are widely known for their terrible economic consequences, another of their oft-ignored implications is that they are a significant check on the growth and expansion of the money supply. Without these episodes purging large chunks of the money supply periodically, currency devaluation would proceed at a much faster pace. These recessions, and the foresight of central bankers, are a major reason why hyperinflation is not such a common occurrence in fiat monetary systems. In a fiat system, credit creation is, to some extent, self-correcting. While

---

19   Friedman, Milton, and Anna Schwartz. *A Monetary History of the United States, 1867–1960*. Princeton, NJ: Princeton University Press, 1963. Print.

there were around sixty hyperinflationary[20] episodes in the past century, and while these episodes are devastating, there is no denying that they have been exceptions rather than the norm during this period, the norm being variable inflation. Hyperinflation has usually appeared after significant government solvency problems and the monetization of government debt through the literal printing of large quantities of paper money.

Data for 167 countries shows that the average annual growth rate of the money supply from 1960–2020 was 29%. Switzerland had the lowest average annual growth rate during this period, at 6.5% per year. The U.S. had the second-lowest annual growth rate, at 7.4%. Sweden had the third-lowest average annual growth rate, at 7.9%, and Denmark the fourth, at 8.2%. Of all the countries surveyed with full datasets, these four are the best poster

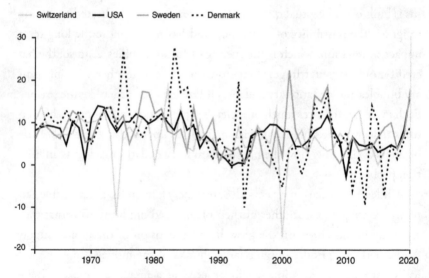

Figure 3. Broad money supply growth rate for the four countries with the lowest average rate between 1960 and 2020.

20   Hanke, Steve H. and Charles Bushnell. "Venezuela Enters the Record Book: The 57th Entry in the Hanke-Krus World Hyperinflation Table." *Studies in Applied Economics* 69 (Dec. 2016), Johns Hopkins Institute for Applied Economics, Global Health, and the Study of Business Enterprise. Web.

children for low monetary inflation in the fiat standard. Looking closely at their monetary supply growth rates from 1960 to 2015, we can see what the best-case scenarios for fiat monetary issuance look like. These countries not only had the lowest annual supply growth rates, but they also had relatively little variability in their growth rates.

Unlike bitcoin's perfectly predictable and auditable declining rate of supply growth, and unlike gold's steady growth rate, which averages around 1–2% every year, fiat's annual growth rate is highly variable. Even for the four best-performing fiat practitioners, the supply can frequently increase by over 10% per year or turn negative at times because of the endless cycles of inflation, deflation, and reflation.

Deflation Phobia

The deflation phobia of modern economists and policymakers has extended beyond just worrying about banking collapses. It has progressed to a pathological level, where even a natural decline in prices caused by productivity increases is viewed as economically catastrophic. There is a huge difference between recession-induced deflation, which is only possible with an inflationary credit collapse, and productivity-driven benevolent deflation. The latter is a healthy, normal, and sustainable feature of a free-functioning market system, where the good with the highest stock-to-flow and the reliably lowest rate of growth is used as money. As the monetary medium grows at the lowest rate of any market asset or commodity, its market price will likely rise relative to most goods over the long term. And as market participants engage in producing more goods, the quantities of all goods available are likely to grow faster than that of the monetary medium. Gold emerged as money because of its hardness, and so it appreciated in the long run against everything else under the gold standard.

Money thus tends to become more valuable in terms of real goods and services, and savers are able to enjoy more goods if they defer consumption. Declining prices are a natural market response to increases in the production of goods and services. Contrary to the argument presented by decades of fiat economists, the normal decline in prices caused by productivity-driven deflation does not have devastating consequences for society (although it does for their fiat jobs). The ability to buy more goods in the future does not stop people from consuming in the present. Time preference is always positive, and people always prefer having something in the present to having it in the future. Humans need to eat to survive, and most expect decent shelter, clothing, and other consumer goods, and so they consume. Deflation will likely cause them to reduce frivolous consumption, but they will consume nonetheless, and whatever they do not consume will be saved or invested, providing demand or goods in the future. Fiat economists understand the direction of the effect of moving to harder money correctly. However, they betray their ignorance of marginal analysis (i.e., comparing marginal costs with marginal benefits) when they conclude that a reduction in spending must somehow be total and catastrophic, rather than marginal and beneficial. People are more likely to hold on to their money if they expect its value to rise, but they will still need to spend it in order to survive. Harder money will result in a reduction in present spending, all else equal, but it will lead to more future spending.

The best example to illustrate this point is the computer industry, which even under inflationary fiat money makes products that become cheaper very quickly. In 1980, a one-megabyte (MB) external hard drive was worth $3,500, but in 2020 that amount of data storage was worth a fraction of a cent. And yet, people have continued to buy and benefit from hard drives for decades, even though their prices continue to decline. When making a purchase, one does not compare the price of the good to its future expected price, but rather the price of the good is measured against the benefit that can accrue from it. Even if the price of the good were to decline, the benefits of buying it today can outweigh the benefits of waiting, and if so, the buyer will make the decision to purchase a good. Every person who buys a phone or laptop today does so even though they would definitely get a lower price if they waited just one year. Yet every year, billions of people globally buy phones and laptops because they need them in the present, not just in the future. Life is finite, time preference is positive, people want to enjoy the benefits of production in the present, and Keynesian inflationary apologia cannot survive five minutes of intelligent inspection.

Human progress is intertwined with the hardening of our monetary media. The harder a monetary medium, the less its supply will be inflated, and the more its owner can expect it to maintain its value, or even have it appreciate over time. The more the money can be expected to hold its value over time, the more reliably an individual can use it to provide for their future self. The more reliably one can provide for their future self, the more they can reduce their uncertainty about the future. The less their uncertainty about the future, the less a person discounts the future, and the more they are likely to plan and provide for it. In other words, hard money is itself a driver of lowered time preference. As our money becomes harder, our ability to save efficiently increases, allowing us to provide for our future more easily and encouraging us to become increasingly future-oriented.

Throughout human history, competition between monetary media has reduced the value of the easier money and increased the value of the harder money. The effect has been a slow demonetization of easier monies and a continual progression to harder alternatives. Seashells, glass beads, rai stones, and salt gave way to metals that were hard to produce, and among the metals, the easier to produce and inflate gave way to the harder metals. Iron was demonetized thousands of years ago, copper hundreds of years ago, and silver began to lose its monetary role in the nineteenth century. By the early twentieth century, almost all of humanity was on a gold standard and able to store the value of its wealth in a money whose supply increases at around 2% per year, and whose value can be reliably expected to appreciate over time.

The introduction of fiat money stopped and reversed this seemingly inexorable progress toward ever harder money. The best money available in the world now increases in supply by around 7% per year. The ability to save value for the future is diminished, and the uncertainty of the future rises significantly. Greater future uncertainty and insecurity inevitably lead to a greater discounting of the future and a higher time preference.

CPI and Unitless Measurement

Fiat money enthusiasts maintain a strange obsession with a metric produced by national governments named the Consumer Price Index (CPI). Government-employed statisticians construct a representative basket of goods and measure the change in the prices of these goods every year as a measure of price increases. There are countless problems with the criteria for inclusion in the basket, for the way that the prices are adjusted to account for technological improvements, and with the entire concept of a representative basket of goods.

Like many metrics used in the pseudoscience that is macroeconomics, the CPI has no definable unit with which it can be measured. This makes measuring it a matter of subjective judgment, not numerical precision. Only by reference to a constant unit whose definition and magnitude are precisely known and independently verified can anything be measured. Without defining a unit, there is no basis for expressing a quantity numerically, or comparing its magnitude to others. Imagine trying to measure anything without a unit. How would you compare the size of two houses if you could not have a constant frame of reference to measure them against? Time has seconds, weight has grams and pounds, and length has meters and inches, all very precisely and uncontroversially defined. Can you imagine making a measurement of time, length, or weight without reference to a fixed unit? The CPI has no definable unit; it absurdly attempts to measure the change in the value of the unit that is used for the measurement of prices, the dollar, which itself is not constant or definable.

The absurdity of unitless measurement covers up the fundamental flaw of the CPI, which is that the composition of the basket of goods itself is a function of prices, which is a function of the value of the dollar, and therefore it cannot serve as a measuring rod for the value of the dollar. As the value of the dollar declines, people will not be able to afford the same products they purchased before and will necessarily substitute them for inferior ones. Market prices result from purchasing decisions, but purchasing decisions are, in turn, influenced by prices. The price of a basket of goods is not determined by some magical "price level" force but by the spending decisions of individuals who can only spend the income they have. Purchasing decisions themselves are price-responsive and will adjust to changes in prices. The main and fatal flaw of the CPI, therefore, is that it is, to a large degree, a mathematical tautology and an infinite referential loop. This point is illustrated with an example in Chapter 8 on fiat food.

Beyond the actual change in the consumer basket of goods as a result of the change in prices, there is also the change in the composition of goods as a result of the judgment and motivations of the people in charge of defining the basket of goods. Economist Stephen Roach, who was starting his career at the Fed in the 1970s, has said then-chairman Arthur Burns fought inflation by removing from the CPI's basket of goods items whose prices were rising, while always conveniently finding a nonmonetary story to explain the price increase. By the time he was done with it, he had eliminated about 65% of the goods in the CPI, including food and oil and energy-related products.[21] The implications of these moves on the food and energy markets will be discussed in detail in Chapters 8, 9, and 10.

One of the most important ways in which the measurement of the CPI has been manipulated is through the removal of house prices from the basket of market goods, under the pretense that a house is in an investment good, an absurd redefinition. Investments produce cash flows, but a person's own home cannot produce an income. On the contrary, it is consumed and it depreciates and requires continuous expenditure to maintain it. The fiat standard first destroyed the ability of individuals to save, then forced them to treat their home as their savings account. With low salability and divisibility, houses constitute terrible savings vehicles, but by excluding it from CPI, and teaching people to treat it as a savings account, inflation magically appears beneficial.

Inflation as a Vector

The CEO of Microstrategy, Michael Saylor, a newly converted bitcoiner, has given the best analysis of measuring inflation that I have come across. His

---

21   Roach, Stephen. "The Ghost of Arthur Burns." *Project Syndicate*. 25 May 2021. Web.

key insight is that inflation cannot be measured as a metric; it can be better understood as a vector.[22] There is no universal inflation rate that measures increases in the prices of all goods and services, as inflation affects different goods in different ways. If inflation is considered as a vector wherein each good has its own price inflation rate, it becomes far easier to identify the impacts of inflation on individuals and their provision for the future.[23]

Saylor's inflation vector allows us to see how inflation rates vary across goods depending on a few key properties, such as their variable cost of production and desirability. Goods that are abundant, not highly sought after, and require a low variable cost of production witness the least price inflation. With modern industrialization and automation driving costs down continuously, these goods are very good at resisting price rises since their supplies can be increased at a relatively small additional marginal cost.

Thinking about goods in terms of their variable cost of production can show their different price inflation rates. Digital and informational goods involve a variable cost of production that is close to zero. As Saylor puts it, if nobody turned up to work at Google tomorrow, their search engine would still continue to work, and the average user would only notice problems later as they stop making upgrades. Digital goods are likely to experience negative price inflation, as they always have done.

Industrial goods that can be produced at scale involve more variable costs than digital and informational goods. However, a very large percentage of their production costs are in original capital expenditure, not in variable running costs. These goods experience price inflation to some extent, albeit not very high. Industrial food is the best example of this. Even through all of the monetary inflation of the past decades, the price of a can of soda, a box

---

22   Ammous, Saifedean, host. "Michael Saylor & Microstrategy Adopt The Bitcoin Standard." *The Bitcoin Standard Podcast*, episode 5, Saifedean Ammous, 24 Sep. 2020, https://saifedean.com/podcast/the-bitcoin-standard-podcast-seminar-5-september-24-2020.

23   Livera, Stephan, host. "SLP213 Michael Saylor—Bitcoin Dematerializes Money." *Stephan Livera Podcast*, episode 213, Stephan Livera, 21 Sep. 2020, https://stephanlivera.com/episode/213.

of cereal, or processed food has increased very little. These goods have a low price inflation rate, in the range of 1–4% per year.

Goods that involve a significant variable cost, such as those involving extensive labor inputs, will be more sensitive to price changes than industrial goods. Organically farmed produce will be more sensitive to inflation than industrial food, and fine dining will be more sensitive to inflation than automated fast-food restaurants. Goods like this will witness higher levels of inflation than digital or industrial goods. As the level of skill involved in producing the good increases, the scarcity of the labor element increases, and the price inflation rate rises. The cost of hiring highly skilled labor increases much faster than the quoted CPI rates.

Another gradient along which the inflation vector manifests is scarcity, and this is where price inflation begins to appear more strongly. Inherently scarce goods manifest price inflation the most. House prices will appreciate faster than the prices of industrial products, and faster than the CPI, particularly as the latter does not include house prices, and the most desirable houses will increase in value the fastest. Property in desirable areas increases at rates that far exceed official CPI measures, and far exceed the price increases of properties in less desirable areas. Tuition in the top-ranked universities increases at similar rates to high-end property, along with luxury goods and artwork. Anything that commands some scarcity premium becomes an attractive store of value under fiat, attracting increasing demand. Whereas industrial goods can easily respond to increased demand with increased supply, scarce goods, luxury goods, and status goods cannot increase in supply and end up continuously rising in price. The price inflation rate for scarce and highly desirable assets is around 7% per year.

To add to Saylor's categories, one could also add durability as a metric, along which the inflation vector varies. Durable goods are more likely to store value into the future, and thus they are more likely to attract store-of-value demand and appreciate. Perishable and consumable goods will likely have lower price inflation than durable goods.

Saylor's most brilliant insight on this issue is to pinpoint that inflation shows up in the cost of purchasing financial assets that yield income for the future. Returns on bonds have declined along with interest rates, reducing the ability of individuals to afford retirement. The market is effectively heavily discounting today's money in terms of tomorrow's real purchasing power as yields disappear. As the future becomes more uncertain, it is no wonder we witness a palpable rise in time preference.

Chapter 5

Fiat Balances: Universal Debt Slavery

The bitcoin monetary system has a neat and simple mechanism for managing user balances. Individual users can opt to run a full bitcoin node, which constantly keeps track of all bitcoins and their ownership among bitcoin public addresses. The network measures the exact number of coins at any point in time with impeccable precision, down to the last satoshi (100 million satoshis = 1 bitcoin). Every ten minutes, all network nodes reach a consensus on the distribution of coins among all addresses. An individual's ownership of a coin is entirely contingent on their command of the private keys of the address containing the coins and cannot be revoked by any authority. In the fiat standard, balances are a far more complicated affair, with significant implications for the way users save and borrow.

Four unique characteristics of fiat balances, outlined in this chapter, set it apart from all other monetary technologies. The fourth will help us understand how the fiat monetary system leads to the proliferation of debt and the destruction of savings.

Unquantifiable

Nobody knows exactly how much fiat exists, and there is significant disagreement over the correct method for calculating the fiat supply. Central banks issue several statistics to measure their money supply according to different definitions, which vary over time and across countries. M0 usually gives the total number of fiat tokens that have been printed into physical paper notes and metal coins that are in circulation. M1 is a measure of M0 and bank checking accounts, allowing for the calculation of all forms of money available to their owner on demand. M2 adds to M1 all savings deposits and certificates of deposits. This is money held by individuals but has not reached maturity, meaning it is not liquid enough for individuals to spend in its current form but can be liquidated quickly. M3 adds to M2 money market mutual funds and other large forms of liquid assets.

There is no clear-cut answer on which measure actually constitutes money, as the nature of fiat is to conflate future fiat with present fiat. As government-guaranteed entities can transform claims on future money into present money for the settlement of current trades, they blur the line between the two. So it is unclear where one should draw the line between the maturity of monetary instruments when counting them as part of the money supply.

To aid the comparison between metals and bitcoin, this book and *The Bitcoin Standard* utilize M2 as a measure of the money supply. M2 is the broadest consistent measure of money supply growth collected by the World Bank and OECD, meaning that it allows us to make international comparisons that are somewhat consistent. The exact quantities of different fiat currencies are not as important for us as their growth rates over the years, and the consistency of the M2 measurement across countries and time allows for better and more consistent comparisons.

Irreconcilable

Unlike with bitcoin, fiat assets cannot be reconciled with their full network issuance. Running the numbers is impossible with fiat. There is no precise way of keeping track of all liabilities, assets, and issuance, which makes financial reconciliation of the overall system impossible. Mining by issuing new debt is done by fiat and can rehypothecate the same collateral several times. Consequently, there is no hard limit on how much lending takes place and no easy way of keeping track of all issuance taking place across all financial institutions in real time.

Tentative and Revocable

Most fiat balances exist on the balance sheets of government-licensed financial institutions, making them at all times revocable by the local fiat node, or the global full node, the U.S. Federal Reserve. If ownership is understood as the ability to command and control something, then one never quite owns fiat in the sense of full sovereign control; one merely holds it tentatively, at the beneficence of the government, which effectively owns all the liquid wealth in its jurisdiction.

There is effectively no final clearance in the fiat monetary system. As monetary inflation has devalued fiat currencies, physical cash notes have declined in real value to the point where they have become extremely inconvenient to use for large value transactions, and holding significant wealth in paper fiat is impractical. Central and commercial banks continue to make it harder for individuals to cash large sums out of their accounts. But even when individuals can withdraw physical notes, they do not confer safe wealth to their holders, as governments can revoke these notes at any time.

Negative

Peculiarly, among all monetary systems known to the author, fiat is the only one where the sum of all balances at any point in time is negative. Because of the enormous incentive to accumulate debt, and the fact that the native token is not physical or scarce in any real sense, financial institutions constantly generate negative balances for their clients. The total sum of all debts far exceeds the quantity of money available. All other media of exchange are present goods, and any debt must be lent by someone who owns it first, so the balances always add up to a positive number.

As explained in the previous chapters, the underlying technology behind the fiat standard is the ability to create monetary units through the process of lending. This monetization of debt has the same effect as the monetization of any market good: it incentivizes the creation of more monetary tokens. This means that the fiat economic system is highly geared toward the creation of more debt, and fiat users are incentivized to get into debt as much as possible.

Fiat is a tiered system. Low-level users are only able to access physical paper money. Higher-level users are able to open bank accounts and secure debt, and the financially responsible ones will get into large amounts of it. For the bottom tier, which constitutes the majority of fiat users worldwide, balances are positive. But the balances of the top tier of users, who constitute the vast majority of global monetary wealth, are usually negative. Under the fiat standard, being rich does not usually mean having many fiat tokens. It rather signifies owing a lot of fiat-denominated debt, which dwarfs the amount of physical fiat and fiat in savings and checking accounts.

Holders of present fiat tokens, whether in cash or bank accounts, are constantly subject to having the value of these tokens diluted by lenders who can create new present tokens by issuing credit based on future receipts of fiat tokens. It therefore makes the most sense for individuals, corporations, and governments not to hold positive balances, as they will be devalued through inflation, but to borrow. Users with negative balances, i.e., those in debt, lack security and risk catastrophic loss. Financial security, in the sense of having a stable amount of liquid wealth saved for the future, is no longer available in the current system. You will either witness the dissipation of your wealth through inflation, or you will borrow and live in the insecurity of losing your collateral if you miss a few payments. Fiat has effectively destroyed savings as a financial instrument, with enormously negative consequences.

Fiat Savings

Saving is the deferral of consumption from the present to the future. An individual forgoes the consumption of a good in the present time to have it, or its monetary equivalent, available at a later date. Holding durable goods was the first form of saving known to humans. With time, the development of money became the most efficient medium of saving, as it gave humanity the ability to save in a liquid and fungible asset that was easy to exchange for any other good. The suitability of money for saving increases with its hardness. Our civilization has progressed through holding ever-harder money, which has provided increasingly reliable mechanisms for transferring value to the future. The harder the money, the more difficult it is to produce new quantities of it in response to increases in demand, and the better the money will be at retaining its value. This has allowed individuals to lower their time preferences and generate more future wealth. The more abundant the savings, the more individuals are likely to invest in capitalist ventures which carry the risk of loss but result in increases in productivity. In short, hard money reduces uncertainty over the future and allows individuals to orient their actions toward the long term.

Saving in physical money has existed for thousands of years. Its pinnacle was the gold coin, which had superior salability across time and space, was recognized the world over, and held its value across millennia. With the gold coin, anyone could save and expect their savings to hold their value relatively well over the long term. Children would start saving the day they were born, as friends and family traditionally gifted them money via their parents. Children were then taught to save from an early age. They learned to work and save money, and as they grew, they were incentivized to be more productive, to earn more and save more. At a certain level of savings, it became possible for individuals to invest in capital goods, increasing the productivity of their own labor, or to invest in someone else's business, which provided income. Once an individual had reached a level of savings that afforded them independence, they married, bought a house, and started a family. Saving continued throughout life and savings were passed on to the next generation.

Human progress consists of providing the next generation with a better life, and savings have played an important role in that process. Only by saving were humans able to lower their time preference and provide for their future. Only by saving first could humans invest and accumulate capital. The more a society saves, the better the lives of its future generations. The development of the concept of saving is a crucial part of the development of human civilization. As money progressively got harder, people started saving more and more, and this became part of culture, religion, and tradition.

We have naturally evolved to use the hardest money so that it can hold its value best. Saving did not require much expertise or effort. Anyone earning a gold coin could hold on to it and see it appreciate by around 1–2% in value per year. Things claiming to be backed by gold would periodically fail, but the physical gold coin never failed. It very rarely depreciated, and when it did, it did not depreciate much or for long.

This outlook that hard money encouraged existed in most of the world until the 1980s and 1990s, by which point fiat money, and the central-bank-led glut of fiat mining, had made debt inevitable and savings pointless for most people. Rather than save for major expenses, people now get into debt to pay for them, accruing a larger negative balance of fiat. People are born to families in debt and spend their entire lives in debt. Success consists of being able to secure ever-growing quantities of debt as you pass through the stages of life: a big college loan that allows you to get into the best paying job, whose salary will allow you a larger loan for a large house and another loan for a car. With more hard work at the company and dedication to its cause, you may succeed in getting an even larger negative balance of fiat for a bigger home and fancier car. Should you succeed even more and start your own business, you do not do it with your own accumulated capital, but rather with a bigger loan. The larger and the more successful the business, the more you are able to borrow. In sum, success in fiat means accumulating larger negative cash balances, and people live their entire lives stacking debt obligations upon themselves.

Once central governments suspended the ability for savers to redeem paper money for physical gold and removed physical gold from circulation, the fiat bank account replaced the gold coin's savings technology. Few held on to paper money for long-term savings; the paper itself could ruin or burn, and the central bank issuing it would usually be expected to engage in inflationary monetary policy, thus reducing its value. The bank account was supposed to offer a rate of interest that would overcome inflation and offer the saver a positive return.

However, as discussed in Chapter 2, removing currencies' gold backing meant more monetary growth and currency devaluation. The ensuing search for yield and monetary inflation create economic bubbles, which are very tempting for the banks to engage in, as happened in the 1920s, resulting in the 1929 stock market crash and ensuing financial crisis, destroying many people's savings.

In 1934, the U.S. Congress passed the Glass-Steagall Act. That act mandated the separation of commercial banking from investment banking, with commercial banking deposits protected by the Federal Reserve. This provided individuals with something close to the old physical gold coin: a guaranteed savings account that offered interest rates intended to beat price inflation. Those who wanted to take on risk in search of profit could then invest in investment banking without government protection.

This arrangement was never workable in the long run because it is not possible for banks to offer real, positive, riskless returns that can keep up with the government's devaluation of its currency. It did work in the immediate aftermath of World War II; however, that was a period in which the U.S. accrued a large influx of gold from all over the world, and in which the majority of the world's countries adopted the dollar standard, buying large quantities of the currency. Add to that the expiration of most of the New Deal's statutes and a large reduction in government spending, and it is understandable how this arrangement seemed to work for most Americans from the 1940s to the 1960s. However, with increasing government spending in the 1960s to finance the Vietnam War and the Great Society welfare programs, and the monetization of government debt, price inflation began to rise noticeably, and savings accounts failed to keep up. When inflation made maintaining the U.S. dollar's gold peg untenable in 1971, fiat savings became unworkable. Those who wanted to save wealth into the future would have to speculate through the shadow banking system and set up an investment portfolio. The stock and bond markets emerged as the pseudo-savings technologies of choice to beat inflation. Retail banking increasingly centered around checking accounts and payment processing, with savings accounts becoming increasingly irrelevant.

From the 1970s until the 1990s, government bonds functioned as the world's savings account, offering inflation-beating returns. However, government bonds are not a useful monetary asset and cannot work as a long-term store of value because there is no effective mechanism restricting their supply from growing. As demand for bonds as a store of value increases, their prices rise and their yields drop, which means their returns eventually stop beating inflation. Bond issuers can borrow on increasingly favorable terms, which encourages them to become less fiscally responsible. By banning the use of gold as money, governments created and amplified demand for their own debt far beyond what their creditworthiness would merit.[24] Increasing demand for government bonds has driven the ever-growing government debt bubbles of the past few decades. By the late 2000s, bond yields in Western economies could clearly no longer beat inflation, and their role as a savings mechanism became less appealing. The stock index emerged as the new savings account in the post-2009 world.

While investment is an essential part of a market economy, it is distinct from and is not a substitute for saving. The two terms have become almost interchangeable in the modern lexicon, and the relationship between them is confused beyond any semblance of reason in modern macroeconomics. The

---

24 A common measure of the creditworthiness of any entity is the ratio of its EBITDA (Earnings Before Interest, Taxes, Depreciation, and Amortization) to its interest payments. Governments are rated far higher than what this ratio would indicate for them had they been operating in the free market. For example, a corporate borrower with an EBITDA/interest ratio of 2.5 would be ranked BB−, but the U.S. government has this ratio, and it is rated AAA. To justify its AAA rating without fiat privilege, the U.S. government would need to have an EBITDA twenty times larger than its interest payment. Its income would need to be eight times higher than what it currently is, or expenditures eight times smaller.

differences between saving and investing are extremely significant. Saving refers to accumulating money in cash balances to hedge against future uncertainty.[25] From a basic accounting perspective, investing is a cash outflow, while savings are held on a balance sheet. Cash is acquired for its salability (the ease with which a money can be sold across time and space). However, the most important distinction between the two is that investment inherently involves more risk. There is no risk-free investment, and any investment can suffer a complete and catastrophic loss of capital. Savings, on the other hand, are kept in the most liquid and least risky assets. The decision to go from saving to investing is the decision to sacrifice liquidity and increase risk in exchange for a positive return.

One should not need to choose between saving and investment, and the two have their place in a portfolio. People would keep a cash balance they would like to have with certainty, and would risk their investment funds in search of returns. Under a hard money standard, such as gold, the hard money itself would be held as saving, given its slight but steady appreciation. In a modern, easy-money economy, cash is trash, as every money manager knows. Instead of holding cash, people hold the equivalent of their savings in government bonds or low-risk investment stocks. Savers need to study financial assets in order to maintain the value they earned and protect it from inflation. This makes it harder to have a stable cash balance and limits the ability of savers to plan for their future.

One of the Keynesian rationalizations given for governments forcing the use of easy money is that devaluing currency encourages people to invest more than they otherwise would, which causes increases in employment and spending. However, this inflationist logic confuses capital for credit. For investments to occur, consumers must defer consumption to direct their resources to production. The devaluation of money does not magically increase the amount of capital and resources available for production. However, it does lead to the perverse scenario in which projects earning even a negative return in real terms are profitable in nominal terms, making them

---

25   Hoppe, Hans-Hermann. "'The Yield from Money Held' Reconsidered." *Mises Daily Articles*, Mises Institute. 14 May 2009. Web.

better than holding cash. The devaluation of a fiat currency is usually also accompanied by credit expansion, which causes a boom-and-bust cycle.

A reliably liquid and low-risk financial asset as a form of saving would be highly valuable for people, as it would allow them to reduce future uncertainty. Being able to secure a specific amount of purchasing power with a relatively high degree of certainty would be financially liberating, and it would allow people to make risky investments proportionately.

Ironically, it might actually be the case that there would be less demand for savings under a monetary system in which money was hard and held its value. If you knew with good certainty that you had ten years' expenditures saved, and that you could reliably expect their value to be consistent over time, you would probably not feel compelled to add more savings and could then take more risks with the rest of your capital. However, when money is a bad store of value, and stocks and bonds involve higher risks, you are less certain about ten years' expenditure stored in investable assets. This might well lead to risk aversion, insecurity, and requiring larger quantities of savings.

The problem with fiat is that simply maintaining the wealth you already own requires significant active management and expert decision-making. You need to develop expertise in portfolio allocation, risk management, stock and bond valuation, real estate markets, credit markets, global macro trends, national and international monetary policy, commodity markets, geopolitics, and many other arcane and highly specialized fields in order to make informed investment decisions that allow you to maintain the wealth you already earned. You effectively need to earn your money twice with fiat, once when you work for it, and once when you invest it to beat inflation. The simple gold coin saved you from all of this before fiat. Why should a doctor, athlete, engineer, entrepreneur, or accountant who is successful in their field have to develop expertise in these many fields just to maintain the wealth they already produced and earned freely on the market?

This arrangement has been a big boon for the investment management industry. Most money in investment accounts is held by people who would rather not take risks with it by investing but would prefer to have a store of value for the future. Without such a store of value, individuals need to hire professionals to help them meet their financial goals. Given the rate of monetary inflation financing wasteful government spending and the high fees charged by the investment management industry, only a small minority of investors can reliably beat monetary inflation. The vast majority must continue to work harder and earn more to not lose wealth.

While many have long believed that index investing or real estate provide reliable ways of beating inflation, this is becoming harder to maintain, particularly over the last year. As interest rates drop to negative territory, it is very difficult to find investments that can beat inflation. Even lending to highly incompetent governments now comes with a negative nominal return, effectively expropriating investors while also subjecting them to serious risks.

Fiat Debt

The correct and successful financial strategy under the fiat standard is to constantly take on as much debt as possible, be meticulous about making all payments on time, and use the debt to buy hard assets that generate future returns. Doing this successively improves your credit score and allows you to borrow at lower rates, while you store your wealth in goods that cannot be inflated as easily as fiat. The fiat system thus taxes savers and subsidizes borrowers. The fiat standard encourages everyone to live fragile lives and take substantial financial risks. The alternative is a slow, continuous bleeding of wealth.

The more irresponsible the risk, the greater your chances of financial success or failure. The path to success ends up necessitating irresponsible decisions along the way. Businesses that are more reckless in taking on debt are more likely to fail than those that do not, but they are also far more likely to grow and drive competitors out. A business whose cash flows grow at a slower pace than the growth in the money supply effectively witnesses a decline of its value in real terms. This is because its cash holdings, assets, and future earnings are all devalued by the monetary issuance. An individual whose income does not increase faster than the rate of monetary issuance sees their standard of living decline. Such companies and individuals need to grow their earnings constantly in order to maintain their economic status.

In the fiat standard, those who choose to hold positive balances are robbed as the purchasing power of their fiat is eroded by all the debt others are creating. Those who are in debt, on the other hand, get to benefit from some of the seigniorage. Not taking on debt is reckless financial irresponsibility. Irish economist Richard Cantillon described the redistributive impact of inflation as benefiting the people who receive the newly created money first at the expense of those who receive it later. In the modern fiat standard, the beneficiaries of the Cantillon effect are the borrowers, and savers are the victims. Spending less than you earn and keeping savings on hand are simply no longer optimal financial strategies; they are expensive luxuries most cannot afford.

Under a fiat standard, users are incentivized to accumulate hard and cash-generating assets instead of accumulating more fiat, which continuously loses value. Whatever wealth one saves in a liquid and internationally redeemable financial asset is continuously and systematically debased. Even saving in gold, the legacy hard money, carries significant transaction costs and spatial salability constraints.

The path to financial success under the fiat standard lies in acquiring hard assets. Financing these acquisitions with debt is even more profitable. Not only is inflation likely to devalue the loan for the asset more than it devalues the asset, but as the lender and borrower are partaking in fiat mining, there is enough benefit in the mining seigniorage to make the purchase cheaper for the borrower. The most profitable route, however, comes from being able to issue fiat and get others into debt. Among the most effective ways to issue debt is to build a business that pivots to providing banking services to its customers, which explains why so many businesses in so many fields offer credit products to their customers.

Under the fiat standard, every business model degenerates into interest rate arbitrage. The purpose behind setting up business is increasingly less about making money from serving customers but establishing a creditor relationship with them. Managing to secure debt at a lower interest rate becomes the most significant market advantage. Businesses live and die by their ability to turn over debt at a healthy arbitrage.

This phenomenon is apparent in many modern companies. Most businesses that provide credit will give their customers very good deals on their products if they use the company's credit card. The incentive for doing so is clear: large corporations can borrow at very low rates, but they can charge their customers interest rates in excess of 20% on their credit cards. Before it went bankrupt, the U.S. department store Macy's was generating about as much revenue from the credit cards it issued its customers as the clothes it sold them.

The consequence of fiat balances being negative is that everyone is constantly in debt. Your homeownership is contingent on you fulfilling your financial obligations for decades. Your future depends on you and many others fulfilling financial obligations in a timely manner. Your future uncertainty is higher than what it would be if you could place your wealth in a hard money, and that causes a rise in time preference. Everyone is less peaceful and more insecure.

In the fiat standard, money becomes a liability rather than future security. Rather than owning dollars that you can use to pay for your future needs, you owe large amounts of dollars, and you need to work for the rest of your life to pay them back. The age-old wisdom of every grandmother has been turned on its head. Instead of saving for the possibility of a rainy day, fiat makes you borrow against all of your future sunny days.

In this absurd mountain of ever-growing debt, one must wonder what would happen if people had the option of placing their wealth in a low-risk store of value with limited upside, similar to a hard money cash balance. Such a hypothetical thought experiment recently became a reality with the failed attempt to build the Narrow Bank.

The Narrow Bank

In 2018, the Narrow Bank applied for a banking license from the U.S. Federal Reserve.[26] It had a unique and very simple business model: it would take money from depositors and deposit it at the Fed, the least risky balance

---

26   Levine, Matt. "The Fed Versus the Narrow Bank: Also Martin Shkreli, Elon Musk, LaCroix, Stock Buybacks and Private Jets." *Bloomberg Opinion*. 8 Mar. 2019. Web.

sheet in the world, where it would collect interest. It would simply pass on the interest rate it received from the Fed to its customers, minus a small fee.

The business model seemed like a great deal for all involved: depositors would get a small return without taking on significant risk, a trade that arguably many would have taken, given the current uncertainty surrounding global capital markets. The bank would make a profit, and the Federal Reserve would have little cause for concern regarding the bank's solvency and liquidity. Tellingly, the bank's license application was rejected.

The fundamental reason the bank was rejected was that its safety and reliability would have endangered the other banks in the financial system. If the safety of the Federal Reserve's balance sheet were easily available to investors, many would have chosen it over traditional financial assets as the bedrock of their portfolios. This is not to say everyone would have put all their wealth in it, but a lot of money, particularly institutional money, would have seen the value in a low-risk, liquid allocation in *savings*. In all likelihood, there is a large demand for about a 2% interest rate with very low counterparty risk. While the rate is not high, it is highly attractive as a savings instrument because of its low risk.

Such a bank would be even more appealing during times of crisis, when everyone searches for wealth protection. The more people seeking out the safety of the Narrow Bank, the fewer there would be investing in traditional financial institutions, and the more precarious the liquidity position of traditional financial institutions would become. The Fed's refusal to grant the Narrow Bank a banking license shows that it recognized that in a free market, many investors would prefer the safety of guaranteed returns over the risky search for a few extra points of yield.

Fiat central banking is built on the fictional idea that devaluing currency will cause people to invest more, thus inducing more economic production. But like all coercive government interventions into markets, there is no free lunch, and the costs are paid in ways that may not appear very clear initially. The Fed's policy to encourage more investment leads to people engaging in riskier investment than their risk profiles would otherwise indicate, leading to financial bubbles and crises.

What would happen if a large percentage of people placed significant portions of their wealth in a financial instrument that offered liquidity and safety but low, or no, returns? Would this reduce the amount of economic production that takes place? Would this reduce the amount of actual capital for investors and entrepreneurs? Arguably, the opposite would be true.

Savings and investment are not competing for a set, fixed pool of money. They are together competing against present consumption. Saving must precede investment, and an increase in savings leads to an increase in investment. Both are driven by, and must be preceded by, lowered time preference and delayed gratification. When money is expected to appreciate, people are more likely to defer consumption and save. If savers can hold cash balances with a high degree of confidence in their value over time, they would have the freedom to take on more risks with their investments. When these savings increase in value, the opportunity for the savers to invest increases. In a world of hard money, the only investments that would make sense would be those that offer positive real rates of return. In a world of easy money, on the other hand, investments are made that accrue positive nominal returns but negative real returns, leading to capital destruction in real terms. The misallocation of capital under an easy monetary system also causes a lot of capital destruction.

The Fed did not stop the Narrow Bank from operating because it was dangerous, but because it would expose just how dangerous the rest of the banking system is and how much demand exists for safe savings. In the third part of this book, the rise of bitcoin is understood in this context. It is a new savings technology that allows anyone in the world to store their wealth, and unlike the Narrow Bank, it does not need a license from the Federal Reserve to operate.

Chapter 6

What Is Fiat Good For?

An economist who has seen the havoc and destruction fiat money has wrought upon the world might be tempted to focus purely on the fiat system's many drawbacks and predictable problems. But in writing this book, I chose instead to think long about the technological advantages that fiat entails. I admit to having acquired an appreciation for the technological improvement the use of fiat money allowed. Rather than a nefarious conspiracy to impoverish the majority to benefit the few, there was an undeniable economic and technological rationale for fiat money, given the technological possibilities of the world in the early twentieth century.

The analytical lens of *The Bitcoin Standard* was salability across time, which can be understood as the degree to which a money holds its value over time. Based on Antal Fekete's work, I argued that the stock-to-flow ratio provides us with a good proxy for intertemporal salability, as it indicates how much supply can be increased to match increasing demand. Historical examples of primitive monies and national currencies demonstrate how monetary goods with higher stock-to-flow ratios displace monetary goods with lower stock-to-flow ratios.

Yet the framework of intertemporal salability alone is insufficient to explain why the world moved from the gold standard to government monies with significantly lower stock-to-flow ratios. This book uses the analytical lens of interspatial salability to explain the technological and economic driving forces behind this change. Fiat's superior salability across space gave it the economic and technological impetus to blanket the planet in the twentieth century. There are two other use cases for fiat that have increased its adoption: unparalleled ability to finance government spending, which was discussed extensively in Chapter 3 of this book and in chapters 6 and 7 of *The Bitcoin Standard*, and the protection of banks engaging in fractional reserve banking, maturity mismatch, and rehypothecation, discussed in this chapter. Understanding how this technology is naturally very conducive to the goals of governments and banks can go a long way toward explaining its mass adoption in the twentieth century.

Salability Across Space

Money is the economic solution to the problem of coincidence of wants, and examining this problem allows us to determine the desirable characteristics of potential solutions. If Alice wanted to buy something from Bob, but Bob did not want what Alice had to offer, the only solution for them would be to engage in indirect exchange: Alice exchanges her good for one that Bob desires, and then exchanges that good with Bob. Alice purchased the intermediary good purely for the purpose of exchanging it for another good, not for its own desirability. As the variety of goods an economy produces grows, indirect exchange is the inevitable solution for facilitating exchange. That some goods will play this role better than others over time is inevitable. The more a good is suitable for performing the function of a medium of exchange, the more *salable* it is.

Carl Menger defines salability as the degree to which a good can be brought to market without a significant loss in market price.[27] A highly salable good

---

27   Menger, Karl. "On the Origins of Money." *The Economic Journal*, vol. 2, no. 6, Jun. 1892, p. 239. Print. Crossref, doi: 10.2307/2956146.

is one with significant market depth and liquidity, making it possible for the holder to obtain the prevailing market price whenever they want to sell it. A good example of a highly salable good today might be the one-hundred-dollar bill, accepted worldwide by merchants and currency exchange shops more than any other monetary medium. A holder of a one-hundred-dollar bill looking to exchange it for goods and services will rarely ever need to sell it for something else to provide to the seller, nor will they ever need to sell it at a discount. They will usually quickly find someone to take it at face value. By contrast, a good with low salability is one for which demand on the market is intermittent and varied, making it difficult to sell the good quickly, and requiring its owner to offer a discount on it in order to be able to sell it. A good example of this is a house, car, or other forms of durable consumer goods. Selling a house is much harder than selling a one-hundred-dollar bill, involving viewings and significant transaction costs, as well as waiting for the right buyer who values the house at the seller's asking price. The seller might need to offer a significant discount to sell the house quickly. In capital markets, the most salable instruments are U.S. Treasury bonds, which at the time of writing are collectively worth around $28 trillion. Most large and institutional investors use U.S. government bonds as their store of value and treasury reserve asset because it is easy to liquidate large quantities without causing large movements in the market.

Central to Menger's analysis of salability is the measure of the spread between the bid and ask prices for assets, where the bid is the maximum price that a buyer is willing to pay, and the ask is the minimum price that a seller is willing to take. Bringing large quantities of a good to market would cause the spread between the bid and ask prices to widen, because as the marginal utility of the good declines with increased quantities, potential buyers begin to offer lower prices. The more a good's marginal utility declines with rising quantities, the less suited it is to the role of money. The smaller the decline in a good's marginal utility, the less the bid-ask spread will widen as larger quantities are brought to the market, the more salable the good is, and the more suitable it is for use as money. We can also understand this process from the perspective of traders buying goods to sell them later. For them, growing stockpiles of a good reduce the chance of each marginal good being sold and increase the risk of price declines hurting the seller. Thus, they will bid at lower levels for increasing quantities of a good. The faster the spread between the bid and ask grows, the less salable the good. Goods for which the spread rises slowly are more salable goods, and these goods are more likely to be hoarded by anyone looking to transfer wealth across space or time.

We can think of salability as existing across three axes: time, space, and scale. Salability across time measures the ability of a good to maintain its market value into the future. As discussed in *The Bitcoin Standard*, the emergence of gold as the world's money was no coincidence but was instead the result of gold having the highest stock-to-flow ratio of all metals. That means gold's supply is the least elastic in response to demand and price shocks. When more market actors turn to gold as a store of value, gold miners have no way to quickly increase the existing stockpiles on the market. This is because annual mining production is always a tiny fraction of global stockpiles, regardless of what new technologies miners deploy in pursuit of more gold. Gold stockpiles have been accumulating over many thousands of years, thanks to gold's physical incorruptibility. Global stockpiles of other metals amount to little more than a few years' worth of production because of their constant degradation. Should monetary demand cause the price of these metals to rise, miners can increase production, thereby significantly increasing existing stockpiles. Gold is the only ancient metal with this property of incorruptibility, and all the other indestructible rare metals, including platinum, palladium, and titanium, have only been discovered in the last few centuries. That means humans have accumulated much smaller stockpiles of these metals in comparison to gold. This discrepancy in historical stockpiles means nongold metals have a much lower stock-to-flow ratio. Silver, the precious metal with the second-highest stock-to-flow ratio, maintained a historical monetary role, particularly for smaller-value transactions for which gold was unsuited, thus addressing gold's limited salability across scales.

Salability across space can be measured as the reduction in the market price incurred by the seller due to the distance between them and the buyer. An immobile house is not salable across space at all, as moving a building would destroy it. Any bulky good will have low space salability because of the heavy cost of transporting it, resulting in a loss of revenue for the seller. Spatial salability helps us understand the success of monetary metals and gold's monetary superiority to other metals.

Metals have a relatively higher value per unit of weight and volume than cattle or crops. Large amounts of value could be minted into relatively small weights of uniform metal to standardize coinage and make these coins recognizable to more people across wider geographies. People using uniform, easy-to-transport coins knew that the coins' purity was relatively easy to verify, allowing for wider geographic dissemination and superior salability across space. The Roman Empire's aureus became the first world money because of its recognizable imprint and standard purity and weight.

Gold's high value per weight made moving value with it cheaper than using silver. In the nineteenth century, gold was fifteen times more expensive than silver, thus making silver more expensive to store and transport. Today that ratio is around seventy to one in favor of gold. Making a payment with gold would thus require transporting a far lighter load than silver, copper, or iron, meaning it would incur a lower cost. Gold's chemical stability and indestructible nature meant that moving it around was relatively safe. More value concentrated in less weight obviously resulted in a currency that was cheaper to transport. As a result, a buyer would expect to lose less value when moving currency long distances for transactions. This spatial salability was key to gold's superiority over other precious metals.

But a gold coin's salability nonetheless declines with distance, as the cost of transporting it rises. Physicality means distance will always result in reduced salability across space. In the late nineteenth century, the steamship, automobile, and railroad spread worldwide, and they were soon followed by the airplane. As transportation costs declined significantly, the possibilities for mutually beneficial trade expanded everywhere. For the vast majority of the world, this meant greater integration and more varied trading with global markets. While gold's salability across space was still the best of all metals, it was still not fast enough to allow for cash settlement of individual trade transactions across cities and national borders. Naturally, banks would work around this problem by resorting to a system of clearance and settlement among one another to save their clients the transaction costs involved in transporting physical gold for every transaction. When Alice would make a payment from her account at Bank A to Bob at Bank B, the two banks would not attempt to move the equivalent sum of gold. Instead, Bank A would debit the sum from Alice's account on a written ledger and send the clearance to Bank B, confirming that Alice has the money to make the payment. Bank B would then credit the sum to Bob's account. Hundreds or thousands of similar transactions can happen between banks before one final clearance.

As the division of labor and international trade expanded, the cost savings of bank gold settlement became more compelling. Banking became a more centralized business because more centralization brought great cost savings. National central banks emerged to settle trade with foreign countries, allowing periodic and regular international settlement between central banks to reduce the cost of transfer, as opposed to the prohibitively expensive international movement of physical gold.

In order to move gold as fast as modern transportation was moving goods, it was increasingly stored in vaults, and financial institutions and individuals traded claims upon that bank-held gold. Over time, market participants moved away from the finality of taking physical custody of gold following a payment, and money increasingly became a liability of financial institutions, which allowed it to move when needed. The more efficient the system, the less gold movement it required, meaning hugely decreased transportation costs. However, the savings achieved through centralization came at the cost of a less secure—and less auditable—financial system.

Although banks could honor their promises to redeem any of their obligations for gold, they could issue more gold liabilities than the gold they had on hand, thanks to its limited spatial salability. Several factors contributed to this early fractional reserve system. For one, there was no easy and convenient place for bank clients to redeem their gold and still use it for settling the increasingly global trades they conducted. With only one monopoly bank in a town, or one central bank in a country, your gold coin had very little spatial salability while it was in your physical possession. In other words, if Bob or Alice wanted to engage in international trade, they could only do so by trusting a centralized bank.

The gold standard's monetary medium was not just the gold underlying it but also the payment and settlement rails that allowed it sufficient spatial salability to move around the world. Gold in the bank effectively carried a spatial salability premium over gold in individual physical possession. Rather than charge individuals a premium for holding their gold with high salability, banks kept gold redeemable at face value but increased the liabilities they issued backed by it. This arrangement was unstable and self-defeating. The more money that flowed into banks, the higher the premium for having gold in banks; the more gold in the banks, the more banks could inflate their liabilities. This dynamic would fuel the bubbles and business cycles that resulted in liquidity shortages and financial crises.

Gold's limited salability across space allowed it to be replaced by government fiat money. The Bank of England had little trouble coaxing gold out of the hands of the British people because without the bank's infrastructure and settlement rails, physical gold coins had very low salability and could not offer their holders final settlement across long distances. In order to achieve greater utility while engaging in international trade, people had to sacrifice the security that came with the physical custody of gold.

Although gold is highly salable across time, its salability across space is very low compared to fiat. This is as significant a flaw as having a low stock-to-flow ratio. Whereas a low stock-to-flow ratio leads to a loss in value when trading the good across time, a high cost of transportation results in a significant loss of value when transacting the good across space. Hard money advocates can deride fiat money for losing its value across time, but they dismiss the reality that an ounce of gold sent across the world will arrive having lost a significant portion of its value to pay for its movement.

In a sane world, a world in which monetary systems were designed by engineers, gold's salability across time would lead to it developing the best salability across space through banking infrastructure. But in the real world of centralized governments, expecting political money to deliver hard money with high interspatial salability is wishful thinking. A hard money that requires brick-and-mortar banks in order to clear it is always liable to government seizure or being replaced with government fiat. Political and engineering realities mean that the low spatial salability of gold and physical monies needs to be considered a feature, not a bug.

Spatial salability also helps us understand why the U.S. dollar continues to garner increasing international demand while other national currencies struggle to maintain their comparative values. The dollar has by far the highest spatial salability of all national currencies, as it is the prime currency for international settlement, and there is a market in U.S. dollars and U.S. government bonds almost everywhere in the world. Other national currencies are rarely accepted outside their national borders, and nondollar paper notes will usually be heavily discounted if sold abroad.

Gold Spatial Salability

The Bitcoin Standard quantified salability across time by using the stock-to-flow ratio. For salability across space, the best metric I can think of is the cost associated with clearing and settling the monetary equivalent of a London Bullion Market Association (LBMA) good delivery gold bar across the Atlantic. Choosing the LBMA good delivery gold bar for this analysis makes sense because it was traditionally the standard unit of settlement for international trade between financial institutions under the gold standard. Further, central banks, financial institutions, and individuals still use LBMA bullion, or similarly sized bars, for gold settlement today.

LBMA bars are the gold standard of gold bars. A good delivery bar weighs around 400 troy ounces, or 12.5 kilograms, and has a market value of around $750,000 in 2021. If the world ran on a gold standard, international financial settlement would likely happen in this unit. That it does not run on a gold standard is a function of how expensive moving this bar really is. One can point to government restrictions on the free movement of gold as the reason for fiat's rise, but that misses the point: if gold had high salability across space, it would not need governments to ensure its monetary role.

We can get an idea of the costs involved in settling gold across the Atlantic at the genesis of fiat by examining the transfer of gold from the Bank of England to the U.S. and Canada, a process we discussed in Chapter 2. In 1919, when the war ended and the Bank of England wanted to repatriate some of its gold from Canada, Osborne reports it hired the Dominion Express Company from St. John's, Canada, to transport it to Liverpool, England, at a cost of $2 per $1,000 of gold carried. We can therefore estimate that in the final days of the gold standard, it cost approximately 0.2% of value transacted to ship gold across the Atlantic.[28]

But the process was often more complicated. One of the many gold shipments from Great Britain to the U.S. in 1917 had 3,211 gold bars, weighing around forty tons, or 1,285,000 ounces, was sent aboard the SS Laurentic from Birkenhead, near Liverpool, to Quebec City in Canada.[29] The gold the Bank of England loaded onto the Laurentic was worth around £5 million at the time, but it would be worth around $2.4 billion in current fiat terms. The Laurentic and its enormous treasure disappeared to the bottom of the ocean after it struck German mines off the northern coast of Ireland.

The Admiralty ordered Captain Guybon Damant to lead a team of divers to salvage the gold. After seven years of diving, Damant's team was able to salvage 3,186 of the 3,211 bars, with only 25 left unaccounted for. Three more bars were to be recovered in the 1930s, but 22 bars remain unaccounted for more than a century after their sinking. The total cost of Damant's salvage operation came to £128,000, around 2–3% of the total value of the gold on board. The salvage operation remains the largest recovery of sunken gold by weight in history.[30]

---

28   Osborne, John. "Gold and Silver." *The Bank of England 1914–21 (Unpublished War History)*. Vol. 2. Bank of England Archive, 1926, p.262. Web. https://www.bankofengland. co.uk/-/media/boe/files/archive/ww/boe-1914-1921-vol2-chapter5a.pdf.

29   Osborne, John. "Gold and Silver." *The Bank of England 1914–21 (Unpublished War History)*, p. 170.

30   Damant, G C. "Notes on the "Laurentic" Salvage Operations and the Prevention of Compressed Air Illness." *Journal of Hygiene*, vol. 25, no. 1, Feb. 1926, pp. 26–49. Print. Crossref, doi:10.1017/s0022172400017198.

A century later, Germany decided to repatriate its gold reserves from New York and Paris. This transaction was for around 54,000 gold bars weighing 12.5 kilograms each, worth around $27 billion at the time. It took four years to complete (2013–2017) and cost $9.1 million, including auditing and authenticating the bars by melting and recasting them.[31] The transaction cost was around 0.03% of the total value. As the cost for shipments from Paris and New York, this estimate is likely lower than the price for the cross-Atlantic trip from New York, which we could estimate as being somewhere around 0.05–0.1% of the value of the gold.

The cost of shipping an individual gold bar across the Atlantic is around $3,000, based on a quote I received from a Swiss gold dealer in Zurich. As the price of a good delivery gold bar is currently around $750,000, the bar would lose around 0.5% of its economic value when shipped across the Atlantic. The transfer would require two to three days to complete, and does not include verification of the gold.

These three data points over a century give us a rough range of the cost of shipping significant amounts of gold across the Atlantic, ranging from 0.05% to 0.5% of the value of the gold. Beyond the cost, moving physical gold carries a serious risk of loss and requires the use of critical reliable physical infrastructure, like airports, seaports, and trains, which governments control. The inability to transport gold across international borders in any significant quantity without the approval of government authorities rendered it increasingly expensive for long-distance economic transactions, especially when compared to the banks' settlement networks. As only central banks could settle trades across long distances and international borders, something gold could not accomplish, these financial institutions' fiat and political decrees came to play the role of money. Governments and their central banks gained unprecedented power to shape society as a direct consequence of the centralized system of international gold transportation.

---

31   Jones, Claire. "How Germany Got Its Gold Back." *Financial Times*. 10 Nov. 2017. Web.

Fiat Spatial Salability

Fiat transactions do not necessitate a lot of physical shipments because they are largely made up of credit obligations, i.e., immaterial entries on balance sheets. The small fraction of fiat money that is physically printed moves around, but this is an increasingly insignificant part of the total money supply. In most cases, settling fiat money involves debiting and crediting ledger entries in different places.

When an individual wants to make an international wire transfer over the fiat network, the sender's bank account issues a payment order to the SWIFT network, a cooperative society based in Belgium and owned by its member financial institutions around the world. SWIFT is a messaging platform, not a platform for transferring funds. It sends payment messages to recipient banks, but it does not send actual money.

The fee to wire funds across the Atlantic is usually in the range of ten to fifty dollars, and it takes around two to five working days for the recipient to receive the payment. But the settlement of funds from the two banks can take significantly longer to finalize, as finality depends on the various banking relationships involved. Should the two banks have a correspondence bank account with one another, they can batch and settle all their transactions at the end of the day, week, or month. But should they need to resort to intermediaries, then the transaction is settled sequentially between intermediaries according to their periodic schedule of settlement. The sending bank credits the account of its correspondent bank, and once the latter receives the money, it credits the account of the recipient bank, or the next intermediary in line. These intermediary correspondent banks will also charge some fees for currency conversion. More fees mean increased costs for the wire transfer, costs that will be absorbed by both the sender and recipient. Despite the individual user seeing a cash credit on their balance sheet after just a few days, the final settlement of the transaction will occur several days, weeks, or months after the transfer has been initiated. Fiat payments over credit cards will involve even more intermediaries, and while the initial payments will be cleared in a matter of seconds, at a fee of around 1–3% of the transaction's face value, the final settlement may take months to complete.

Distinguishing between the costs of making a payment and those of making the final settlement is important when examining the fiat system. Gold banking no longer exists in any meaningful sense, as there are no banks holding accounts in gold or allowing international payments to be made with gold, which makes comparing gold and fiat not a like-for-like comparison. Unlike gold shipments, fiat consumer payments are not final settlement transactions. Final settlement in fiat does not necessarily offer much improvement in speed over shipping physical gold, but it is significantly cheaper, as it involves little more than the transfer of electronic data.

As gold standard payments increasingly became credit payments and not cash settlements, the payment rails of banks and central banks became an increasingly important part of the monetary infrastructure that made payments possible. That the operators of the rails would favor a diminished role for physical gold seems obvious and inevitable in hindsight. Without cheap and fast gold settlement outside the banking system, there was little to deter them from this step. The Faustian bargain of fiat money appears inevitable this way, as the ability to save for the future was compromised to transact quickly across space. The technology of fiat strongly benefits governments and banks, as will be discussed below, but it was the spatial salability of fiat that allowed them to take advantage of it to their own ends.

Spatial salability is the key to understanding the fiat monetary system's evolution and survival and the most important criterion by which to assess bitcoin's competitive threat to government central banks. Bitcoin's ability to settle hundreds of thousands of transactions worldwide regardless of the distances involved gives it a far superior spatial salability to gold, and its ability to cross borders and perform final settlement in a matter of hours is not contingent on the fiat of political authority.

Bank Profitability

The fiat standard's second "killer app" is enabling fractional reserve banking, the dubious practice of holding deposits on demand without having their corresponding value available in cash on hand. Under a fiat monetary system, banks issue loans and create deposits for clients many times their cash reserves. This system is spectacularly profitable for banks since it allows them to keep their money in one place while lending in another location, the fiat version of a bitcoin double-spend transaction. A bank can operate on fractional reserves perfectly fine unless and until a critical mass of its customers all come calling for their holdings. But even in such an event, the bank knows it will have the safety net of the central government and central bank as lenders of last resort. Should the fractional reserve house of cards begin to collapse, as it inevitably will, the banks know that the government will simply conjure credit out of thin air to bail them out. Under the gold standard, by contrast, banks were kept on a relatively tighter leash in terms of their ability to generate financial obligations. Bank clients could at any time ask for the redemption of their banknotes and checking accounts in physical gold, and if the bank was short of gold, there was no authority that could print gold on demand to meet the bank's obligations. The many booms and busts under the gold standard suggest this mechanism was not perfect, but it was far less severe than under fiat.

The U.S. Congress passed, and President Woodrow Wilson signed, the Federal Reserve Act into law in 1913 in response to the financial crisis of 1907, in which overextended fractional reserve banks faced a liquidity crisis. During that crisis, J.P. Morgan, Wall Street's leading banker, relieved that liquidity crisis by acting as the lender of last resort for banks facing insolvency. The episode motivated banks to seek the establishment of the Federal Reserve Bank to alleviate future liquidity crises and not make the economy depend on the bailout of its biggest banker. Proponents of this legislation provided two reasons for the federal bank to create central banks: to protect the banking system from bank runs or financial crises and to stabilize the value of the U.S. dollar. That these two goals were directly contradictory is the kind of blatantly obvious fact only noticed by economists like Friedrich Hayek:

> I would emphasize that bank deposits could never have assumed their present predominant role among the different media of circulation, that the balances held on current account by banks could never have grown to

ten times and more of their cash reserves, unless some organ, be it a privileged central bank or be it a number of or all the banks, had been put in a position, to create in case of need a sufficient number of additional bank notes to satisfy any desire on the part of the public to convert a considerable part of their balances into hand-to-hand money.

...The fundamental dilemma of all central banking policy has hardly ever been really faced: the only effective means by which a central bank can control an expansion of the generally used media of circulation is by making it clear in advance that it will not provide the cash (in the narrower sense) which will be required in consequence of such expansion, but at the same time it is recognised as the paramount duty of a central bank to provide that cash once the expansion of bank deposits has actually occurred and the public begins to demand that they should be converted into notes or gold.[32]

Inevitably, the goal of protecting the value of the cash conflicted with the goal of protecting banks from bank runs, and central banks have almost always favored the financial system at the expense of the currency's value. The fiat standard, and the moral hazard of having a lender of last resort, has served as a giant boon for the global banking industry. The Federal Reserve Act effectively gave banks a license to create money out of thin air and a safety net to protect them from the consequences.

Is Fractional Reserve Banking Necessary for a Growing Economy?

The argument for the necessity of fractional reserve banking ultimately boils down to the same arguments that Keynesians, inflation apologists, and monetary cranks of all hues use for monetary expansionism in general: an increase in the supply of money will lead to more economic production. By this logic, banks that can create loans in excess of the capital they hold in

---

32   Hayek, Friedrich. *Monetary Nationalism and International Stability.* London: Longmans, Green, and Company, 1937: 12. Print.

reserve can mobilize more capital and finance more projects, resulting in less unemployment and increased prosperity. Conversely, if banks are prevented from engaging in fractional reserve banking, a shortage of credit would hamper economic activity, reduce production, and reduce living standards. By using fractional reserve banking to decouple available credit from savings, society benefits overall. At least, that is what Keynesians believe.

The problem with this logic is the same as with all inflationist arguments: money and credit, by themselves, are not productive assets. They merely represent receipts that allow their holders to purchase productive assets. An increase in the supply of money or credit will no more increase the stock of productive assets in an economy than an increase in printed football stadium tickets will increase the capacity of the stadium itself. The ticket is merely a proxy for a seat in the stadium, and money and credit are but claims on final products and the capital goods used in their production. Should a football team wish to increase the maximum number of tickets it sells, it cannot do so by simply increasing the number of tickets it prints; instead, it would have to increase the stadium's capacity, which requires engineers, workers, and heavy capital equipment to complete. Printing tickets beyond the capacity of the stadium would result in more spectators than seats and a conflict over these seats, but it cannot, under any circumstance imaginable, cause an increase in the number of seats.

There can be no such thing as a shortage of money or a shortage of credit. Whatever supply of money an economy is using is always sufficient to supply all the needs of the economy, provided the money itself is divisible enough. The demand for money is always higher than the supply, because people desire more things than they produce and because desiring is far easier than producing. In the fiat standard, it appears that these desires can be satisfied with more money, but the creation of money to meet these desires does nothing to produce the objects of desire. The sought-after good can only be created by dedicating scarce resources to its production. In a free market, people dedicate their time to production in order to make money, and as the number of goods and the number of economic production increases, the supply of money need not increase, but its value will naturally rise.

Fractional reserve banking does not magically create more capital, labor, or resources; it merely entrusts their allocation to central banks rather than the productive conscientious people who produce and save them. Fractional reserve banking is a form of central planning that impoverishes society overall but enriches banks and politically connected individuals. Without fractional reserve banking and the fiat that protects it, capital and labor would flow to the highest bidder, and that will always tend to be the entrepreneur who uses capital and labor most productively. This would encourage people to save, as free-market forces work to efficiently allocate resources according to the most productive and valuable endeavors. With the bank credit creation of the fiat system, capital allocation becomes increasingly political and centrally planned, and failed users of capital can still continue to control it if they are allowed to create credit. The market's natural process of creative destruction and reallocation of resources is thwarted the more that credit is politically manifested rather than generated from savers.

Can Fractional Reserve Banking Survive in a Free Market?

Fractional reserve banking is not necessary for an economy to function, but such systems nonetheless remain prevalent the world over. How can we explain this apparent contradiction? In particular, how can we explain that economies that have used it seem to prosper and that the majority of banks employing it do not fail? To answer these questions, we must examine the role central banks play as the lenders of last resort for banks operating with fractional reserves.

In a free market, a bank that engages in fractional reserve lending will find its assets and liabilities mismatched. For instance, it may owe a depositor one hundred dollars, available to them on demand, but will simultaneously loan out a fraction of that money to a borrower. Should the depositor request all their money when the borrower still has it, the bank has a problem. But since the bank has more than one borrower and depositor, returning money back to the depositor by giving him another depositor's cash keeps the system afloat. As the amount of lending increases (along with the fraction of deposits lent out), the bank's position becomes increasingly precarious and vulnerable to a bank run. To make matters worse, once depositors and borrowers discover the increasing amount of unbacked credit issued by the bank, they become more concerned about the safety of their deposits and thus more likely to demand their withdrawal. If the amount of cash depositors demand exceeds the bank's reserves on hand, the bank has a "liquidity problem." This is viewed as distinct from a solvency problem because the bank does have enough assets to meet all its depositors' withdrawal demands, but it does not have them on hand.

There are a few different ways to address liquidity problems. For one, banks can simply satisfy withdrawal requests on a first-come-first-serve basis until they run out of cash. Another way is for the bank to redistribute the problem to all customers by taking a percentage haircut off each depositor's balance until the bank's total reserves match the total of all depositors' newly adjusted balances. In effect, both methods transition the bank to full-reserve banking, which then allows all depositors to withdraw their total balance simultaneously. Both options imply the bank's bankruptcy, as its assets cannot meet its liabilities to depositors and lenders. While these options can be devastating for both the bank and its depositors, they are in fact the healthiest way to deal with this problem; at a bare minimum, both depositors and bankers learn not to engage in such activities again. And if they don't, they are left with less capital and reputation with which to attempt it.

The alternative option introduced over the last century is the creation of a government-mandated central bank to "inject liquidity" into the struggling bank and allow it to meet its obligations to depositors. Now, with a monopoly on the issuance of money, the central bank can effectively monetize the obligations of the bank and offload the risk of the bank's reckless actions onto all the holders of the nation's currency, not just the bank's depositors. Full reserve banks then become unprofitable in comparison, as they bear the burden of responsible risk management, limiting their upside relative to their fractional reserve counterparts.

The emergence of modern central banking cannot be understood separately from the problems caused by fractional reserve banking. As Guido Hulsmann put it,

Fractional reserve banking is not unrelated to central banking, fiat paper money, and international monetary institutions such as the International Monetary Fund. Ultimately, these institutions are abortive attempts to solve the problems of fractional reserve banking by centralizing cash reserves or by refusing redemption of money titles.[33]

Shadow Fractional Reserve Banking

Fractional reserve banking, in the institutional manner discussed in the old works of Mises and the Austrian economists, is no longer the serious problem it once was. As mentioned above, the tension between banking solvency and currency hardness was resolved in favor of the former. With time, the Federal Deposit Insurance Corporation (FDIC) and its international equivalents came to play the official role of lender of last resort. Laws like Glass-Steagall segregated banking from investment banking and endowed only the former with the protections of a lender of last resort. Supposedly, strict lending criteria were implemented to prevent too much credit expansion, and the central bank became the primary determinant in setting interest rates. As discussed previously, this highly complex edifice of central planning did not work too well: currencies continuously lost value, and business cycles were a constantly recurring phenomenon. For many years, however, major economies' haphazard attempts at reining in fractional reserve banking have succeeded in averting major crises by putting some limit on credit expansion.

---

33 Hülsmann, Jörg Guido. "Banks Cannot Create Money." *The Independent Review*, vol. 5, no. 1, Summer 2000, pp. 101–10. Web. For more readings on the topic of fractional reserve banking, see de Soto, Jesús Huerta. *Money, Bank Credit, and Economic Cycles*. 3rd ed. Translated by Melinda A. Stroup. Auburn, AL: Ludwig von Mises Institute, 1998. Print; H de Soto, Jesús Huerta. "A Critical Analysis of Central Banks and Fractional-Reserve Free Banking from the Austrian School Perspective." *The Review of Austrian Economics*, vol. 8, no. 2, Sep. 1995, pp. 25–38. Print. Crossref, doi:10.1007/BF01102290; Hülsmann, Jörg Guido. "Free Banking and the Free Bankers." *The Review of Austrian Economics*, vol. 9, no. 1, 1995, pp. 3–53. Print. Crossref, doi:10.1007/BF01101880.

But this arrangement is less stable than it appears, for its illusion of stability contains the seeds of its collapse.

That banks would not abuse the exorbitant privilege of government protection from failure is unthinkable. Of course, they would press the limits in search of profits, knowing all the while that a government-backed lender of last resort was ready to bail them out. Those who fail to see this dynamic misunderstand human nature and how humans respond to basic incentives. In the era of modern banking, banks have abused the exorbitant privilege of government protection in several ways. To understand how this has happened, we must examine a relatively new and not well-known phenomenon: *the shadow banking system.*

The shadow banking system is the dirty little secret that the banking sector has used to work around financial regulations. The sector may have ring-fenced retail banking into a highly regulated industry to prevent bank runs, but they have branched out into other models of banking and finance. The shadow banking system comprises financial firms created to take financial risks with fewer regulations and restrictions, and without a formal lender of last resort like the FDIC. They include investment banks, mortgage companies, money market funds, repurchase agreement markets, asset-backed commercial paper, securitization vehicles, and more arcane financial tools. Nonetheless, time has shown that when push comes to shove, the Federal Reserve will act as a lender of last resort to the shadow financial system, in many different ways.

First, these financial institutions can secure funding at a lower interest rate than other businesses. The availability of lower interest rates is what led financial companies to acquire larger and larger sectors of the economy. These low interest rates are the reason even nonfinancial companies have adopted elements of the shadow banking system into their business models. By permitting the institutions that comprise the shadow banking system to access lower rates than outsiders, central governments implicitly subsidize their operations. This implicit subsidy is itself a taxpayer-funded handout because access to lower interest rates allows these institutions to profit relatively easily from interest rate arbitrage.

Second, the U.S. central government and the Federal Reserve have repeatedly illustrated that massive financial corporations can engage in wild risk-taking while avoiding any downside. Politicians and Federal Reserve officials have given life to the "too big to fail" idea by repeatedly bailing out financial institutions that engage in risky behavior. The bailout rationale is always the same: we are so big, so intertwined in the global economy, so systemically interconnected into every facet of financial life, that *not* forcing taxpayers to pay for our mistakes will result in economic calamity and pain for not just us, but also for all the responsible people who did not take risks and who never stood to gain a penny from our recklessness.

As far back as 2004, Gary H. Stern and Ron J. Feldman warned of the pervasiveness of a bailout mentality in the financial system in *Too Big to Fail*, arguing that "not enough has been done to reduce creditors' expectations of [too-big-to-fail] protection."[34] Stern and Feldman outlined several episodes that had, over two decades, fostered creditors' bailout expectations. The first episode occurred following the failure of Continental Illinois National Bank and Trust Company in 1984, which at the time was the largest bank failure in U.S. history. The Federal Reserve bailed out Continental Illinois's creditors. Shortly after, C. T. Conover, the comptroller of the currency, testified to Congress that policymakers would also protect creditors of the eleven largest banks in the country since they were too systemically connected to fail.

The message to banks was clear, incentivizing them to become too big and too interconnected to fail by taking excessive risks. Several other banks and savings and loans associations failed in the subsequent years, and federal protection seemed to become more generous toward creditors and depositors with time, going beyond its legal requirements under the pretext of guarding against systemic effects. Stern and Feldman argued that the Federal Deposit Insurance Corporation Improvement Act of 1991 (FDICIA) was insufficient to counter the growing bailout expectations. Further, increased bailouts for debtor countries, as well as the government-induced rescue of Long-Term

---

34   Stern, Gary, and Ron Feldman. *Too Big to Fail: The Hazards of Bank Bailouts.*
     Washington, DC: Brookings Institution Press, 2004. Print.

Capital Management (LTCM) in 1998, all contributed to heightened expectations of creditor protection. In time, their warnings have proved prescient.

Third, yet perhaps even more important than the first two factors, was the growing deployment of monetary policy as a means of rescuing failed institutions and forestalling creative destruction. Under what came to be known as "Greenspan's put," former Federal Reserve board chair Alan Greenspan repeatedly lowered the official federal funds rate in response to asset price decreases and large firms' solvency problems. This politically motivated manipulation of monetary policy allowed large corporations to borrow on favorable terms to save themselves. The Federal Reserve cut the federal funds rate following the 1987 stock market crash, Russia's 1998 debt default, the 1998 collapse of LTCM, and the 2000 bursting of the dot-com bubble. Over and over again, the government used politically expedient cash bailouts and monetary manipulation to protect well-connected insiders from the consequences of their rash and irresponsible behavior. Investors and creditors had found a way of privatizing their gains while socializing their losses. Straightforward solvency problems—market losses—were now treated as liquidity problems, which a lender of last resort could alleviate.

Fourth, financial corporations have gone beyond merely exploiting existing laws; they have actively wielded tremendous political influence to bring about favorable regulatory environments. In 1990, individuals and groups associated with the financial sector contributed more than $71 million to the campaign coffers of U.S. federal office holders, according to Federal Election Commission records analyzed by OpenSecrets.com. By the 2020 election cycle, that number had swelled to nearly $2 billion.

The financial sector's rent-seeking behavior achieved many successes for the industry, one of the biggest wins being the wholesale repeal of the Glass-Steagall Act. With Glass-Steagall stricken from the U.S. legal code, retail banks could once again enter into investment banking. Rather than being the main culprit of this episode, the repeal of Glass-Steagall was more of a symbolic confirmation of the reality that had crept in over decades of government-controlled banking: a giant shadow banking system was now responsible for creating far more of the U.S. dollar money supply than the government or the formally regulated retail banking system. The shadow banking system's ability to increase the supply of credit is hard to measure or understand, as its many organs move in many different ways.

All of this means that today, inflationary money creation and business cycles are not mainly generated in the traditional or retail banking system, as was the case during the eras of most Austrian economists. Analyses of fractional reserve ratios, lending criteria, and interest rates for depository institutions are becoming increasingly quaint irrelevancies in the modern economic system, where far more money is created outside the traditional retail banking system than inside it. The layers and degrees to which maturity mismatching and fractional reserve banking can exist in the shadow financial system are not easy to survey.

If you thought fractional reserve banking was complicated for bank reserves, it is nothing compared to the complexity of performing the equivalent of fractional reserve banking for all financial assets and instruments held by the shadow financial system. Stocks, bonds, commodities, and all different kinds of debt are now part of mismatched maturity lending, which effectively means the claims for ownership of these assets dwarf the assets. The 2008 financial crisis was merely the collapse of this fractional reserve shadow banking system, sparked by an acute crisis in housing and mortgage markets. By bailing out most financial institutions directly, and by letting them borrow at lower rates, central banks played the role of lenders of last resort, allowing these banks to profit from mismatched maturity lending in the financial markets.

PART II

Fiat Life

Chapter 7

Fiat Life

Fiat against Nature

Nature offers humans a reality they must learn to deal with to survive. You must sow to reap, you must work to be rewarded, and you will suffer from want by not working. This is the nature of life for all living beings. Every creature needs to spend its day searching for food and trying to avoid becoming food. This is the natural survival instinct without which we would not have survived to be here today.

As a monetary system whose constituent units are easy to produce for governments, fiat disrupts this natural order, as it severs the connection between work and reward. Rather than the market offering individuals the reward for their work as valued by the others they serve, fiat money makes monetary reward highly dependent on political obedience and connections. Instead of learning to be productive, fiat teaches you to play politics. Instead of work being rewarded based on its productivity, it is rewarded based on artificial status games.

When you start to think deeply about the distortionary effects of a centrally planned monetary system, you start to see them everywhere. Money, after all, is one half of every economic transaction. Money is the main vehicle with which we can trade with our future selves through the act of saving. The development of money allows humans to think of the future and make plans to provide for it. The harder the money, the more reliably we can provide for the future; the less uncertain the future is, the easier it is to think and plan for it, and the less it is discounted.

Money is the medium for the communication of information in a market economy. Profit and loss are the signals that ensure the most productive continue to profit and receive the resources needed to produce more, while those engaged in unproductive work lose their resources and stop wasting them. In a sound money economy, the only way for a business to survive is to produce something of value to others. At any point in time, all operational businesses must be productive, and the only exceptions would be the businesses on their way to shutting down. When money is controlled by government, this process is perverted, and the profit-and-loss mechanism is sabotaged. The requirement for survival is no longer productivity, but political acceptability and obsequiousness. Unproductive but politically favored firms can survive for decades, continuing to waste resources, while productive and politically unfavored firms can go out of business. At any point in time, the businesses that are operational will likely contain a large number of zombie parasites, draining resources away from productive members of society.

By devaluing the monopoly currency, government essentially forces everyone to raise their time preference. At the same time, the devaluation of currency allows government to meddle with all aspects of life. This chapter focuses on the impact fiat money has had on time preference, architecture, capital, the environment, and the family. The next chapters will explore the effect that raised time preference, limitless government spending, and overbearing government intervention have had on a few very important aspects of modern fiat life: food, education, science, energy, and security. Other important consequences of fiat money were discussed in *The Bitcoin Standard*: government finance, war, tyranny, and business cycles.

After a century of the fiat standard, wherein government fiat mandated citizenry use debt as money, it is now possible to discern some clear societal and economic consequences of the widespread use of this technology. Money can be thought of as the operating system for society, as it is involved in every economic transaction, and so it will have a pervasive influence on the nature of economic choices that individuals make and the values that motivate them.

Fiat Time Preference

Money as a technology is heavily intertwined with our time preference, i.e., the degree to which we discount the future. As humans develop the capacity to store economic goods for future use, their ability to provide for their future increases. An economically primitive man can provide for his future self by saving consumption goods for future use. As their degree of economic sophistication increases, humans can develop durable consumption goods that they maintain and use over time. As money develops as a mechanism for conducting trade, it can be saved to transfer economic value in the future, allowing for a more compact and reliable transfer of value across time. The better we are at providing for the future, the more we become aware of it and plan accordingly.

The process of lowering time preference is inextricably linked to money. Having money allows humans to delay consumption in exchange for something that can hold value well and can be exchanged easily. Without money, delaying consumption and saving would be more difficult, because the goods could lose their value over time. You could store grains to grow, but the chance of them ruining before the next season is higher than the chance of a gold coin ruining. If you can sell the grain for gold, you are able to exchange it back to grain whenever you need to, and you can use it to purchase something else meanwhile. Money naturally increases the expected future value of deferring consumption, compared to a world with no money. This incentivizes future provision. The better the money is at holding on to its value into the future, the more reliably individuals can use this money to provide for their future selves, and the less uncertainty they will have about their future lives.

The history of money is a natural progression from easier to harder media over time. Salt, cattle, glass beads, limestone, seashells, iron, copper, and silver have all been used as money in various times and places, but by the end of the nineteenth century, the entire globe was practically on a gold standard. The use of an easier monetary medium would lead to its overproduction, and thus a decline in its value and the dissipation of its monetary premium. Throughout history, and through global trade, money would always tend to be the hardest good to produce. As money progresses from easier to harder media of exchange, individuals' time preference will naturally decline, as their discounting of the future declines. We can understand the process of human civilization as the process of lowering time preference, as Hans-Hermann Hoppe explains.[35] As people value the future more, they begin to invest in improving it. Their actions are carried out with regard to their consequences over a longer and longer time frame. As more and more people cooperate and trade within a market order, creating more economic value, and planning for the future, capital is accumulated and the productivity of work increases. Material living conditions improve over time, and successive generations have a better standard of living than their forebears. With time, humans are able to direct their attention and labor away from the drudgery of basic survival to more elevated and elevating concerns.

According to Austrian economists, and as discussed in more detail in my *Principles of Economics* textbook,[36] time preference is the driver and determinant of interest rates. In *The History of Interest Rates*, Homer and Sylla show a 5,000-year process of decline in interest rates, intertwined with significant increases during periods of war, diseases, and hardship.[37] The move toward harder monies with better salability across space and time can be viewed as a contributor to the epochal decline in time preference by allowing humans

35   Hoppe, Hans-Hermann. "On Time Preference, Government, and the Process of Decivilization." *Democracy: The God That Failed*. Rutgers, NJ: Transaction Publishers, 2001. Print.

36   Ammous, Saifedean. "Principles of Economics." *Saifedean Ammous*. Web. 3 Oct. 2021.

37   Homer, Sidney, and Richard Sylla. *A History of Interest Rates*. Hoboken, NJ: John Wiley & Sons, 2005. Print.

better savings technology, making the future less uncertain for them, and thus making them discount it less.

With the gold standard of the late nineteenth century, the majority of the world had access to a form of money that could hold its value well into the future, while also being increasingly easy to transfer across space. Saving for the future became increasingly reliable for more and more of the world's population. With the ability to save in hard money, everyone is constantly enticed to save, lower their time preference, and reap future rewards. They see the benefits around them every day in falling prices and in the increased wealth of savers. Economic reality is constantly teaching everyone the high opportunity cost of present spending in terms of future happiness.

The twentieth century's shift to an easier monetary medium has reversed this millennia-old process of progressively lowering time preference. Rather than a world in which almost everyone had access to a store of value whose supply could only be increased by around 2% a year, the twentieth century gave us a hodgepodge of government-provided abominations of currencies growing at 6–7% in only the best examples, usually achieving double-digit percentage growth and, occasionally, triple-digit.

Rather than expecting money to appreciate and thus having a reliable way to retain value into the future, fiat returned humans of the twentieth century to far more primitive times, when retaining value into the future was far less certain and the value of their wealth was expected to be reduced in the future, if it survived at all. The future is hazier with easy money, and the inability to provide for the future makes it less certain. This increased uncertainty leads to a higher discounting of the future and thus a higher time preference. Fiat money effectively taxes future provisions, leading to a higher discounting of the future and an increase in basic present-oriented behavior among individuals. Why delay consumption today when you are unsure what will happen to your property tomorrow?

The extreme of this process can be seen when observing the effects of hyperinflation, i.e., the move to a very easy and rapidly devaluing currency. A look at the modern economies of Lebanon, Zimbabwe, or Venezuela through their recent hyperinflationary episodes provides a good case study, as do the dozens of examples of hyperinflation in the twentieth century. Adam Ferguson's *When Money Dies* provides a good overview of the effects of hyperinflation in interwar Germany, a society that was one of the world's most advanced a few years earlier.

In each of these hyperinflationary scenarios, as the value of money was destroyed, along with it went any concern for the future. Attention turns instead to the short-term quest for survival. Saving becomes unthinkable, and people seek to spend whatever money they have as soon as they secure it. People begin to discount all things which have value for the long run, and capital is used for immediate consumption. In hyperinflationary economies, fruit-bearing trees are chopped down for firewood in winter, businesses are liquidated to finance expenditure, and the proverbial seed corn is eaten. Human and physical capital leave the country to go where savers can afford to maintain and operate them productively. With the future so heavily discounted, there is less incentive to be civil, prudent, or law-abiding, and more incentive to be reckless, criminal, or dangerous. Crime and violence become exceedingly common as everyone feels robbed and seeks to take it out on whoever has anything. Families break down under financial strain. While more extreme in the cases of hyperinflation, these trends are nonetheless ever-present, in milder forms, under the yoke of the slow fiat inflationary bleed.

The most immediate effect of the decline in the ability of money to maintain its value over time is an increase in consumption and a reduction in saving. Deferring consumption and delaying gratification requires one to give up immediate pleasure in exchange for future reward. The less reliable the medium of exchange is for transforming value into future reward, the lower the expected value of the future reward, the more expensive the initial sacrifice becomes, and the less likely people are to defer consumption. The extreme of this phenomenon can be observed at the beginning of the month in supermarkets of countries witnessing very fast inflation. People who get their paycheck will rush to the supermarket to immediately convert it into groceries and essentials, knowing that the quantities they can acquire by the end of the month will be far smaller due to the destruction of the value of the currency. Fiat's low and steady inflation does something similar, but it is more subtle.

The culture of conspicuous mass consumption that pervades our planet today cannot be understood except through the distorted incentives fiat creates around consumption. With the money constantly losing its value, deferring consumption and saving will likely have a negative expected value. Finding the right investments is difficult, requires active management and supervision, and entails risk. The path of least resistance, the path permeating the entire culture of fiat society, is to consume all your income, living paycheck to paycheck.

When money is hard and can appreciate, individuals are likely to be very discerning about what they spend it on, as the opportunity cost appreciates over time. Why buy a shoddy table, shirt, or home when you can wait a little while and watch your savings appreciate to allow you to buy a better one. But with cash burning a hole in their pockets, consumers are less picky about the quality of what they buy. The shoddy table, home, or shirt becomes a reasonable proposition when the alternative is to hold money that depreciates over time, allowing you to acquire an even lower quality product. Even shoddy tables will hold their value better than a depreciating fiat currency.

The uncertainty of fiat extends to all property. With government emboldened by its ability to create money from thin air, it grows increasingly omnipotent over all citizens' property, able to decree how they can use it, or to confiscate it altogether. *In The Great Fiction*,[38] Hoppe likens fiat property to a sword of Damocles hanging over the head of all property owners, who can have their property confiscated at any point in time, increasing their future uncertainty and reducing their provision for the future.

Fiat Architecture

Fiat's high time preference is perhaps most apparent when examining the longest-lived consumption good humans have: buildings. As industrial technology has made construction cheaper and easier than ever before, the quality

---

38   Hoppe, Hans-Hermann. *The Great Fiction: Property, Economy, Society, and the Politics of Decline*. 2nd ed. Auburn, AL: Ludwig von Mises Institute, 2021, p. 174. Print.

of buildings worldwide has declined, along with their longevity—an astoundingly curious fact until you consider how the increased discounting of the future affects fiat construction planning. Time preference changes have the most significant effects on goods that survive longer, as they offer the most scope for trading-off future for present-day utility. As time preference rises, the discounting of the future increases, and the value of a house surviving for many decades declines markedly. As this happens, architecture has moved from optimizing for quality and longevity to optimizing for present-day cost reduction.

Under the gold standard, homes were built to last. The owner would have saved since their childhood to build their home, and they usually built it with the intention of living in it for the rest of their life. But in the twentieth century, homes were built cheaply, with very little regard for the building's long-term prospects. Twentieth-century architecture is uglier and less permanent than nineteenth-century architecture, and one might be tempted to think this is so because the uglier modern buildings are more economical. But this is likely only true if one discounts the future heavily. While it is likely cheaper to build one of today's modern modular homes in the short run, it is more expensive in the long run, given the regular maintenance costs needed to keep it operational, and the fact that it will need to be replaced far sooner than a nineteenth-century building.

A stroll through any city with parts built in both the nineteenth and the twentieth century shows a very marked difference in the architecture produced in each era. An entire book could be written contrasting nineteenth- and twentieth-century building styles and discerning all the ways in which rising time preference has influenced design and construction. This chapter will only use one illustrative example: the Boston Public Library's two buildings constructed almost a century apart. The first building, the magnificent McKim building, was built between 1888 and 1895 in the classical tradition, at the cost of $2.268 million, in gold-backed dollars, equivalent to $70.2 million in 2020 fiat dollars.[39] A century and a quarter after its construction, the

---

39   Willis, Catherine. *Images of America: Boston Public Library*. Mount Pleasant, SC: Arcadia Publishing, 2011, pp. 8–10. Print.

building is still one of the most beautiful in Boston and one of the city's most important landmarks, attracting locals and tourists to enjoy its splendid interior. Its structure has needed little construction or maintenance to remain standing and beautiful.

The second building, the Johnson building, is a brutalist modernist abomination nicknamed "the mausoleum" by those unfortunate enough to have experienced the gloom of entering it. Built in 1971, it reached such a degree of disrepair and dysfunction that it needed a complete overhaul in 2013, which cost $78 million and took three years to complete. The cost of maintaining the ugly Johnson building, only 40 years after its construction, exceeded the cost of building the magnificent McKim building, which has not required major maintenance after 125 years of uninterrupted and reliably functional beauty, at least according to official CPI statistics.

Our technology today is far superior to what existed in the late nineteenth century, and it is only natural that the cost of construction has gone down with technological improvements. Poverty did not drive the city of Boston to switch from building beautiful monuments to ugly concrete boxes; it was the high time preference that heavily discounts the future costs of renovation, implied by the modern quick-to-build and quick-to-decay construction. The millennia-long tradition of classical architecture was not displaced by modern abominations because the latter were cheaper, but simply because they defer their costs to the future which the twentieth century taught us to discount heavily.

Fiat Capital Destruction

The fiat system's strong incentives to engage in credit creation makes borrowing an attractive proposition for most people, allowing their lenders to mine new fiat tokens into existence. The result is a society where everyone is indebted and few have savings for the future. The wealthy can protect themselves in these situations by holding most of their wealth in hard assets, but the majority of the population will usually have most of its wealth in liquid assets which are constantly devalued, removing the motivation to work for a better future.

This dissaving is not just reflected in the negative fiat balances everyone keeps; it pervades all forms of capital. Temporally and cognitively, saving is the necessary predecessor to investment and capital accumulation. Individuals have to first decide to defer gratification and delay consumption. In other words, they have to save before they are able to accumulate any capital. The reduction in the incentive to save will lead to a reduction in the availability of capital to invest.

Fiat enthusiasts will respond to this point by arguing that central bank credit expansion amplifies the incentive to engage in productive business rather than hoard cash unproductively. But if we understand saving as the necessary prelude to investing, then the reduction in savings will lead to a reduction in real investments backed by real savings. The investments financed through credit expansion without requisite savings are not a free gift from government that allows us higher productivity without sacrifice; they are simply miscalculations and malinvestments that lead to business cycles, inflation, and crises.

As discussed in chapters 6 and 7 of *The Bitcoin Standard*, central banks manipulate their monopoly currencies, distorting the ability of entrepreneurs to perform economic calculations. This leads to systematic errors in the allocation of capital, which are exposed when a credit expansion recedes, leading to the recessionary bust part of the business cycle. Each business cycle causes large amounts of capital misallocation into unprofitable and unproductive ventures that effectively consume capital rather than increase it. Credit unbacked by savings cannot generate new capital for investment; it can only misallocate existing capital to sectors where self-interested individuals operating in a free market would not have allocated it.

Another way to understand the destructive impact of inflation on capital accumulation is that the threat of inflation encourages savers to invest in anything they expect will offer a better return than holding cash. When cash holds its value and appreciates, an acceptable investment will return a positive nominal return, which will also be a positive real return. Potential investors can be discerning, holding on to their cash while they wait to find the best opportunity. But when money is losing its value, savers have a strong impetus to avoid the devaluation of savings by investing, and so they become frantic to preserve their wealth and are less discriminating. Investments that offer a positive nominal return could nonetheless yield a negative real return. Business activities that destroy economic value and consume capital appear economical when measured against the debasing monetary unit and can continue to subsist, find investors, and destroy capital. The destruction of wealth in savings does not magically create more productive opportunities in society, as childish Keynesian fantasists want to believe; it simply reallocates that wealth into destructive and failed business opportunities.

Fiat's consumptive and destructive impetus is also reflected in natural capital and the environment. As the possibility of providing for the future becomes less certain due to money's inability to maintain its value, economic actors discount more heavily the future services provided by soil, rivers, forests, beaches, and water aquifers, which makes depleting these resources a more rational strategy. The desire to conserve these parts of nature wanes when individuals do not value their future services, and the inevitable outcome is depletion and overuse. The next chapter, on fiat food, discusses the impact this has on agriculture and diets.

Related to the general rise in time preference and the heavy discounting of the future is the rise of interpersonal conflict between individuals and the degradation of the manners and mores that make human society possible. Trade, social cooperation, and the ability of humans to live in close contact with one another in permanent settlements are dependent upon them learning to control their base, hostile, animal instincts and responses, and substituting them with reason and a long-term orientation. Religion, civic, and social norms all encourage people to moderate their immediate impulses in exchange for the long-term benefits of living in a society, cooperating with others, and enjoying the benefits of the division of labor and specialization. When these long-term benefits seem far away, the incentive to sacrifice for them becomes weaker. When individuals witness the dissipation of their wealth, they rightly feel robbed, and they question the utility of living in a society and respecting its mores. Rather than a way to ensure more prosperity for all, society appears as a mechanism for an elite few to rob the majority. Under inflation, crime rates soar and more conflict emerges. Those who feel robbed by the wealthy elite of society will find it relatively easier to justify aggressing against others' property. Diminished hope for the future weakens the incentive to be civil and respectful of clients, colleagues, and acquaintances. As the ability to provide for the future is compromised, the desire to account for it declines. The less certain the future appears to an individual, the more likely they are to engage in reckless behavior that could reward them in the short term while endangering them in the long term. The long-term downside risk of these activities—such as imprisonment, death, or mutilation—are discounted more heavily compared to the immediate reward of securing life's basic goods.

Fiat Family

The family itself is also a victim of the onslaught of fiat inflationism on time preference. In all cultures, people invest their youth and resources into building a family with a life partner, sacrificing present resources to provide a safe fostering environment for children. In return, they get a family to care for them in their old age. Starting a family is a low time preference decision that requires the individual to highly value the future and sacrifice for it. With hard money, the burden of sacrifice is lightened by the ability to save in a money that appreciates in real terms. But when monetary hardness was compromised in the twentieth century, the ability of family members to provide for one another was also compromised. With fiat's loose supply growth resulting in continuous price increases, and savings becoming ineffective, the financial pressures of fiat have resulted in a large increase in families with two wage earners, resulting in far less time for them to spend together. As the stored monetary savings of individuals are depleted to finance the state, along with it goes the ability to provide. The ability of the state to provide undermines the individual's incentive to sacrifice to start a family. As education, childcare, healthcare, and retirement become the responsibility of the state, the need for a family decreases, and the sacrifices required for it become less compelling. All the bonds of family will weaken when the state appropriates the power of provision.

In the world in which fiat did not finance the welfare state, family was one's only hope for surviving childhood and old age, and so everyone had a strong incentive to invest in familial relationships. Children had little choice but to listen to their families, and adults had little choice but to be devoted to their families, as straying away from a family was far more consequential without a welfare state to care for you in your old age.

Throughout history, most humans understood that if you spent your youth building a healthy family, you stood a good chance of having loving company in your later years and someone to take care of you. The urge to have children is instinctive for most people, and the happiness kids provide makes many want them, but few think of getting children as a great way to prepare for old age. It is very common to see people extend their adolescence indefinitely and waste their youth on inconsequential nonsense, offering fleeting pleasures but little lasting security, satisfaction, or fulfillment.

Even if government is still there to provide for you financially in your old age, it cannot caress and love you as you grow old and frail. Humans have needs beyond just the financial. The need for connection, love, and familiarity is very strong, and long-term investment in family is the most reliable method known for obtaining this. Being relieved from having to provide for the long term by the fiat credit machine, individuals end up investing less in the families that would give them joy and satisfaction in their later years. Nothing in our psyche has changed over the past one hundred years to allow us to overcome this need and sacrifice family. What has changed is our ability to think long term and care for our future selves.

Armed with the advanced and dangerous technologies of his ancestors from the golden age, fiat man finds himself approaching the world with a progressively shorter horizon, stumbling along from one short-term fix to another, depleting his capital stock, devaluing the age-long institutions, mores, and traditions that have allowed his modern existence. Fiat man finds himself descending back into the barbarism of his distant ancestors. By providing a monetary standard built on a hard money that resists debasement, bitcoin is allowing people worldwide to provide for their future selves more reliably, decreasing their uncertainty about the future, lowering their time preference, and offering us the intriguing possibility of reversing the twentieth century's rise in time preference, and its many attendant catastrophes.

Chapter 8

Fiat Food

Money, being a part of every economic transaction, has a pervasive effect on most aspects of life. The mechanics of fiat money outlined in the first section of this book create several distortions significant to food markets. This chapter focuses on examining two particular distortions: how fiat's incentives for raising time preference affect farmland production and food consumption choices, and how fiat government financing facilitates an activist government role in the food market through interventionist farm regulations, food subsidies, and dietary guidelines.

Fiat Farms

The closing of the gold-exchange window in 1971, discussed in Chapter 2, relieved the U.S. government from the restraint of having to redeem its fiat in physical gold, and thus allowed it a larger margin of inflationary expansion. The inevitable result of the expansion in the quantity of money was price increases for goods and services—the hallmark of the world economy in the

1970s. As runaway inflation ensued, the U.S. government did what every inflationist government in history has done: it blamed it on a multitude of factors—the Arab oil embargo, evil speculators on the international capital markets, natural resources reaching their limits, etc.—but it never accepted the culpability of its own monetary policy.

Each expansion of government credit and spending develops a dependent group, which uses its political influence, i.e., its votes and its money, to perpetuate the spending, making the job of any politician who would urge restraint in government spending very difficult. The path to success in fiat politics lies in abusing the printing press, not reining it in. Whether it is welfare checks, pandemic stimulus checks, housing assistance, food stamps, free college, or free healthcare, the politician who wants to spend fiat money will always find support from a certain segment of the population. On the other hand, the politician who favors fiscal restraint is unlikely to become popular and will more likely be branded as an enemy of the poor. As food prices became the pressing political question of the day, there was little chance of reining in the price increases through reversing inflationary policies. Instead, governments and their leaders chose the path of centrally planning the food market. The disastrous consequences of that choice continue to unfold to this day.

In 1971, U.S. President Richard Nixon appointed longtime government bureaucrat Earl L. Butz to serve as secretary of the U.S. Department of Agriculture. Butz was an agronomist who also sat on the boards of various agribusiness companies. His stated goal was to bring food prices down, and his methods were brutally direct: "Get big or get out," he told farmers as low interest rates flooded farmers with capital to increase their productivity. This was a boon to large-scale producers but the death knell for small farmers. Butz's strategy killed small-scale agriculture and forced small farmers to sell their plots to large corporations, consolidating the growth of industrial food production, which would in due time destroy America's soil and its people's health. While increased production did lead to lower prices, they came at the expense of the nutritional content of the foods and the quality of the soil.

The large-scale application of industrial machinery can bring down the price of industrial foods, which was what Butz sought. Mass production leads to an increase in the size and quantity of the food and its sugar content, but it is much harder to increase its nutrient content as the soil gets depleted of nutrients from repetitive intensive monocropping, requiring ever-larger quantities of artificial fertilizer to replenish the topsoil.

The quality of food has degraded over the fiat years, as has the quality of food included in governments' favorite broken measure of inflation, the Consumer Price Index, the invalidity of which is discussed in Chapter 4. The absence of an objective definable unit makes the measure meaningless and hides the fact that the composition of the basket of goods used as the reference will change in response to changes in the value of the currency it purports to measure. Food provides the best example of this dynamic.

As prices of highly nutritious foods rise, people are inevitably forced to replace them with cheaper alternatives. As the cheaper foods become a more prevalent part of the basket of goods, the effect of inflation is understated. To illustrate this point, imagine you earn ten dollars a day and spend it all on eating a delicious ribeye steak that gives you all the nutrients you need for the day. In this simple (and many would argue, optimal)[40] consumer basket of goods, the CPI is ten dollars. Now imagine one day hyperinflation strikes, and the price of your ribeye increases to one hundred dollars while your daily wage remains ten dollars. What happens to the price of your basket of goods? It cannot rise tenfold because you cannot afford the one-hundred-dollar ribeye. Instead, you make do with the chemical shitstorm that is a soy burger for ten dollars. The CPI, magically, shows zero inflation. No matter what happens to monetary inflation, the CPI is destined to lag behind as a measure because it is based on consumer spending, which is itself determined by prices. Price rises do not elicit equivalent increases in consumer spending; they bring about reductions in the quality of consumed goods. The change in the cost of living cannot, therefore, be reflected in the price of the average basket of goods, since the basket declines in quality with inflation. This gives

40   See Michael Goldstein's highly informative website *Just Eat Meat*, justmeat.co.

us an understanding of how prices continue to rise while the CPI registers at the politically optimal level of 2–3% per year. If you are happy to substitute industrial waste sludge for ribeye, you will not experience much inflation!

This move toward substituting industrial sludge for food has helped the U.S. government understate the extent of the destruction of value in U.S. dollars and the devastating consequence this has had on its unfortunate users. By subsidizing the production of the cheapest foods and recommending them to Americans as the optimal components of their diet, the extent of price increases and currency debasement is less obvious.

A closer look at the historical trend of the U.S. government's suggested dietary guidelines since the 1970s shows a continuous decline in the recommendation of meat and an increase in the recommendations of grains, legumes, industrial oils, and various other nutritionally poor foods that benefit from industrial economies of scale.

The industrialization of farming has created large conglomerates with significant political clout that have become a powerful part of the political landscape in the U.S. According to OpenSecrets.org, a website that tracks political contributions in U.S. elections, large agribusinesses gave federal office seekers more than $193 million in the 2020 election cycle. Perhaps this helps explain why, for seven decades, industrialized farming operations have had so much success lobbying for increased subsidies and dietary guidelines that encourage Americans to buy their products.

Fiat Diets

The second link between nutrition and monetary economics pertains to the impact of government dietary guidelines. The rise of the modern nanny state, which role-plays as caretaker of its citizens and attempts to provide all the guidance they need to live their lives, could not have been possible under the gold standard, simply because governments that start making centralized decisions for individual problems would quickly cause more economic harm than good and run out of hard money to keep financing their operation. Easy government money, on the other hand, allows for government mistakes to accumulate and add up significantly before economic reality sets in through the destruction of the currency, which generally takes much longer. It is thus no coincidence that the government-approved dietary guidelines came into existence shortly after the Federal Reserve's creation had begun the U.S. federal government's transformation into the nation's iron-fisted, gun-toting nanny. The first such guideline, focused on children, was issued in 1916, and the next year, they issued a general guideline.[41]

The shortcomings of centrally planned economic decisions have been thoroughly detailed by Mises and the Austrian School, primarily in the economic context, but the logic is equally applicable to nutritional decisions. Mises explained that what coordinates economic production, and what allows for the division of labor, is the ability of individuals to perform economic calculation over their own property. When an individual can weigh the costs and benefits of different courses of action they might undertake, according to their own preferences, they are able to decide the most productive course of action to meet their own ends. On the other hand, when decisions on using economic resources are made by people who do not own them, there is no possibility of accurately calculating the real alternatives and opportunity costs, particularly as they pertain to the preferences of the individuals using and benefiting from the resources.

Humans, like all animals, have an instinct for eating, as anyone who has seen a baby approach food will know. Humans have developed traditions and cultures around food for thousands of years which help people know what to eat, and individuals can experiment themselves and study the work of others to decide what to eat to meet their goals. But in the century of fiat-powered omnipotent government, even the decision of what to eat is increasingly influenced by the actions of central governments.

Government agents making decisions about food subsidies and dietary and medical guidelines are, like the economic central planners Mises critiqued, not making the decisions from the perspective of every individual

---

41   "Food and Nutrition through the 20th Century: Government Guidelines." *University of North Carolina, Health Sciences Library*. 20 Aug. 2021. Web.

eating in the country. They are, after all, employees with careers heavily influenced by the government fiat that pays their salary. That political and economic interests would influence their supposedly scientific decisions is only natural. Three main driving forces have created today's modern government dietary guidelines: governments seeking to promote cheap industrial food substitutes to hide the price increases of real foods, the revival of a nineteenth-century movement that sought to massively reduce meat consumption for religious reasons, and industrial agricultural interests trying to increase demand for the high-margin, nutrient-light industrial sludge.

In *The Great Inflation and Its Aftermath*, Robert Samuelson recounts the story of how desperately President Lyndon Johnson had attempted to fight the rising prices of many economic goods.[42] Of the many harebrained and economically destructive ideas he had, what was most striking was that in the spring of 1966, he called on the U.S. surgeon general to issue a phony warning against the consumption of eggs when their prices spiked. In other words, Johnson asked a federal bureaucrat to concoct a fraudulent health scare around perfectly nutritious food for reasons that had nothing to do with science.

For theological reasons outside the scope of this book, the Seventh-day Adventist Church has for a century and a half been on a moral crusade against meat. Ellen G. White, one of the founders of the church, had "visions" of the evils of meat-eating and preached endlessly against it (while still eating meat secretly, a very common phenomenon among antimeat zealots even today). There is, of course, nothing objectionable about religious groups following whatever dietary visions they prefer, but problems arise when they seek to impose those visions on others. Under a fiat standard, the political process allows for enormous influence on national agricultural and dietary policies. Seventh-day Adventists are generally influential members of American society, with significant political clout, and many successful individuals are in positions of power and authority.

---

42   Samuelson, Robert. *The Great Inflation and Its Aftermath: The Past and Future of American Affluence*. New York: Random House, 2010. Print.

The Soyinfo Center proudly proclaims on its website:

No single group in America has done more to pioneer the use of soyfoods than the Seventh-day Adventists, who advocate a healthful vegetarian diet. Their great contribution has been made both by individuals (such as Dr. J.H. Kellogg, Dr. Harry W. Miller, T.A. Van Gundy, Jethro Kloss, Dorothea Van Gundy Jones, Philip Chen) and by soyfoods-producing companies (including La Sierra Foods, Madison Foods, Loma Linda Foods, and Worthington Foods). All of their work can be traced back to the influence of one remarkable woman, Ellen G. White.[43]

Another member of the Seventh-day Adventist Church, Lenna Cooper, went on to become one of the founders of the American Dietetics Association (ADA), an organization that still holds significant influence over government dietary policy. The ADA is responsible for licensing practicing dietitians. In other words, anyone caught handing out dietary advice without a license from the ADA could find themselves thrown into jail, financially ruined, or both. One cannot overstate the influence that such a catastrophic policy has had: the government granted a monopoly on dietary advice to zealots with a religiously motivated agenda that was totally divorced from the human body's needs and the entire planet's dietary traditions. The result has been the complete distortion of many generations' understanding of which foods are healthy.

Even worse, the ADA is responsible for formulating the dietary guidelines taught at most nutrition and medical schools worldwide, meaning it has shaped the way nutritionists, doctors, and chefs (mis)understand nutrition for a century. American adults interested in eating a healthy diet, as opposed to the diet recommended by official government-approved guidelines, are free to ignore the decrees of federal bureaucrats posing as scientists, although they will still be influenced by the economic distortions. American schoolchildren,

---

43   Shurtleff, William and Akiko Aoyagi. "The Seventh-Day Adventists and Ellen G. White: Diet, Health & Vegetarianism." *History of Soybeans and Soyfoods, 1100 B.C. to the 1980s.* Lafayette, CA: Soyinfo Center, 2004. Web. 3 Oct. 2021.

however, are not. In the government-run schools of America, following federal health guidelines is a legal requirement, and school cafeterias adhere to them religiously. At the same time, politicians have made schools responsible for feeding children not just lunch, but also breakfast, dinner, and even summer meals. Millions upon millions of American kids are being compelled by the government to consume a fiat diet. While statists proudly believe they are fighting poverty by having the state supply this fiat food for children, they are actually impoverishing them long term by setting them up for years of health problems in adulthood. While American children pay the price with their bodies, industrial food producers soak up taxpayer-funded profits.

The reader should not be surprised that the ADA, like all the other main institutions that support the government's control of the economy and its citizens, was established in 1917, around the same time as the Federal Reserve. Another organization, the Adventist Health System, has been responsible for producing decades' worth of shoddy "research" that advocates of industrial agriculture and meat reduction use to push their religious visions on a species that demonstrably can only thrive by eating animal proteins and fatty acids.

The messianic antimeat message might have been drowned out in a sane world, but it was highly palatable to the agricultural industrial complex who could cheaply produce the crops which were to replace meat in the fevered visions of the Adventists. It was a match made in heaven. Agroindustry profited enormously from producing these cheap crops, governments benefited from understating the extent of inflation as citizens replaced nutritious meat with cheap slop, and the Adventists' crusade against meat provided the mystic romantic vision that would make this mass poisoning appear as if it were a spiritual step forward for humanity.

The confluence of interests around promoting industrial agriculture products is a great example of the "Bootleggers and Baptists" nature of special interest politics, described by economist Bruce Yandle.[44] While Baptist

---

44   Smith, Adam and Bruce Yandle. *Bootleggers and Baptists: How Economic Forces and Moral Persuasion Interact to Shape Regulatory Politics*. Washington, DC: Cato Institute, 2014. Print.

priests were evangelizing the evils of alcohol and priming the public to accept these restrictions, it was the alcohol bootleggers who lobbied and financed politicians to impose prohibition, as their profits from bootlegging would increase with the severity of the restrictions on alcohol sales. In so many matters of public policy, this pattern repeats: a sanctimonious quasireligious moral crusade demands government policies, the most important consequence of which is to benefit special interest groups. This dynamic is self-sustaining and self-reinforcing and does not even require collusion between the bootleggers and Baptists!

With fiat inflation causing both the cost of nutrient-rich food to rise and the increased power of government to meddle in dietary affairs, with a religious group attempting to commandeer government diet policy for its own antimeat messianic vision, and with an increasingly powerful agricultural industrial complex able to shape government food policy, the dietary Overton window has shifted considerably over the past century. What

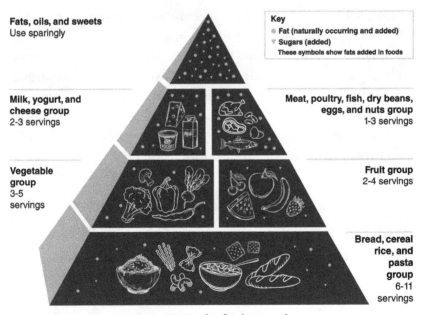

Figure 4. The fiat food pyramid.

Source: "Food Guide Pyramid—Graphic Resources." *U.S. Department of Agriculture.* 30 Oct. 2014. Web.

passed for healthy food came to include a long list of toxic industrial materials. It is entirely inconceivable that the consumption of these "foods" would have been as popular without the distortions generated by fiat money.

By the end of the 1970s, the U.S. government and most of its international vassals were recommending the modern food pyramid. The fiat subsidized grains of the agricultural industrial complex feature heavily in this pyramid, which advertises them as the base of the diet, recommending six to eleven servings a day. This food pyramid is a recipe for metabolic disease, obesity, diabetes, and a plethora of health problems that have become increasingly common in the intervening decades, to the point most people think of them as a normal part of life. The next section will focus on listing the most damaging industrial substances that have been marketed as food by the fiat system, while the next chapter examines the scientific process behind it.

Fiat Foods

Industrialization has made it possible to use plants to mass-produce substances that humans had never before digested. But just because something can be produced does not mean it should be eaten. However, since these foods are cheap, there will always be a strong financial incentive to convince large groups of people to eat them. The most successful of these products are highly palatable and addictive. These drugs and toxic industrial products have been foisted upon the world through a century of heavy propaganda and government policy—all financed by fiat money.

1. Polyunsaturated and Hydrogenated "Vegetable" and Seed Oils

A century ago, the majority of fats humans consumed consisted of healthy animal fats like butter, ghee, tallow, lard, and schmaltz. Today, most fat consumption comes in the form of toxic, heavily processed industrial chemicals misleadingly referred to as "vegetable oils." These are mainly soy, rapeseed, sunflower, and corn, as well as the abomination that is margarine. The diet change that would likely cause the largest improvement in a person's health with the least effort is the substitution of these horrific industrial chemicals for healthy animal fats.

Most of these chemicals did not exist one hundred years ago, and those that did were mainly deployed in industrial uses, such as lubricants. As industrialization spread and the government stoked hysteria against animal fats, these toxic chemicals have been promoted worldwide by governments, doctors, nutritionists, and their corporate sponsors as the healthy alternative. The spread of this sludge across the world, replacing all the traditional fats used for millennia, is an astounding testament to the power of government propaganda hiding under the veneer of science. The late Dr. Mary Enig of the Weston Price Foundation has written extensively on the different kinds of fat and their impact on health.[45]

2. Processed Corn

In the 1970s, government policy pushed the mass production of corn and used policies to make its price very cheap. As a result, American farmers had a large surplus of corn crops. This abundance of cheap corn led to the development of many creative ways to use it in order to benefit from its low price. The overproduction of corn has become so excessive that the cheap inferior products of the corn plant are now used where other substances would be a far better, healthier, or more efficient option. Sweeteners, gasoline, cow feed, and countless industrial processes all deploy heavily subsidized corn for its cheapness, when far superior alternatives exist.

One of the most destructive uses of corn is the production of high fructose corn syrup (HFCS), which has replaced sugar as a sweetener in the U.S. because it is so cheap, and because tariffs on sugar in the U.S. make sugar very expensive. In 1983 the FDA blessed this new substance with the classification of "Generally Recognized as Safe," and the floodgates opened in an unbelievable manner. Since then, American candy, industrial food, and soft

45   Fallon, Sally, and Mary G. Enig. "The Skinny on Fats." *The Weston A. Price Foundation.* 1 Jan. 2000. Web.

drinks have become almost universally full of HFCS, which is arguably even more harmful than regular sugar, on top of being nowhere near as appetizing or desirable. If you have ever wondered why candy and soft drinks taste much better everywhere other than in the U.S., now you know why: the rest of the world uses sugar while the U.S. uses its digestive systems and cars to consume the corn that is depleting its soil, degrading its engines, and destroying the health of its people with obesity, insulin resistance, diabetes, liver damage, and much more.[46]

3. Soy

Historically, soy was not an edible crop; it was used to fix nitrogen in the soil. The Chinese first figured out how to make it edible through its extensive fermentation in products like tempeh, natto, and soy sauce. Famines and poverty later forced Asian populations to eat more soybeans and soybean-based products. Modern-day soy products come from soybean lecithin. The squeamish may want to skip this, but here is how the Weston Price Foundation described the process by which this abomination is prepared:

> Soybean lecithin comes from sludge left after crude soy oil goes through a "degumming" process. It is a waste product containing solvents and pesticides and has a consistency ranging from a gummy fluid to a plastic solid. Before being bleached to a more appealing light yellow, the color of lecithin ranges from a dirty tan to reddish brown. The hexane extraction process commonly used in soybean oil manufacture today yields less lecithin than the older ethanol-benzol process, but produces a more marketable lecithin with better color, reduced odor and less bitter flavor.
>
> Historian William Shurtleff reports that the expansion of the soybean crushing and soy oil refining industries in Europe after 1908 led to a problem disposing the increasing amounts of fermenting, foul-smelling sludge.

---

46   Sanda, Bill. "The Double Danger of High Fructose Corn Syrup." *The Weston A. Price Foundation*. 19 Feb. 2004. Web.

German companies then decided to vacuum dry the sludge, patent the process and sell it as "soybean lecithin." Scientists hired to find some use for the substance cooked up more than a thousand new uses by 1939.[47]

While there are many great uses for soy in industry, its use as food has largely been an unmitigated disaster, as the above article makes clear. But the overwhelming evidence attesting to the destructive nature of soy foods is no match for the motivated reasoning of special interest groups that have effectively captured government regulators. Government-approved dietary guidelines continue to push such toxic plant matter as a substitute for meat.

4. Low-Fat Foods

The insane notion that animal fats are harmful has spurred the creation of many substitutes for fatty foods that contain low or no fat. Without delicious animal fat, these products all become tasteless and unpalatable. Food producers quickly discovered that the best way to make them palatable was to introduce sugars. Those who try to avoid animal fat because of dietary guidelines will find themselves hungry more often. They need to binge on endless doses of sugary snacks all day, junk food that contains lots of chemicals and artificial, barely edible (or pronounceable) compounds. As the consumption of animal fat declined, the consumption of sweeteners, particularly HFCS, increased as a flavor substitute. But the addictive nature of these substitutes means that people deprived of wholesome, satiating animal fats end up being constantly hungry and are more likely to resort to eating large quantities of the cheap industrial alternatives.

The popularization of fat-free skim milk has been one of the most destructive battles in the crusade against saturated fats. In the early twentieth century, American farmers used the leftovers from the production of butter to fatten their pigs, as combining it with corn provided the quickest way to fatten a hog. Through the magic of the fiat scientific method, corn

---

47 "Soy Alert!" *The Weston A. Price Foundation*. Web. 3 Oct. 2021.

with skimmed milk ended up being the human breakfast recommended, promoted and subsidized by fiat authorities, with the same fattening result. John Kellogg, another devout Seventh-day Adventist and a follower of Ellen White, viewed sex and masturbation as sinful, and his idea of a healthy diet was one that would stifle the human sex drive. He was correct and astoundingly successful in marketing his favorite breakfast to billions worldwide.[48]

5. Refined Flour and Sugar

Whole grain flour and natural sugars have been consumed for thousands of years. Whole grain flour, produced from the whole grain, contains the germ and bran, which contain all the nutrients in the wheat. As Weston Price documented, elaborate rituals existed for preparing whole wheat, and it was eaten with ample animal fat. Industrialization changed things drastically for these two substances, effectively turning them into highly addictive drugs. Goldkeim, producers of whole flour, explain:

> An important problem of the industrial revolution was the preservation of flour. Transportation distances and a relatively slow distribution system collided with natural shelf life. The reason for the limited shelf life is the fatty acids of the germ, which react from the moment they are exposed to oxygen. This occurs when grain is milled; the fatty acids oxidize and flour starts to become rancid. Depending on climate and grain quality, this process takes six to nine months. In the late 19th century, this process was too short for an industrial production and distribution cycle. As vitamins, micronutrients and amino acids were completely or relatively unknown in the late 19th century, removing the germ was an effective solution. Without the germ, flour cannot become rancid. Degermed flour became standard. Degermation started in densely populated areas and took approximately one generation to reach the countryside. Heat-processed flour is flour

---

48   "The Surprising Reason Why Dr. John Harvey Kellogg Invented Corn Flakes." *Forbes*, 17 May 2016. Web.

where the germ is first separated from the endosperm and bran, then processed with steam, dry heat or microwave and blended into flour again.[49]

In other words, industrialization solved the problem of flour perishing and ruining by industrially removing the nutrients from it. Sugar, on the other hand, existed naturally in many foods. In its pure form, however, sugar was rare and expensive, since its processing required large amounts of energy, and its production was almost universally done by slaves because few would choose to work that exhausting job of their own volition.[50] As industrialization and capital accumulation allowed for slave labor to be replaced with heavy machinery, people were able to produce sugar in a pure white form, free of all the molasses and nutrients that accompany it, and at a much lower cost.

Refined sugar and flour can be better understood as drugs, not food. Sugar contains no essential nutrients, and flour only contains very few, in small amounts. The pleasure of consuming them is akin to the pleasure you get from a hit of an addictive substance. In *Bright Line Eating*, Susan Thompson explains how the process of refining sugar and flour is similar to the refining process that has made cocaine and heroin such highly addictive substances.[51] Whereas chewing on coca leaves or eating poppy plants will give someone a high and an energy kick, it is nowhere near as addictive as consuming purified cocaine or heroin. Many cultures consumed these plants for thousands of years with adverse effects far less severe than the damage their refined and processed descendants do to their modern consumers. The industrial processing of these plants into their modern, highly potent drug form has made them extremely addictive. It allows those consuming them to ingest large quantities of the pure essence of the plant without any of the rest of the plant matter that comes with it. The high is intensified, as is the withdrawal that follows it and the craving for more. Thompson makes a compelling case that

---

49   "Flour." *Goldkeim, Systains*. Web. 3 Oct. 2021.
50   Whipps, Heather. "How Sugar Changed the World." *Live Science*. 2 Jun. 2008. Web.
51   Thompson, Susan. *Bright Line Eating: The Science of Living Happy, Thin, and Free*. Carlsbad, CA: Hay House, 2017. Print.

the processing of these drugs is very similar to the processing of sugar and flour in how addictive it makes them, citing studies that show sugar is eight times more addictive than cocaine.

The Harvest of Fiat

Seed oils and soy products have legitimate industrial uses. Corn, soy, and low-fat milk are passable cattle feed, though certainly not as good as letting cattle graze. Processed flour and sugar can be used as recreational drugs in tiny quantities, but none of these products have a place in the human diet and must be avoided for humans to thrive and be healthy. Yet as technology and science continue to advance and make them cheaper, and government increasingly subsidizes their production, we find people consuming them more and more, to an extent that is truly unbelievable. Faster and more powerful machines can reduce the cost of producing these materials very significantly, and as industrial technology has advanced, producing these foods has become increasingly less expensive.

Industrialization can do little to improve the cost of nutritious red meat, which is produced by allowing livestock to walk freely on large areas of land, grazing, and getting sun, and which also perishes quickly. But the fiat foods of monocrop agriculture have a stable shelf life, allowing them to remain in storage or on display for years and to spread far and wide. Worse, their shelf stability allows them to be manufactured into highly processed foods engineered to be artificially palatable and addictive. The ubiquity of these cheap, heavily subsidized, highly tasty and toxic foods has been an unmitigated disaster for the health of the human race.

Another way of understanding the impact of rising time preference is in the food choices individuals make. As depreciating money drives people to prioritize the present, they are more likely to indulge in foods that feel good in the moment at the expense of their future health. The shift toward short-term decision-making invariably favors more consumption of the junk foods mentioned above. Eating cookies and candy bars, for example, might yield short-term pleasure, but doing so on a longer timescale will almost certainly come at a cost to the consumer's health. Modern fiat medicine is highly unlikely to mention the obvious dietary drivers of modern diseases, as prevention makes for bad business. Why prevent someone from eating themselves into diabetes when you are the one who will sell them insulin for the rest of their shortened life? The prevalent religious faith in the power of modern medicine to correct all health problems further encourages individuals to believe eating industrial waste has no consequences.

Government subsidies for the production of unhealthy foods—and government scientists recommending and requiring we eat them—have been extremely effective in altering Americans' food choices. In the years between 1970 and 2014, Americans' per capita consumption of red meat declined by 28%, whole milk by 79%, eggs by 13%, animal fats by 27%, and butter by 9%. By contrast, the consumption of toxic "vegetable" oils increased by 87%, and grains increased by 28%. In a show of exemplary compliance with government guidelines, Americans have also increased their consumption of fresh fruits and vegetables significantly, which is an important indicator that the driver of obesity is not the absence of vegetables and fruits, but the decline in meat consumption, particularly red meat. Overall meat consumption stayed relatively constant, rising by 2%, but that happened because American meat-eaters began substituting inferior, cheap, mass-produced poultry for highly nutritious essential red meat. Overall, Americans' calories from animal foods declined by 21%, while calories from plant foods increased by 14%.

Nina Teicholz estimates the average American ate around 175 pounds of meat per year in the nineteenth century, predominantly from highly nutritious red meat. Today, the average American eats around 100 pounds of meat per year, but half of that comes from poultry. A century of technological progress and ever-increasing economic growth has somehow not translated to an increase in the consumption of the most sought-after and nutritious food. Instead, Americans are increasingly having to make do with inferior and cheaper sources of food. The impacts of this dietary transition on Americans' health have been calamitous. Obesity has been increasing steadily since the 1970s, along with many chronic diseases which modern nutrition science and its corporate sponsors have done everything to pretend are unrelated to diet.

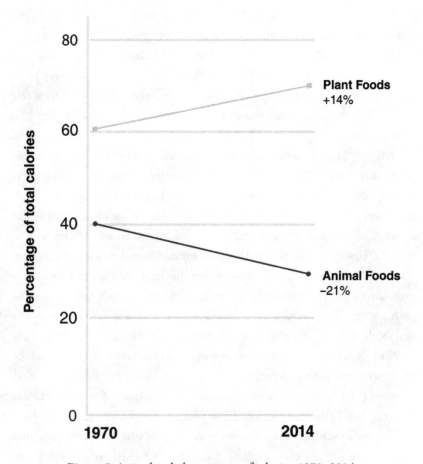

Figure 5. Animal and plant sources of calories, 1970–2014.

Source: Teicholz, Nina. "Dietary Guidelines & Scientific Evidence." Low Carb Denver 2019 Conference, Denver, CO. 9 Mar. 2019. Presentation. https://www.youtube.com/watch?v=qXtdp4BNyOg.

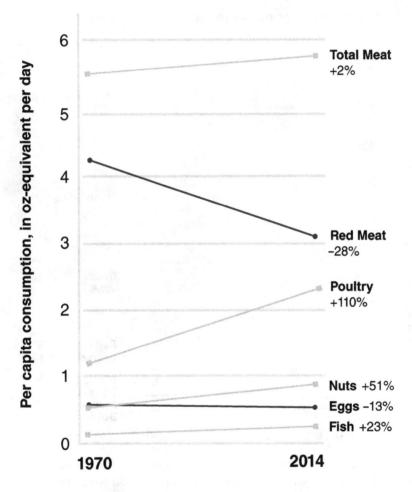

Figure 6. Changes in protein sources, 1970–2014.

Source: Teicholz, Nina. "Dietary Guidelines & Scientific Evidence." Low Carb Denver 2019 Conference, Denver, CO. 9 Mar. 2019. Presentation. https://www.youtube.com/watch?v=qXtdp4BNyOg.

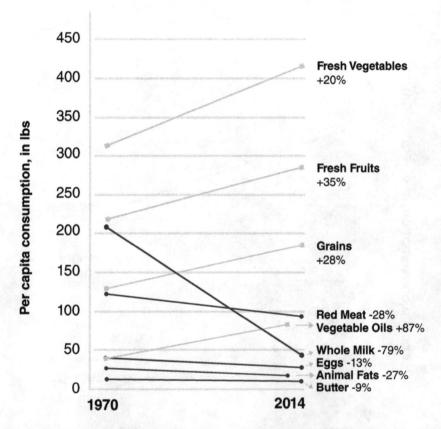

Figure 7. Change in foot per capita consumption, 1970–2014.

Source: Teicholz, Nina. "Dietary Guidelines & Scientific Evidence." Low Carb Denver 2019 Conference, Denver, CO. 9 Mar. 2019. Presentation. https://www.youtube.com/watch?v=qXtdp4BNyOg.

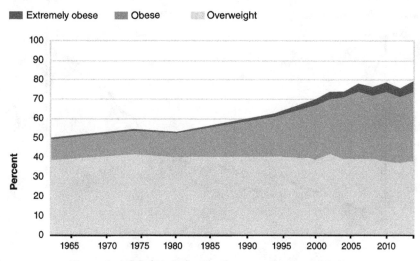

Figure 8. Adult (20–74) male obesity in the United States.

Source: Fryar, Cheryl D., Margaret D. Carroll, and Cynthia L. Ogden. "Prevalence of Overweight, Obesity, and Extreme Obesity Among Adults Aged 20 and Over: United States, 1960–1962 Through 2013–2014." *National Center for Health Statistics*, Center for Disease Control and Prevention. 5 Sep. 2018. Web.

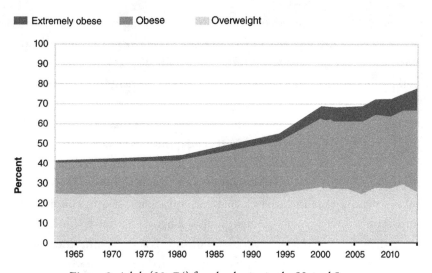

Figure 9. Adult (20–74) female obesity in the United States.

Source: Fryar, Cheryl D., Margaret D. Carroll, and Cynthia L. Ogden. "Prevalence of Overweight, Obesity, and Extreme Obesity Among Adults Aged 20 and Over: United States, 1960–1962 Through 2013–2014." *National Center for Health Statistics*, Center for Disease Control and Prevention. 5 Sep. 2018. Web.

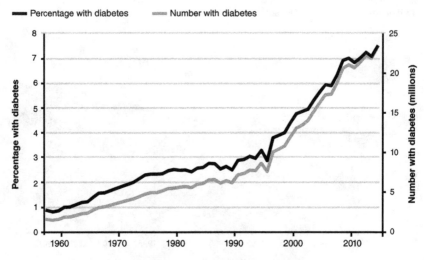

Figure 10. Number and percentage of US population
with diagnosed diabetes, 1958–2015

Source: "Long-term Trends in Diabetes." *United States Diabetes Surveillance
System*, Center for Disease Control and Prevention. Apr. 2017, p. 3. Web.

One cannot find a more apt representation of the impact of inflation and unsound money: the paper wealth of Americans is increasing and the statistics show that their quality of life is rising. In reality, however, the quality of their food is degrading because the quantity of nutrients they consume is declining, and their mental and physical health are deteriorating. Instead of nutrients, Americans are increasingly subsisting on drugs and toxic industrial products. The ever-growing variety and quantities of flavored industrial sludge filling Americans' refrigerators is not food, nor is it a satisfactory substitute. Americans' increasing obesity is not a sign of affluence but a symptom of deprivation. The level of spending and income in America may be increasing according to government statistics, but if Americans work longer hours than they ever did and their basic nutrition is deteriorating, there must be something seriously wrong with the money they are using, both as a store and measure of value. The Faustian bargain of fiat money did not deliver the free lunch its cheerleaders promised. Instead, it brought industrial concoctions of soy sludge and high fructose corn syrup, light on nutrients, high on empty calories, and extremely costly to the health and well-being of its consumers. The ever-increasing cost of medication and healthcare cannot be understood without reference to the deterioration of health, diet, and soil, and the economic and nutritional system that promoted this calamity.

The modern world suffers from a crisis of obesity unprecedented in human history. Never before have so many people been so overweight. Modernity's tragically self-flattering misunderstanding of this crisis is to cast it as a crisis of abundance: it is the result of our affluence that our biggest problem is obesity rather than starvation. The flawed paradigm of nutrition—another field of academic inquiry thoroughly disfigured by government funding and intervention—emphasizes the importance of obtaining a necessary quantity of calories, and that the best way to secure the needed calories is by eating a diverse and "balanced" diet that includes hefty portions of grains. Animal meat and fat are viewed as harmful, best consumed in moderation, if at all. From this perspective, obesity occurs when too many calories are consumed, and malnourishment occurs when too few calories are consumed. This view is as overly simplistic and ridiculous as Keynesian textbooks' insistence that the state of the economy is primarily determined by the level of aggregate spending, with too much spending causing inflation, and too little spending causing unemployment.

In reality, nutrition is about far more than caloric intake. It is about securing sufficient quantities of essential nutrients for the body, which come in four categories: proteins, fats, vitamins, and minerals. The fats are primarily used to provide the body's energy, the proteins for building and rebuilding the body and its tissues, and the vitamins and minerals are necessary for vital processes that take place in the body. The other major food group, carbohydrates, is not essential to the human body but can be utilized to provide energy. In the absence of essential nutrients, the body begins to deteriorate, with negative consequences manifesting as diseases. In particular, the absence of animal proteins and fatty acids cause the body to enter starvation mode: energy expenditure is reduced, manifesting in physical and mental lethargy, and the body begins to convert its intake of carbohydrates into fatty acid deposits for storage for future use (in other words, fat). Rather than a sign of affluence and overfeeding, obesity is actually a sign of malnutrition. The ability to digest sugars and convert them into stores of fatty acids is an extremely useful evolutionary strategy for dealing with hunger in the short run, but when the deprivation of essential nutrients becomes a lifestyle, the fat storage turns into the debilitating sickness of obesity. Americans are not fat because of prosperity and abundance; Americans are fat because they are malnourished and nutritionally impoverished.

Sound Food

Many people worldwide, including me, have improved their health immeasurably by simply avoiding fiat foods. The exact diet plans people follow may differ, but the hallmark of successful diets is the elimination of processed fiat foods. As the internet has allowed people to share their experiences outside of the fiat science establishment's dogmas, what emerges from real human experience is markedly different from what fiat authorities advertise. Nutrition departments, medical schools, and government guidelines continue to rationalize the consumption of toxic industrial sludge under the guise of "balance." But outside of this government-controlled system, online communities have helped millions worldwide regain their health by guiding them to avoid these fiat foods and ignore the fiat recommendations.

The state of nutrition research is analogous to the state of economic research: a fiat-financed mainstream heavily invested in arriving at the conclusions conducive to its fiat financing. Much as economics has its Austrian alternatives, such as Mises, Rothbard, and Hoppe, nutrition also has its heretics. As the field has degenerated into just another junk food marketing gimmick, as will be discussed in the next chapter, some renegades have for long attempted to counter the prevailing narrative. John Yudkin's heroic but doomed struggle against sugar is particularly noteworthy. But perhaps the most comprehensive framework for studying nutrition comes from the work of Weston Price, a Canadian dentist who worked a century ago.

Price is mainly known today as both a dentist and a pioneer in the discovery and analysis of several vitamins. His 1939 magnum opus *Nutrition and*

Physical Degeneration is largely ignored by the mainstream of academia and nutrition science,[52] as his conclusions fly against the politically correct dogma taught in the medical and nutrition schools of modern universities. Price provides a rigorous and clean exploration of the horrible damages caused by modern industrial foods whose producers are the main benefactors of nutrition schools everywhere today. On top of being methodologically thorough and well documented, Price's research is unique and likely impossible to replicate. He spent many years traveling the world when airplanes had just been invented and closely observed the diet and health of people from cultures across all continents, meticulously documenting their diets and their overall health, particularly their dental health. Since flight was so novel, he was able to visit many areas which were still largely isolated from global markets and thus reliant on their own local, traditionally prepared food items. All of these places have become far better integrated into global trade and their diets are quickly degenerating into the appropriately acronymed Standard American Diet (SAD). Price took thousands of pictures of the people he studied as well as countless samples of their foods, which he then sent to his laboratories in Ohio for analysis.

Across the world, Price compared the diets of genetically similar separate populations. The major difference between the populations he compared was that, in each comparison, one population was integrated into global trade markets with access to industrial foods, while the other was isolated and eating its local, traditionally prepared foods. Price studied Inuits in northern Canada and Alaska, Swiss villagers in isolated valleys, herdsmen in central Africa, Pacific Islanders, Scottish farmers, and many other populations. No matter where in the world you come from, Price visited your ancestors or people not too far from them. The results were as stark as they are edifying, and Price arrived at several important conclusions. While it is really impossible to do justice to this momentous work in a few paragraphs, there are some important conclusions worth discussing.

---

52   Price, Weston. *Nutrition and Physical Degeneration: A Comparison of Primitive and Modern Diets and Their Effects.* Great Barrington, MA: Keats, 1939, p. 311. Print.

One purpose of Price's trip was to find "native dietaries consisting entirely of plant foods which were competent for providing all the factors needed for complete and normal physical development without the use of any animal tissues or product."[53] But after scouring the globe, Price did not find a single culture that subsisted on plant foods exclusively. All healthy traditional populations relied heavily on animal products. The healthiest and strongest populations he found were the Inuit of the Arctic and African herders. Almost nothing about the environment and customs of those two populations is similar in any way except for their reliance almost exclusively on animal foods. Price came to see the sacred importance of animal fats across all societies and analyzed the lengths to which populations went to secure it. Price found many nutrients that cannot be obtained from plants and conclusively demonstrated that it is simply not possible to be healthy for any significant period of time without ingesting animal-based foods. To the extent that plant food was eaten, its role seemed primarily to be a vessel for ingesting precious fats.

Since Price's research, nobody has managed to produce evidence of a single indigenous human society anywhere whose diet excludes animal foods. All human societies, from the arctic to the tropics, on every continent, throughout history have based their diet around animal foods. The internet has allowed dietary knowledge to escape the grip of fiat science, and so more humans have learned about Price's work. Countless other scholars, doctors, dietitians, and physical trainers have also become willing to counter the fiat dogma.

Thanks to the spread of dietary knowledge outside of the politically correct, government-sanctioned channels, we are beginning to see a very clear pattern emerge from people who shift their diet from one based on fiat garbage to one based predominantly on animal foods: a huge reduction in

53   Price, Weston. "Studies of Relationships Between Nutritional Deficiencies and (a) Facial and Dental Arch Deformities and (b) Loss of Immunity to Dental Caries Among South Sea Islanders and Florida Indians." *The Dental Cosmos: A Monthly Record of Dental Science*, vol. 77, no. 11, Nov. 1935, p. 1038. Print.

their desire for junk and ultraprocessed food. The need to constantly be eating junk food is not just a product of its engineered hyperpalatability and addictive properties. Junk food cravings are also a result of deep malnutrition caused by not eating enough meat. No wonder the antimeat message is blared out relentlessly by mainstream media, academia, and other industrial food marketing outlets. The less meat people eat, the more highly profitable, subsidized junk they must replace it with. One can only imagine how different modern nutrition science would be if its purpose was to inform humans of how to be healthy rather than manipulate them into eating poisons for the profit of food corporations.

Another important conclusion from Price's work is that the diseases of civilization that we have accepted as a normal part of life largely began to appear with the introduction of modern processed foods, in particular, grains, flours, and sugars. Here is but one of many examples to illustrate the point, drawn from chapter 21:

> The responsibility of our modern processed foods of commerce as contributing factors in the cause of tooth decay is strikingly demonstrated by the rapid development of tooth decay among the growing children on the Pacific Islands during the time trader ships made calls for dried copra when its price was high for several months. This was paid for in 90 per cent white flour and refined sugar and not over 10 per cent in cloth and clothing. When the price of copra reduced from $400 a ton to $4 a ton, the trader ships stopped calling and tooth decay stopped when the people went back to their native diet. I saw many such individuals with teeth with open cavities in which the tooth decay had ceased to be active.[54]

Price closely studied how various cultures prepared their plant foods and extensively documented the methods needed to make most grains and plants palatable and nontoxic. These heavily complex traditional rituals of soaking, sprouting, and fermenting are necessary to remove the many natural toxins

---

54 Price. *Nutrition and Physical Degeneration*, p. 311.

that exist in plant foods, and they allow the body to absorb the nutrients in these foods. In the high time preference age of fiat, nobody has time for these rituals, and instead, the majority prefer the industrial food-processing methods which rely on maximizing the sugar and palatable ingredients at the expense of nutrients.

Price contributed massively to our understanding of nutrition and health, but like Menger and Mises in economics, his teachings are largely ignored by the paper-pushing, government-employed bureaucrats pretending to be scientists. Not coincidentally, listening to these government employees and ignoring Price has come at a devastating cost not just to the health of individuals but also in bloated healthcare spending, which has saddled productive citizens with onerous tax burdens. With a better understanding of nutritional science, resources currently dedicated to diabetes and other obesity-related diseases could instead be applied to more productive endeavors.

Price's research shows that the trends most responsible for malnutrition, obesity, and some diseases of modern civilization are directly related to the economic realities of the twentieth century. The nutritional decline Price documented happened around the turn of the twentieth century, which, coincidentally, was when the modern world economy moved away from the hard money of the gold standard and toward easy government money.

It is unquestionable that a large part of the problem of modern industrial diets lies in the availability of modern high-powered machinery capable of efficiently and quickly processing plants into hyperpalatable junk food. Yet, given everything discussed above, it is very difficult to argue that the fiat money experiment of the last century has not massively exacerbated the impact of modern industrial foods by heavily subsidizing them, and subsidizing the miseducation of generations of nutritionists and doctors who promote them. On a hard money standard, we would still have these industrial foods. But without fiat subsidies, they would not have been so ubiquitous in modern diets. Fiat has facilitated the growth of the managerial state and the production of mass propaganda "research." Fiat has given us unscientific dietary guidelines tailored to normalize the consumption of industrialized food sludge. Fiat has paid credentialed types in white coats to warn against the dangers of healthy, wholesome, nonindustrial (but low profit-margin) foods, like meat. In the absence of this fiat-driven dynamic, most people's understanding of nutrition would be very different and far more similar to the traditions of their ancestors, which revolved heavily around animal foods.

Fiat Soils

The heavily discounted future that the fiat system incentivizes, discussed in the previous chapter, is not only reflected in the increased indebtedness of capital markets, but also anywhere people can trade off the future for the present, most notably the natural environment and the soil.

As individuals' time preference rises and they start to discount the future more heavily, they are less likely to value the maintenance of a healthy future state for their natural environment and soil. Consider the effect this would have on farmers: the higher a farmer's time preference, the more they will discount the future health of their soil, and the more likely they are to care about maximizing their short-term profits. Indeed, this is exactly what we find with soil depletion leading up to the 1930s, the time of Price's writing.

The introduction of modern industrial production methods, thanks to the utilization of hydrocarbon energy, has allowed humans to increase the intensity with which they utilize land, and consequently the number of crops they grow on a given patch of soil. The story of increasing agricultural productivity is often touted as one of the great successes of the modern world, but the heavy cost it has imposed on the soil goes largely unmentioned. It is very difficult to grow plants on most agricultural topsoil in the world today without the addition of artificial, industrially produced chemical fertilizers. The nutritional content of the food grown on such soil is steadily degrading compared to food grown on rich soil.

Price's study begins with a discussion of the quality of soil in modern societies, which he found was quickly degrading. The degradation of farmland, Price found, was causing severe nutrient deficiencies in food. Price published his book in the 1930s, and he had pinpointed the few decades prior as a time of particular decline in the nutrient content of land. While he does not explicitly draw a connection with fiat money, the development is perfectly consistent with the analysis of fiat and time preference discussed in Chapters 5 and 7.

Soil, being the productive asset from which all food comes, is capital. And as fiat encourages the consumption of capital, it will encourage the consumption of soil. We can understand the drive of industrial agriculture as the high time preference stripping of productive capital from the environment. Heavily plowed industrial agriculture is an object lesson in high time preference, as is well understood by farmers worldwide, and well-articulated on the website of the Natural Resource Conservation Service of the U.S. Department of Agriculture:

> The plow is a potent tool of agriculture for the same reason that it has degraded productivity. Plowing turns over soil, mixes it with air, and stimulates the decomposition of organic matter. The rapid decomposition of organic matter releases a flush of nutrients that stimulates crop growth. But over time, plowing diminishes the supply of soil organic matter and associated soil properties, including water holding capacity, nutrient holding capacity, mellow tilth, resistance to erosion, and a diverse biological community.[55]

The work of Alan Savory on the topic of soil depletion is very important here. The Savory Institute has been working on reforestation and soil regeneration across the world with spectacular success. Their secret? Unleashing large numbers of grazing animals on depleted soil to graze on whatever shrubs they can find and fertilize it with their manure. The results, visible on their website,[56] speak for themselves and clearly illustrate a strong case for keeping soil healthy by holistically managing the grazing of large mammals. Agricultural crop production, on the other hand, quickly depletes the soil of

55   "Breaking Land: The Loss of Organic Matter." *Soil Quality for Environmental Health.* 19 Sep. 2011. Web.
56   "Holistic Management." *Savory Institute.* Web. 3 Oct. 2021.

its vital nutrients, making it fallow, and requiring extensive fertilizer input to be productive. This explains why preindustrial societies worldwide usually rotated their land from farming to grazing. After a few years of farming a plot whose output had begun to decline, the land was abandoned to grazing animals, and farmers moved to another plot. After that one was exhausted, farmers moved on to another plot, or returned to the earlier one if it had recovered. Cattle grazing increases the soil's ability to absorb rainwater, allowing it to become rich with organic matter. After a few years of grazing, the land becomes ready once again for crop farming.

The implication here is very clear: low time preference approaches to managing land would prioritize the long-term health of the soil, and thus entail the management of cropping along with the grazing of animals. A high time preference approach, on the other hand, would prioritize an immediate gain and exploit the soil to its fullest with little regard for long-term consequences. The mass production of crops, and their increased availability in our diet in the twentieth century, can also be seen as a consequence of rising time preference. The low time preference approach involves the production of a lot of meat, which usually has small profit margins, while the high time preference approach would favor the mass production of plant crops, which can be optimized and scaled drastically with the introduction of industrial methods, allowing for significant profit margins.

As industrialization introduced heavy machinery to plow the soil, and as fiat money discounted the utility of the future, the traditional balance between crop farming and grazing was destroyed and replaced with intensive agriculture that depletes the soil very quickly. Rather than regenerate the soil naturally with cattle manure, industrial fertilizers are applied in ever-increasing amounts, often with devastating unintended consequences. For example, the impact of industrial fertilizer runoff in the Mississippi River Delta and the Gulf of Mexico is well documented.[57] Industrial food conglomerates chasing quick profits saturate the land with chemical fertilizers, which in

---

57 "Farm Runoff in Mississippi River Floodwater Fuels Dead Zone in Gulf." *PBS News Hour*. 18 May 2011. Web.

turn enter the Mississippi River and kill fish, cause algae blooms, and even make the water unfit for human consumption.

Industrial farming allows farmers to strip nutrients from their soil rapidly, maximizing output in the first few years, at the expense of the long-term health of the soil. Fertilizers allow this present orientation to appear relatively costless in the future, since depleted soil can still be made fertile with industrial fertilizers. After a century of industrial farming, it is clear that this trade-off was very costly, as the human toll of industrial farming grows larger and clearer. By contrast, maintaining healthy soil through rotating cattle grazing and crop farming will offer less reward in the short run, but it will maintain the health of the soil in the long run. A heavily plowed field producing heavily subsidized fiat foods would allow the farmer a large short-term profit, while careful management of the soil would allow the farmer a more sustainable income into the future. Just because industrialization allows for the quick depletion of the soil, it does not mean that people are obliged to engage in it any more than access to cliffs should compel people to jump off them. Understanding the distortions of fiat and high time preference helps us understand why this style of agriculture has become so popular in spite of its massively detrimental effect on humans and their soil.

It is remarkable to find that within the field of nutrition, and without any reference to economic or monetary policy, Price had identified the first third of the twentieth century as having witnessed immense soil degradation and a decline in the richness of nutrients in the food that farms produced. The great cultural critic Jacques Barzun, in his seminal history of the West, *From Dawn to Decadence*,[58] precisely identified 1914 as the year in which the decline of Western civilization began, when art began its shift toward the less sophisticated modern forms, and when political and social cultures shifted from liberalism to liberality. Like Price, Barzun made no mention of the shift in monetary standards and the link it might have to the degradation he identified. In the work of these two great scholars,

---

58   Barzun, Jacques. *From Dawn to Decadence: 500 Years of Cultural Life, 1500 to the Present*. New York: HarperCollins, 2000. Print.

prime experts in their respective fields, we find compelling evidence of a shift toward more present-orientated behavior across the Western world in the early twentieth century.

As with his architecture, art, and family, fiat man's food quality is constantly declining, as well-marketed, addictive, and toxic fiat "food" replaces the healthy, nourishing, traditional foods of his ancestors. The soil from which life and civilization spring continues to get depleted, and its essential nutrients are replaced by petroleum-derived chemical fertilizers marketed as soil by fiat.

Chapter 9

Fiat Science

The last chapter examined how fiat affects the human body by distorting food markets. This chapter will examine how fiat's influence on markets for education and science have influenced the human mind. Fiat money allows governments to play a pervasive role in these markets, at all levels, from primary education to cutting-edge scientific research. By suspending the normal workings of the market economy in education and science, government can decree who gets to be a teacher and what passes for science. Education no longer needs to meet the needs and aspirations of the student or help them succeed in life. Instead, education in government-run, government-subsidized schools need only meet the political goals of the source of fiat. Fiat's influence on scientific research undermines open inquiry; scientific truth no longer stands on its own, open to scrutiny and debate. What passes for science in today's fiat world has descended into blindly followed mantras that cannot be questioned by anyone who wants to be called a scientist.

Fiat Schools

There are few causes that sound more deserving of fiat funding than children's education. In the first decade and a half or so of life, humans aren't able to provide for themselves sufficiently and must rely on the provision, protection, guidance, and education of older people. These years are critical for forming the habits and temperament that will shape a person's life. A good education can open a world of possibilities, whereas truancy and lack of guidance and education could ruin a person for life. Letting a child's entire future hinge on whether their parents are able to provide them an education in their early years appears like a dangerous proposition for society, as it could lead to a large number of misguided, uneducated, unskilled, unproductive, and dangerous citizens. With government able to effectively conjure money at will, there seem no apparent downsides to spending some of that money to educate children.

Like most ideas financed by fiat, free public schooling only appears good when ignoring the many unintended consequences and unseen effects it has on the very people it is meant to help. As funding for education becomes centralized, flowing from the government's money printer rather than the children's parents, the providers of education have more of an incentive to appease their funders rather than their beneficiaries. As funding education becomes a matter of policy, the process inevitably becomes politicized, providing incentives for the providers of the service to toe the political line that the fiat funders prefer, relegating the interests of the children to an afterthought.

As funding is enshrined in law and provided by an authority with virtually limitless money, there is little need for the providers to worry about the quality of the education they provide to students. In a free market, that accountability is enforced through customers walking out of a business and bankrupting it if it fails to meet their needs. In most of the world, students are required by law to attend schools and/or are forced to attend a particular school based on where they live. This completely undermines parents' ability to hold schools accountable by leaving a failing school for a better one. Public schools cannot go out of business, regardless of how poor student outcomes become, and teachers almost never get fired thanks to all-powerful teachers' unions.

Since children's education is the perfect kind of story to elicit popular approval for increased government financing, government-run schools have operated with virtually no limitations on funding and with no accountability for teachers and administrators. Infinite cash for public education is a curse, not a blessing. Public schools operate in an alternative universe where scarcity does not exist, which prevents accountability from taking hold and allows producers to get away with vast incompetence.

Corey DeAngelis, a scholar and education policy researcher, has successfully highlighted how catastrophic the impacts of fiat education have been on schoolchildren. Astonishingly, DeAngelis finds that the average private school tuition in Washington, DC, is $23,959,[59] while the average DC government school spends $31,280 per student. Even though they spend 81.3% as much as is spent on public school students, private school students still significantly outperform those from public schools. Clearly, the issue is not in the lack of funding but in the way that funding is used. Money spent by parents holding schools accountable, i.e., private schools, will be far more productively deployed than fiat from government printers with no opportunity cost. Private schools will go out of business if parents decide that their kids aren't getting a good education. No similar mechanism exists to enforce accountability in government-run schools.

This is a very common theme in the world of fiat: the distortion of basic incentives is often worse for society than the inflation increased government spending causes. Very often, fiat's most catastrophic effect is not price increases but the myriad distortions—and outright destruction—of incentives it brings to many areas of human life. In government-run institutions, fiat leads people to operate as if their agency or office is immune from the ironclad economic laws of nature. The consequences of living in this fiat-enabled delusion are often severe.

---

59 "District of Columbia Private Schools by Tuition Cost." *Private School Review*. Web. 3 Oct. 2020.

DeAngelis has compellingly advocated for an important economic reform to public education: instead of spending government money on public schools which are protected from market competition, governments should simply hand the money to parents and allow these parents the freedom to choose for themselves where their children go to school. Unsurprisingly, his ideas are met with vehement opposition by the many vested interests in the educational system whose jobs and privileges depend on collecting government fiat directly, without having to be accountable to the students and their parents.

The most vivid example I know of the economic distortion caused by public financing of education comes from Egypt, where an entire private education system takes place in the afternoon, where the teachers are paid a decent wage and the students pay a decent tuition fee, leading to productive learning. A friend told me that in some cases, entrepreneurs would rent the public schools to host the classes, leading to the surreal situation of the same students and the same teacher meeting in the same classroom twice on the same day. In the morning, the government is paying and the teacher is getting negligible pay, and so no education happens. But in the afternoon, in the privately organized schooling system, actual education takes place.

Fiat Universities

Fiat's distortion of the university system is similar to that of the grade school system, with the added consequence of ruining entire educational disciplines, notably the hard sciences, with disastrous economic impacts. The most common misconception about modern universities is that they are private, when they are almost all reliant on government financing. Governments provide universities with a sizable portion of their income in the form of research funding. Perhaps more importantly, governments provide students with subsidized low-interest loans to attend university, heavily skewing young adults' choice in favor of attending university and causing a large misdirection of resources in that direction. That tuition costs have risen in concert with larger subsidies for a college education is no coincidence.

After a century, it is fair to say fiat has successfully destroyed the modern university as a center of learning and research, transforming a once noble institution into a make-work welfare program for nerds, a highly over-priced credential mill, an inescapable debt trap, a country club experience, a political indoctrination camp, and a corporate advertising agency. He who pays the piper calls the tune, and as students are not the main source of income for universities, they are increasingly turning into the product universities offer to their various governmental and private sponsors, rather than the consumers.

In a free market where universities had to compete for tuition fees, universities would have to remain moored to the real world and receptive to students' need to learn useful skills and become productive members of society. Universities that offer students a good education would see these alumni graduate to achieve high earnings in their professional careers. This would attract young students to these universities, and the alumni would donate to the university, helping it prosper and advance. A free market would ensure that universities remain true to their mission of educating and advancing knowledge, because if they diverged from it, they would be quickly punished by market forces. In other words, universities that do not offer superior education would become unattractive to potential students, and alumni would have neither the means nor the desire to donate.

University research would also have to remain relevant to the needs of the real world in a free market, as universities could only keep financing projects that offer significant material benefits to the world. Even highly theoretical and abstract research must demonstrate some real-world relevance for universities and their donors in order to remain funded. Fiat upends this reality. With financing for universities increasingly dependent on the judgment of bureaucrats with access to an infinite credit printer, the discipline of the free market is replaced with the whims and desires of politicians, bureaucrats, and the hoard of administrators and deans that have multiplied on university campuses. Success for a university is no longer primarily based on meeting the students' demand to learn productive skills, but instead, on satisfying the wishes of the bureaucrats who finance the university.

Altering the incentive structure in the higher education industry has led
to the perversion of the university's purpose. Educational excellence, free and
open inquiry, acquiring the knowledge necessary to be free—none of this is
important for the modern university. These honorable ideals have been sup-
planted by irrelevant pontificating, unproductive waste, and political indoctrination. The only thing today's university students are learning well is the
ideology of allegiance to government, and universities actively export this
same ideology to society at large.

With students afforded cheap credit to engage in university education,
the opportunity cost of spending four years in university is reduced significantly by being deferred to a future that fiat money increasingly discounts.
Large subsidies and economic thinking that discount the future mean universities don't need to worry as much about delivering quality education. In
such a system, students don't treat going to college like it is an economic
decision. Instead, higher education is merely the next stop on the government-approved path of life. This thinking insulates colleges from the basic
market signals that otherwise would enforce accountability. As a result, university education has increasingly changed from an investment in a capital
good into a consumption good.

Universities increasingly resemble country clubs, where students borrow money to live like aristocrats, doing little work while partying, socializing, and enjoying themselves. The heavy opportunity cost of university
only becomes apparent when one looks at the future, something newly
graduated high school kids are not accustomed to doing. Instead, most
of them will realize all too late that they squandered their precious time.
Student loan debt accumulated in university country clubs cannot be dis-
charged, even if the debtor files for bankruptcy, and students will spend the
rest of their lives paying for the fun they had when they could have been
learning. In the United States, it's not uncommon for college graduates to
carry more than $100,000 in student debt, bills they will still be paying in
their thirties and forties. Instead of beginning their adult lives by earning
and accumulating capital and deferring the country club experience until
they achieve financial independence and can afford it, young adults are

getting the country club experience first and spending the rest of their lives working to pay it off.

Fiat Academics

The role of government in universities increased drastically in the United States in the 1930s after the Great Depression. With increased economic problems engulfing universities, and with fiat allowing government practically limitless spending, governments naturally began encroaching on universities' financial and intellectual output, particularly as governments needed the help of universities in determining how to manage the modern fiat economy and direct spending toward achieving government goals.

Perhaps the most pernicious effect of the fiatization of the modern university is the destruction of the scientific method. What passes for science now is a mix of government propaganda, corporate advertising, make-work welfare programs for nerds, and research papers that amount to meaning-free irrelevant gibberish. This sad state of affairs persists and survives because government intervention has removed the market test for success.

With funding for research primarily coming from government bureaucrats, academics don't need to worry about real-world, profitable applications of their work. Irrelevant research bears no cost for the researcher or his institution. And with universities afforded an effective subsidy through subsidized loans for their consumers, the market test for success is removed, and universities, and the geeks populating their offices, are free to drift into a world of insignificance and corruption—a world with little regard for truth. The most obvious manifestation of this is the mushrooming of entire fields and departments specialized in producing completely inconsequential and incoherent noises and marketing them as scholarship.

What passes for humanities in the modern university has degenerated into an endless sea of angry grievances and rabid victimology, consisting almost entirely of politically correct platitudes and zero substance. The end result is heaps of graduates with zero marketable skills but a strong talent for finding ways to take offense at everything. These departments continue to grow, and the professors in them continue to get paid, because they face no real market test and can continue to secure financing from the world's biggest money printer while railing against inconsequential, imaginary, and historical evils.

Unsurprisingly, these departments are heavily populated with semiliterate intellectual midgets of the Marxist variety, as that ideology is perfectly conducive to the furthering of government power and the anointing of a parasitic, unproductive class to control the lives of the productive. For all of the nonsense that Marxists spout about oppression and opposition to the power of capital, it's worth remembering that Marx's entire worldview rested on the need for governments to take over the function of credit and money creation and for a revolutionary vanguard to be in charge of all economic and social decisions for society at large. It makes perfect sense that parasites who live off government money pillaging the world via inflation continue to promote this criminal ideology even after all the massive death and destruction it has brought the world. For all the victimhood and self-righteous chips on their shoulders, Marxists are just the useful idiots and foot soldiers for fiat money printing.

Entire books could be written about the degeneration of humanities education in the modern university, but for our purposes, we will simply invoke one highly illustrative story. A physicist by the name of Alan Sokal had long suspected that most humanities' scholarship was nonsense, so he chose to test this theory himself by submitting a paper of incomprehensible gibberish for publication at a leading journal of critical studies.[60] The paper was accepted for publication. These are the same journals in which publication is necessary for academics to keep their jobs and advance in their career. By publishing deliberately fashionable gibberish, Sokal showed us the true nature of fiat academia: nonsense devoid of meaning, churned out by the bucketload to tick bureaucrats' boxes.

---

60   Sokal, Alan D. "Transgressing the Boundaries: Toward a Transformative Hermeneutics of Quantum Gravity," *Social Text*, no. 46/47, 1996, p. 217. Print. Crossref, doi: 10.2307/466856.

Fiat Science

Scholars in the hard sciences are accustomed to laughing at their colleagues in the humanities, but they should remember that both of these broad fields of scholarship come from the same universities, financed by the same fiat printers, subject to the same incentive structures. There is nothing inherent in humanities that makes them liable to degenerate into nonsensical politically motivated drivel. Rather, the economic and institutional framework into which they are placed enables the degeneration, and the humanities share this framework with the natural sciences. Why would the same universities giving tenure to innumerate Marxists who write fashionable nonsense be expected to give tenure to genuine scholars in the hard sciences? One cannot help but wonder whether the natural sciences have been similarly compromised, and whether the reason they aren't as derided as the humanities is that their sophisticated methods make the nonsense less obvious to the nonspecialist.

To answer this question, we must look at the root of the problem: the academic publishing industry. With government spending an increasingly important part of universities' budgets, the freedom of each university to determine for itself how to allocate its own resources to better meet the needs of its students is compromised in favor of central planners who decide on financing, credit, and benefits for the entire university system, which is now protected from the consequences of market competition. But how can these planners allocate resources and assess the success of different universities, programs, and departments?

Over time, the answer to this question increasingly came to be publications in academic journals. Successful researchers are those who get their papers published in the most important journals, and university funding came to heavily reflect that. Consequently, academics' career prospects became increasingly tied to publication in academic journals, to the point where teaching skills are an afterthought in hiring decisions. Students the world over complain about professors who are unable and unwilling to put effort into teaching, but most universities do not and cannot care about this because the students are not the customers they are seeking to please as long as government grant money and subsidized student loans continue.

The fixation with academic publication has led to the complete corruption of the academic publication industry, and professors worldwide complain about the current abomination. Academic publishers are the kingmakers of the entire university system, as their journals are the basis for determining who gets hired, promoted, and tenured in their university. Academic publications have been consolidated into a handful of academic publishing houses that are far more akin to a cartel than beacons of knowledge. If you think the cartel comparison is hyperbolic, consider the case of the late Aaron Swartz. Swartz was an American computer programmer who was arrested, threatened with prison time, and ultimately driven to suicide after he was caught downloading journal articles from JSTOR, a digital archive of academic publications.

As long as university funding is tied to publication in supposedly prestigious, accredited, and ranked journals, these journals can exploit the labor of professors who need them to secure their livelihoods. Academic journals do not pay academics for writing articles, nor do they pay them for reviewing articles or editing journals. In fact, many journals even charge academics for publishing their articles! The entire production of the journal costs the publishers approximately zero dollars, and yet, these journals are sold back to the universities at exorbitant prices, as is access to their articles online. As academic gatekeepers, publications determine who gets published and, thus, who gets promoted and who gets funded. Academic publishers have successfully maneuvered themselves to become the prime beneficiaries of the fiat education system.

The facade of relevance and coherence was easier for modern academic journals to maintain before the internet, when producing physical copies and corresponding between editors and journals cost time and money. The occasionally expensive paper used for printing might have made the exorbitant prices university libraries paid for these journals appear justified. But as the internet has practically reduced the cost of producing journals close to zero, and access to academic articles has become mostly digital, the costs of these journals have gone up, not down. Universities now pay thousands of dollars to access a digital journal, and an individual needs to pay more than twenty dollars to access a single article, all when the publisher has incurred almost no cost for publication, since the writing, editing, and reviewing was done with modern academia's professor slaves.

All along, the content of the journals has continued to deteriorate to the point where it is predominantly unreadable academic masturbation with no link to the real world, which nonetheless adheres to the correct political, grammatical, and methodological guidelines needed to keep up the pretense that actual scholarship is taking place. Almost nobody normal or productive in the real world ever bothers reading academic journal articles, nor do they have any reason to. The only real readership of most journals consists of the academics in the very narrow field looking to build on the papers in it so they can get published. Rather than communicate important ideas to the world and advance society's understanding of the state of the art in modern fields of research, academic publication has been reduced to a circle jerk which only has consequences for the academic careers of those in the circle.

For an academic to publish in the journals that guarantee them a job, their language and methods need to be so niche, arcane, esoteric, and absurd that their work would be incomprehensible for most readers. They tailor to the demands of journal editors who are completely detached from the real world. Publication in academic journals is so agonizingly time-consuming with endless rounds of review and quibbling back and forth—all for no discernible benefit to anyone. As you make the tenth nitpicking revision to the same paragraph in the eighteenth month of peer review, it begins to dawn on you that you are wasting your life typing something nobody will read or benefit from, like Jack Nicholson's character in *The Shining*, who had lost his mind spending many months at a typewriter working on a novel, only for his wife to discover all his work had consisted of repeatedly typing the same single sentence over and over for hundreds of pages.

Fiat academia is the enormously wasteful redirection of the talents of masses of intelligent and conscientious people into the production of nonsense nobody will ever read. Being able to come up with something useful and intelligent to say about the world requires being up to date with the real world and its developments. Creating valuable research requires constantly evolving with the times. Rather than scholars being involved in the real world, where their knowledge is applied, today's scholars are isolated in ivory towers, working on increasingly obscure and irrelevant minutia, constructing elaborate mental Rube Goldberg machines purely to impress other socially isolated individuals. Anyone who reads an academic's article does so in the same way a parent goes to their child's soccer game. The draw is not the entertainment value of watching your son and his fat eight-year-old friends attempt to play soccer; the draw is your love for your son and your desire to encourage him and make him feel like he's significant. In private, and sometimes in public, academics will joke about the complete lack of relevance of their work to the real world, and how they need to add a few lines to the conclusion of each study to attempt to shoehorn some relevance. Almost all academics understand this and joke about it, as the only academics who survive in the field are those that have accepted the lack of relevance of their work. Those who cannot accept this life of irrelevance will leave to work in the real world, liberated from indentured servitude to multinational academic paper mills.

When you understand how academic publications operate, you start to read them in an entirely different light. Rather than a place for our smartest minds to engage in discourse about important things, you start to see academic publications as primarily aimed at helping the author (and enriching the publisher). An assessment of the economics of academic research would clearly explain why this is the case. Academic research today is not a product of a free market; it is a product of a central plan, decided by a committee. It suffers from the problems of economic production familiar to anyone unfortunate enough to have lived under socialist regimes or fortunate enough to have read Mises's monumental works on socialism.

In his excellent book *The Economic Laws of Scientific Research*, biochemist Terence Kealey provides a masterful counternarrative to the prevailing wisdom in fiat academia that science needs public funding.[61] Kealey observes

---

61   Kealey, Terence. *The Economic Laws of Scientific Research*. London: Macmillan Press, 1996. Print.

how private enterprise and a free market in scientific research spurred the industrial revolution that happened in the eighteenth and nineteenth centuries in Great Britain. Government funding simply did not exist during that period, and would only emerge during World War I, which, coincidentally, was the same time Britain went off the gold standard.

In a free market for science, free of the intervention of fiat, research is intimately tied to the needs of the market, and any misdirection of resources results in a loss for the investor, either forcing him to learn his lesson or eventually bankrupting him. Either way, what is wasteful will cease. But with a fiat standard, the waste can continue for as long as the government's currency can be devalued.

Government scientific and research bodies are central planning boards, able to decree by their fiat what is legitimate science, which researchers get funded, which scholars get to call themselves scholars, and which get banished as heretics. Like central planners in socialist economies, as Mises explained, these bureaucrats are unable to perform a rational economic calculation with their resources, as they do not own the resources they allocate and cannot estimate the correct opportunity costs for their different uses. There is no real feedback from the market to the decision-makers in the form of profits for productive applications of capital and losses for wasteful applications. Without the feedback mechanism of profit and loss, any bureaucracy is deaf, dumb, and blind. Whereas in the production of agricultural commodities, central planning boards led to the creation of catastrophic shortages and surpluses, in the context of scientific research, these boards have led to an enormous shortage in proper scientific research. Instead, government intervention has left us a glut of largely pointless research papers.

Without a real market test of research decisions, the bureaucrats must assess contributions using imperfect metrics. Free from the test of the market, researchers must focus on the metrics themselves, and eventually, only the best at achieving these metrics succeed. The goal is to get published, not to arrive at important conclusions. Scholars want to publish as much as possible to get more funding, while journals want to publish as much as possible to sell more subscriptions to universities. Research funding bodies also want to support as much research as possible, as that allows them to draw on larger budgets and there is no real opportunity cost. Without the real budget constraints that would be enforced by a hard money, this academic system can only head in the direction of ever-increasing amounts of research papers and ever-decreasing relevance and usefulness.

John Ioannidis has published some very compelling research to show why the majority of scientific research findings are likely false, and his conclusions are intimately tied to the fiat system's decoupling of science from market incentives and feedback.[62] With such strong incentives to publish, the likelihood of a false result getting published increases drastically. With the enormous number of experiments that can be carried out, only the experiments with desirable results get published. With tolerable margins of error around results, there will inevitably be a growing number of scientific papers published with false findings.

Testing novel hypotheses that can attract media attention is a good way to get published, and testing many of these will inevitably lead to many statistically significant results even when the studied relationship does not exist. With the ever-increasing number of scientific journals out there, there is always a market for papers. Perhaps the most profound problem with the incentive structure of fiat science was captured by the remarks of Brian Nosek: "There is no cost to getting things wrong. The cost is not getting them published."[63] With little opposition to getting things published, one would expect most research findings to be irrelevant and wrong. Anyone who follows science news in mainstream media with a decent memory will notice how "scientists found" that pretty much every single thing on the face of the earth causes cancer and also protects from cancer. The requirements to

62   Ioannidis, John P. A. "Why Most Published Research Findings Are False." *PLoS Medicine*, vol. 2, no. 8, 30 Aug. 2005, p. e124. Print. Crossref, doi:10.1371/journal. pmed.0020124.

63   Nosek, Brian. "Unreliable Research: Trouble at the Lab." *The Economist*. 18 Oct. 2013. Web.

produce a study that implicates coffee, meat, wine, or electronics with causing cancer is so low that it is equally plausible to find an opposite conclusion.
Any sponsor of a study can "find" the result they want by hiring enough creative researchers.

The Science Industrial Complex

Science inevitably becomes very ripe for capture by special interests when
funding is removed from the realm of market competition. The government
boards handing out funding, loans, and titles are made up of scholars who
can assess the work at hand, an arrangement that places the universities and
the scholars in charge of their own regulation. Imagine the same governing
structure of fiat science was applied to the production of cars. A govern-
ment-appointed board staffed by car producers licenses car producers, judges
their output and rewards them accordingly, and assigns the cars to consumers. Clearly such an arrangement would be in favor of the car producers and
not the car consumers, who have no ability to influence car production with
their preferences, choices, and purchasing decisions.

With this institutional arrangement, government agencies become ripe
for capture by private interests who stand to gain enormously from having
"The Science" issue decrees in their favor. It is only natural to expect to see
significant rent-seeking and well-funded attempts to influence and control
governments' relationship with scientific researchers.

In his farewell address, U.S. President Dwight Eisenhower warned his
countrymen about the dangers of the emergence of a military-industrial
complex, and these remarks have become fairly well known today. Far less
known are the remarks that immediately followed, warning of what may be
called the scientific-industrial complex:

> The prospect of domination of the nation's scholars by Federal employ-
> ment, project allocations, and the power of money is ever present and is
> gravely to be regarded. Yet, in holding scientific research and discovery
> in respect, as we should, we must also be alert to the equal and opposite

danger that public policy could itself become the captive of a scientific technological elite.[64]

The Science Says

Science is a name given to a systematic method for asking questions and experimenting to answer these questions. Science relies on demonstrable experimentation precisely because it relies on the word of nobody. Under the fiat standard, science has instead become a set worldview with pre-scribed statements and commandments. When the practice of science and all universities are captured by a single authority with infinite fiat at its dis-posal, the experiments are turned into ritual exercises carried out behind closed doors, whose results are to be believed by relying on the author-ity of the experimenters and the bodies that regulate them. The scientific method is perverted to its exact opposite when government channels relay the supposed results. Rather than a process, "Science" has become an ide-ology or religion.

One indication of the state of disrepair in which modern science finds itself is the normalization of the completely absurd phrase "the science says," very commonly repeated by academics, journalists, politicians, and the pub-lic at large. The use of this phrase indicates an understanding of science as if it is a predetermined list of unquestionable and immutable pronouncements and declarations. But science is not a sentient being capable of saying things, and science cannot refer to a set of institutions or scientists' conclusions, no matter how much they promote them, or how much fiat they have at their disposal. The implications of this bait and switch have been ruinous for sci-ence as well as for society at large, in various fields.

Another powerful example of the depths of the degradation and corrup-tion of modern academic sciences comes from studying the science of nutri-tion, mentioned in the previous chapter.

---

64   Eisenhower, Dwight. "Farewell Address." *Dwight D. Eisenhower Presidential Library, Museum & Boyhood Home.* 17 Jan. 1961. Web. 3 Oct. 2021.

Fiat Nutrition Science

The research certain activists and evangelicals use to tout the benefits of meat avoidance has always been based on poor statistical techniques interpreted with cavalierly motivated reasoning which would be laughed out of any freshman statistics class. The main problem with these studies is that they are observational studies, and there are always many confounding factors to take into account. The most popular studies promoted by Seventh-day Adventists focus on comparing Seventh-day Adventists to the general population. They find that since Seventh-day Adventists are healthier, reduced meat consumption must be responsible. But that ignores that Seventh-day Adventists also avoid smoking and drinking, are more affluent than the general population and thus able to live in cleaner and healthier environments, and usually have a stronger sense of community, all of which are factors that are very helpful for longevity. These studies also rely on self-reporting of food intake, and it is well established that this is not an accurate way of assessing food intake, as people generally report what they would like to have eaten, not what they have actually eaten, particularly when the religious group to which you are reporting has a strong stigma around the consumption of meats.

More general observational studies, such as the terrible reports bureaucrats at the World Health Organization rely on, find that people who eat more meat suffer from more diseases than people who eat less meat and therefore conclude that meat must be to blame. But on a population level, the consumption of meat is very strongly correlated with the consumption of all other kinds of foods. In other words, the same people who eat a lot of meat also eat a lot of sugars, grains, flour, and all manner of industrial sludge. A proper statistical observational study would try to control for these factors, but antimeat studies never do that because they are based on trying to validate religious visions and not the scientific method. Yet, even an observational study that controls for many factors cannot be viewed as definitive.

The John Maynard Keynes of nutrition science is Ancel Keys: a man as politically skilled as he is intellectually vacuous, a man who knew how to play politics to serve the special interests that have popularized and mandated his juvenile and borderline criminal "research" as gospel in universities around the world. Making nutrition science a closed guild protected by the state, tasked with peddling state propaganda, has allowed it to be easily captured by special interest industries who use it to promote their products unopposed, as all dissenting voices were silenced and marginalized by not having access to the government's printing presses. Nina Teicholz's modern book *The Big Fat Surprise* offers a detailed accounting of the extent of corruption in modern science that has made the world eat so much poison.[65]

The work of Ancel Keys and many generations of Harvard "scientists" was the Trojan horse with which agro-industrial businesses managed to inject their poisonous industrial sludge into the bodies of billions around the world, resulting in the disastrous consequence of the spread of diabetes, obesity, cancer, heart disease, and many other fatal ailments which most people accept as a normal part of life, completely oblivious to the fact that they are only a normal part of a life spent consuming fiat foods. One of the most shocking and discomforting realizations of one's life is that Keys and the scientists who peddled his ridiculous research have likely been responsible for more unnatural deaths around the world than anyone, even more than all communist regimes combined.

Keys's ridiculous research was based on travels he did around Europe after World War II. He collected unreliable data on the consumption of meat across seven countries, and then plotted that against rates of heart disease. After inexplicably eliminating France from the data, Keys found a correlation between heart disease and meat consumption, which he interpreted as evidence that meat causes heart disease, and from that was born the famous Seven Country Study, popularized to the heavens by mass media and mass education as the definitive and final word on nutrition. Conveniently enough, Keys had also ignored data from fifteen countries that would have made his study show different results. That France has low rates of heart disease in spite of consuming large quantities of meat is still viewed as a paradox

---

65   Teicholz, Nina. *The Big Fat Surprise: Why Butter, Meat, and Cheese Belong in a Healthy Diet*. New York: Simon & Schuster, 2014. Print.

by modern nutritionists, when there is nothing paradoxical about it except if one buys Keys's unsubstantiated conclusions.

Keys did not stop at cherry-picking countries but also used the consumption of margarine, a toxic industrial waste, as part of the consumption of fat along with healthy and essential animal fats. With this simple trick, the increasing health problems caused by margarine were attributed to animal fats, helping lend credence to his conclusion that saturated fat was the problem, and resorting to processed plant oils was the solution.

Keys also popularized the ridiculous idea that a Mediterranean diet is one low in animal fats and high in plant fats, an idea that has been used to heavily market poisonous seed oils (like "heart-healthy" canola oil which no human should feed to their dog, let alone eat). Keys's travels came after the destruction of Europe during World War II, at a time when people were severely impoverished and relied heavily on olive oil. But the people of the Mediterranean, like all *Homo sapiens*, rely on animal fats primarily for cooking, resorting to plant-based fats after calamities like World War II or Harvard nutritional advice have befallen them. Teicholz shows countless sources illustrating how Mediterranean diets relied heavily on animal fats for cooking, as the basis of the diet, with olive oil used primarily for soap, lighting, skin, hair, and food dressing. Even after many years of Teicholz publishing her book, and many other researchers pointing out the absurdity of Keys's conclusions, fiat science and all its official organs continue to tell people to eschew animal fats for highly profitable processed industrial waste.

Beyond just the vilification of natural fats in favor of toxic industrial waste, Harvard University played a big role in the mass promotion of sugar. *The New York Times* reports:

> The documents show that in 1964, John Hickson, a top sugar industry executive, discussed a plan with others in the industry to shift public opinion "through our research and information and legislative programs."
>
> At the time, studies had begun pointing to a relationship between high-sugar diets and the country's high rates of heart disease. At the same

time, other scientists, including the prominent Minnesota physiologist Ancel Keys, were investigating a competing theory that it was saturated fat and dietary cholesterol that posed the biggest risk for heart disease.

Mr. Hickson proposed countering the alarming findings on sugar with industry-funded research. "Then we can publish the data and refute our detractors," he wrote.

In 1965, Mr. Hickson enlisted the Harvard researchers to write a review that would debunk the anti-sugar studies. He paid them a total of $6,500, the equivalent of $49,000 today. Mr. Hickson selected the papers for them to review and made it clear he wanted the result to favor sugar.

Harvard's Dr. Hegsted reassured the sugar executives. "We are well aware of your particular interest," he wrote, "and will cover this as well as we can."

As they worked on their review, the Harvard researchers shared and discussed early drafts with Mr. Hickson, who responded that he was pleased with what they were writing. The Harvard scientists had dismissed the data on sugar as weak and given far more credence to the data implicating saturated fat.

"Let me assure you this is quite what we had in mind, and we look forward to its appearance in print," Mr. Hickson wrote.[66]

The role of Harvard in this crime against humanity cannot be chalked off as a private institution being corrupt. Harvard, like most American universities, is heavily funded by government research grants. It maintains its prestige and importance through the very heavy influence it exerts on public policy. The founder of Harvard's School of Nutrition, Fredrick Stare, was practically a living, breathing advertisement for the worst trash concocted by American junk food producers. An article from 1978 on his school is absolutely mind-blowing in the level of downright shamelessness with which he enjoyed getting rich by using his and his university's name and

66   O'Connor, Anahad. "How the Sugar Industry Shifted Blame to Fat." *New York Times*. 12 Sep. 2016. Web.

his government connections to ram industrial junk down people's throats.[67] Wikipedia summarizes some of the most shocking facts about this man:

> As an adviser to the US government, Stare rejected the idea that "the American diet" was harmful; stating for example that Coca-Cola was "a healthy between-meals snack" and that eating even great amounts of sugar would not cause health problems.
>
> In his autobiography, *Adventures in Nutrition*, Stare states that in 1960 he obtained a grant of $1,026,000 from General Foods for the "expansion of the School's Nutrition Research Laboratories" and that in the 44-year period as a nutritionist he raised a total of $29,630,347. For instance, Kellogg's funded $2 million to set up the Nutrition Foundation at Harvard. The foundation was independent of the university and published a journal *Nutrition Reviews* that Stare edited for 25 years.
>
> Stare also co-founded and served as chairman of the Board of Directors for the American Council on Science and Health. In 1980, during his tenure as Chairman, he sought funding from US tobacco giant Philip Morris USA for ACSH's activities.[68]

It's important to note that this new paradigm of nutrition science is based on popularizing the managerial state's attempts at economically and efficiently mass-feeding soldiers during the Second World War. After the success of British and American soldiers in defeating Nazism, the managerial state in both countries sought to apply the successes in managing the wartime effort to managing civilian life, and the result was the modern dietary guidelines. These are written with the aim of producing the cheapest way of feeding masses of humans. Instead of allowing nutrition to be an individual choice and food production a free-market process, modern governments have treated their societies as industrial lot-feeds and tasked third-rate

---

67   Hess, John. "Harvard's Sugar-Pushing Nutritionist." *The Saturday Review* (Aug. 1978): 10–14. Print.

68   "Frederick J. Stare," *Wikipedia*. 27 Jul. 2021. Web. 4 Oct. 2021.

scientists and terrible statisticians with devising the cheapest way of feeding them enough calories. Humans' natural instincts were to be overridden by government-employed charlatans profiting from telling them how much to eat of each kind of food, and whose prime directive (as in the war years) was economy. Consequently, the biggest beneficiaries from government nutritional guidance were the producers of the cheapest sources of calories and proteins: grains and legumes. But the nutrition mandarins failed to notice, or mention, that grains are largely nutrient-free, while pulses contain inferior nutrients to those contained in animal meat.

A monetary system built on a pyramid of unsound debt money gave us a food system built on a pyramid of unsound grains and carbohydrates. In one of the most catastrophic scientific errors of all time, detailed thoroughly in the work of Nina Teicholz and Gary Taubes, carbohydrates were given a free pass and became the foundational basis for nutrition while animal meat and fat, the highest quality and most nutritious food available, were vilified as the cause of modern diseases and illnesses. Modern medicine took the word of slimy politicians pretending to be scientists, like Ancel Keys and Fredrick Stare, and spread the gospel worldwide. Astonishingly, to this day, even the least health-conscious people still worry about their consumption of animal fats, while finding nothing wrong with eating large quantities of "healthy" grains, sugars, processed foods, and soft drinks.

The result of this catastrophic mistake has been that people the world over have massively increased their consumption of cheap, nutrient-deficient grains and all manners of toxic industrial "foods" while drastically cutting down on meat and animal fats. Grains may be more abundant in our modern world, but they are not more nutritious, and eating them does not satisfy people's nutritional requirements. Instead, the government-approved diet causes more hunger and cravings, motivating them to eat more and more. The obesity of the modern world has its root in a very real lack of necessary nutrients in favor of eating highly addictive and nonnutritious junk, while the truly nutritious food, fatty meat, has been deemed dangerous by modern governments' diet dictators. The reason that the obese of today eat too much is not that they are affluent. Rather, it is that they are utterly deprived of nutrients and are constantly hungry, and the grain and sugar which form the vast majority of today's diet provide close to no nutrition.

The role of the government as the nanny state responsible for dictating the diets of the entire population is a natural outgrowth of the totalitarianism that fiat money engenders. When government has the ability to generate any money it needs for whatever purposes it deems necessary, any nice-sounding ideal will eventually come to be viewed as a prerogative of the state. What started off as a well-meaning religious attempt to save people from the "envisioned" damages of eating meat devolved into a government bureaucracy captured by large agro-industrial food interests motivated to sell food that can easily scale industrially and provide the highest margins.

Fiat Hysteria

The skewed incentives of science go beyond just publishing an endless stream of trivialities that are likely untrue. The quest for publication is strengthened by researching something that attracts a lot of attention, and a very good way to attract attention is to focus on areas that invoke fear. Academics are strongly incentivized to overemphasize risks and potential catastrophes in their work, because that significantly increases the chances of publication. More importantly, perhaps, findings that are "concerning" and "troubling" are far more likely to successfully attract more funding in the future.

In fiat science, there is a very strong incentive for researchers to warn of impending calamity. If their warnings prove unfounded, they face no consequences for being wrong. Like the central planners who order up expensive government projects, scholars warning about impending doom from their offices will not be the one to foot the bill for the many precautions they ask governments to impose on citizens. There is no market test that would punish a scholar for misleading people into misdirecting resources over a manufactured crisis, and government research boards have no incentive to introspect, criticize, or punish their own financing of inaccurate scaremongering research.

With the incentives aligned for panicking and little downside to it, it is no wonder many modern researchers resemble Chicken Little more than scholars. One need not invoke any grand conspiracy to push scare stories in science to understand why so many scientists are constantly so terrified of the natural world; the simple reality is that without a market test, and with unlimited government fiat ostensibly dedicated to research topics in the public good, there will naturally be more funding available for scary conclusions, and the more panicky scientists are likely to thrive and achieve prominence than their more reasonably sober colleagues. By separating researchers from the consequences of their research and action, fiat naturally selects for and magnifies the hysterical conclusions. The next chapter discusses one of the most prominent of these examples.

Chapter 10

Fiat Fuels

One of the most notable consequences of the closing of the gold-exchange window in the 1970s was the significant and unprecedented increase in the price of oil, the first significant increase in the costs of energy after centuries of steady decline had immensely improved the lives of people.[69] The economic shock was very significant for Americans whose modern lives were increasingly reliant on high energy consumption: gasoline for cars and electricity for a growing number of household appliances.

As with food, government attempted to fix the problem of rising prices by manipulating the market for oil rather than addressing its underlying monetary cause. Instead of reducing inflationary credit expansion and government spending, bureaucracies sought to find cheaper and better alternatives to oil.

---

69   For a detailed treatment of the economics of energy, and as a prelude to this chapter, see my forthcoming textbook: *Principles of Economics*, https://www.saifedean.com/principles-of-economics.

Most fiat academics and textbooks continue to this day to blame the energy crisis on the Arab oil embargo of 1973, an astonishingly absurd explanation for several reasons. The shortages had started in 1972, before the embargo. The embargo failed to reduce the imports of oil to the United States in any meaningful sense, as the oil market was liquid and large enough for the U.S. to find oil from other sources.[70] Further, oil prices continued to rise long after the Arab-Israeli War and the embargo had ended.

The U.S. Department of Energy was set up in 1977, and the central planning of energy markets was to proceed along a half-century quest for an elusive "alternative energy," which has resulted in a very expensive and highly destructive mission to replace oil and hydrocarbons with inferior alternatives through subsidies, favorable lending, and government mandates. For an ever-shifting variety of reasons, government agents viewed the market selection of oil as a failure, and correct and better fuels had to be imposed by fiat. Since then, the seemingly indomitable power of governments with a money printer has been at war with the laws of thermodynamics and the basics of engineering.

Centuries of human engineering progress and quality of life improvement had been based on channeling hydrocarbons' high power—high quantities of energy per unit of time—as well as their high energy density per unit of weight, which made them nature's cheap, powerful, and ubiquitous batteries. But to avoid the rise in oil prices, the U.S. government's fiat sought to ignore half a millennium of technological advancement and build the modern world using premodern solar, wind, and biofuel energy. With their low power, low weight density, intermittency, unreliability, and massive bulk, these sources were only ever predominant in primitive societies precariously living on the brink of survival, at the mercy of nature, with very little in the way of technological progress. Against all logic and reason, the fuels of preindustrial poverty were designated by government fiat to be the fuels of the industrial future.

---

70 Ball, Ben, Richard Tabor, and Thomas Lee. *Energy Aftermath: How We Can Learn from the Blunders of the Past to Create a Hopeful Energy Future*. Boston: Harvard Business School Press, 1990, p. 78.

For the first time in history, centrally planning the sources of energy humans use became viewed as a legitimate function of government, and it led to the emergence of large industries reliant on government subsidies, mandates, and subsidized credit to operate, while constantly making promises of achieving technical and economic success in a few years. The consequences of this megalomaniacal quest to override the laws of thermodynamics are predictable for anyone familiar with the inevitable fate of all attempts to centrally plan market outcomes. Yet, as is the custom for failed central plans, fiat universities and academics spend little time dwelling on them, and those who do are largely ignored. Perhaps the best treatment of the episode comes from *Energy Aftermath*, a good overview book published in 1990 by Ben Ball, Thomas Lee, and Richard Tabors.[71]

The authors of this book detail how the U.S. government sought to promote five main sources of energy in response to the "energy crisis" (actually just an inflation crisis) of the 1970s, and these sources were synfuels, photovoltaics, biofuels, natural gas, and nuclear energy. Synfuels were never produced commercially, and photovoltaics failed commercially. Biofuel policies succeeded in initiating a large wealth transfer of fiat holders to corn farmers and biofuel producers, but the fuels came nowhere near replacing oil for cars. And with nuclear and natural gas, the authors detail how the crushing embrace of regulatory fiat actually hampered the development of these energy sources. The authors concluded, "The major portion of this blunder was assuming that it was possible, in effect, to dictate the supply-demand relationship in advance and that by having the government establish the market through forced, prestated quantity purchases, it would be possible to drive the price of the technology down." The second problem was the assumption that it was possible to predict the advancement of technology and the cost curve for the future. As the price inflation of the 1970s subsided and hydrocarbon prices dropped in the 1980s, the economic rationale for

---

71   Ball, Ben, Richard Tabor, and Thomas Lee. *Energy Aftermath: How We Can Learn from the Blunders of the Past to Create a Hopeful Energy Future*. Boston: Harvard Business School Press, 1990.

replacing oil with fiat fuels became less pressing, and many of these projects diminished in importance. But by the 1990s, the fiat fuel industry found fresh winds in its sails from the threat of catastrophic global warming and in marketing its fiat fuels as salvation.

The drive for environmental panic, like the drive for industrial junk fiat foods, represented a confluence of interests. The "alternative energy" industries that sprang up in the 1970s stand to benefit from promoting any narrative that supports the replacement of hydrocarbon fuels with their inadequate alternatives, justifying more government subsidies for these energy sources. But there is also a religious element to this environmentalism, based on pagan conceptions of the earth as pristine and humans as a destructive consuming force. The undertone of much of modern environmental hysteria is the idea that earth left alone and free from human influence is something good and desirable for its own sake. What philosopher Alex Epstein astutely calls antihuman environmentalism views humans as a burden on earth and seeks to minimize this burden to allow the earth to thrive.[72] Epstein analyzes this viewpoint and persuasively argues that any assessment of environmental issues needs to be understood from the perspective of humanity, with the goal of increasing human flourishing. Viewed in that regard, humans are not a destructive force on earth; our actions are what make the earth habitable for us, allowing us to survive, prosper, and flourish.

With modern industrialization picking up in the twentieth century, the environmentalist movement long warned about the dangers of human consumption and industry to the planet and the likely devastating consequences it would cause. These warnings came to a head in the 1970s, where the inflationary rise in the price of most commodities was presented as evidence that earth had reached carrying capacity, and conflicts, famines, and destitution were the inevitable fate awaiting humanity. Throughout the 1960s and 1970s, leading environmentalists made dire predictions of the horrific fate awaiting humanity from the depletion of resources, and as inflation increased, these environmentalists became increasingly popular.

---

72 Epstein, Alex. *The Moral Case for Fossil Fuels*. New York: Portfolio / Penguin, 2014. eBook.

But as inflation waned in the 1980s, all of these claims became suspect. How could we be running out of oil, steel, nickel, and various industrial materials when their prices had begun a steady decline in real, if not nominal terms, while consumption continued to rise unabated. The environmental doomsday cults had a major branding problem on hand, and they only successfully resolved it by pivoting the existential threat to humanity away from the depletion of resources to the overconsumption of resources. We were no longer doomed because we were going to run out of oil and essentials; we were now doomed because we consume so much oil and essentials, and that consumption is going to destroy the atmosphere and boil the oceans. The reasoning had pivoted to its diametrical opposite, but the conclusion remained the same: apocalypse by fiat.

Fiat Apocalypse

The previous chapter examined the underlying distortions to the scientific method caused by fiat money providing governments with outsized influence on the direction and results of scientific research. As funding decisions end up under the control of bureaucrats isolated from market feedback and consequences, the incentives of researchers are skewed toward publication and bureaucratic metrics and away from truth and relevance to the real world. Further, with public funding of science motivated primarily by notions of the public interest, it is more likely to be granted to researchers who identify potential catastrophes than those who arrive at comforting conclusions. Fiat science is optimized for panicking, and the more concerning a scientist's finding, the more likely they are to receive more funding and grow their department. Since funding has no opportunity cost to the funder, there is no rational calculation of the costs and benefits of constant hysterical Chicken Littleism as the scientific method. In a free market, scientists would have to demonstrate the validity and value of their research to justify free people paying their hard money to finance it.

Only with this context can one understand the astonishing phenomenon of many intelligent and educated people worldwide hysterically concerned about carbon dioxide causing the destruction of the planet. Carbon dioxide is a gas that is an essential component of all living creatures, and it has always existed as part of the earth's atmosphere in trace amounts, currently at a concentration of around 418 parts per million, or 0.0418%. Preindustrialization, the concentration of carbon dioxide in the atmosphere was closer to 280 parts per million, and modern climate science has been converted into a weird monomaniacal cult that attributes every single problem in the natural environment to the increase of the concentration of this trace gas.

The greenhouse effect, upon which most of this hysteria is based, is an effect that is well demonstrated in laboratory settings. But try as they may, fiat scientists have completely failed to demonstrate, using the scientific method of testable hypotheses, what the increase in CO_2 is causing in the real world. The initial hysteria was primarily concerned with increasing global temperatures, with many decades of doom-mongering predictions about the temperatures of the world rising to the point that large parts of the world would be rendered uninhabitable. And yet, the instrumental record of temperatures worldwide shows very little upward trend over the last century, and whatever variation exists is well within the range of the normal variation experienced by earth before industrialization.

In the early years of carbon hysteria, there was a general consensus around the idea that global temperatures had begun rising in the shape of a hockey stick, coinciding with the beginning of industrialization, and the fear was that continued increases in CO_2 emissions would lead to runaway temperature increases that would have devastating consequences for the planet and the humans that inhabit it. Based on a highly publicized scientific study by highly prestigious fiat scientific research centers, the hockey stick captured the world's imagination, and was used in Al Gore's panic porn flick An Inconvenient Truth. Gore famously got into an elevator that raised him to track the rises in temperature on a giant wall to drive home the point that industrialization was changing the planet irreversibly.

But in 2010, one of the most eye-opening episodes of modern fiat science took place, when hackers managed to expose the emails of the researchers who were working on producing this study. In very clear terms, fiat scientists discussed applying different tricks with the data in order to "hide the decline" in temperatures witnessed in the second half of the twentieth century. This being fiat science, of course, nobody involved in this blatant fraud suffered any consequences for it. They all continue to promote hysteria worldwide. But the exposition of this fraud has thankfully led to the disappearance of the "hockey stick" as the totem and talisman of the carbon hysterics.[73] Contrary to fiat scientists' illusions, there is very little reason to believe that atmospheric CO_2 levels are earth's thermostat knob.

Ocean acidification is another common supposed impact of increased concentration of CO_2. Dozens of academic papers discussed this effect. But as scientists tried to replicate the findings of these papers, it became apparent they were based on extremely liberal methodology to arrive at the desired results.[74] When fiat scientists studied the fish in fish tanks, they noticed the fish were not thriving. But when researchers tested them in the sea, they found little preference among fish for water with lower levels of CO_2.

Without a clear demonstrable effect of increased CO_2 emissions world-wide, carbon hysteria has moved on to promoting an endless list of natural phenomena as being the product of CO_2. The panic survives from one field to another, with the conclusion foregone, but the theories and mechanisms a constantly shifting variety of motivated reasoning by fiat. Since our earth is moving, not static, it is constantly oscillating between night and day and four seasons, and since it is surrounded by a complex atmosphere, nothing is constant in weather and climate, so the hysterics never run out of changes to attribute to CO_2, in the same way witch doctors and shamans have always blamed extreme weather on their followers, demanding they sacrifice to fix it.

Blaming carbon dioxide has reached pathological levels of delusion at this point. A website has collected hundreds of press articles based on scientific

---

73 Steve McIntyre, an independent scientist, has done a terrific job documenting the entire episode, as well as countless other problems with fiat climate science, on his independent blog: ClimateAudit.org.

74 Enserink, Martin. "Sea of Doubts: Dozens of Papers Linking High Carbon Dioxide to Unsettling Changes in Fish Behavior Fall Under Suspicion." *Science*. 6 May 2021. Web.

studies blaming CO_2 for an endless list of bad things happening worldwide.[75]
These range from increases in cases of depression among pets, to earthquakes,
cancer, declines in bird populations, the creation of ISIS, traffic jams, earlier
squirrel reproduction, increased aggression by polar bears, floods, sea-level
rise, hurricanes, and decline in whale populations. This is just a random sam-
pling of the many horrors attributed to the increase in the concentration of a
gas essential to all living things from 0.028% to 0.042%.

Once it has been established that "the science says" carbon dioxide emissions are bad and a cause to panic, the fiat scientific method is set in motion:
the path to publication, promotion, research grants, and increased importance goes through magnifying the panic, finding more reasons for it, and
asking for more funding. The path to irrelevance and career suicide comes
from soberly assessing the evidence and finding little cause for concern.

All of the "evidence" for the link between carbon dioxide and these
calamities comes entirely from observational studies. All of these things are
changing while the concentration of carbon dioxide is rising, and since there
is research money to be made from assuming causality, the causality is always
concluded, and any doubters are immediately dismissed as heretics. In fact,
a closer look at the studies behind these sensationalist headlines shows that
the causal link between CO_2 emissions and the phenomenon concerned
is usually assumed as a given, and the paper does not make any attempt to
prove it but will instead switch to discussing the details of the phenomenon
observed. These papers continue to provide the grist for the mill of news
items constantly beating the drums of fear. It is well known to fiat academics
that including a few paragraphs with a tangential link to global warming in
your paper increases its chances of securing publication and funding.

What would a proper scientific study need to do to convincingly illustrate a
causal link between carbon dioxide emissions and these various phenomena? It
would need to posit a testable hypothesis based on the impact of carbon dioxide
emissions, and test whether the predictions of the hypothesis accurately map

---

75   "A (Not Quite) Complete List of Things Supposedly Caused by Global Warming."
      What Really Happened. Web. 3 Oct. 2021.

against reality, and continuously fail to reject the null hypothesis that there is no link between CO_2 and the phenomenon. In other words, a proper scientist would measure bird populations, sea levels, or temperature and make a testable prediction conditional on CO_2 emission levels along the lines of: "If CO_2 emissions increase by X% over the period between Year X and Year X+10, there will be no impact on bird populations/sea levels/temperature." Repeatedly rejecting the null hypothesis, and then developing accurate numerical predictions for the studied relationship would go a long way to establishing the credibility of the evidence linking carbon dioxide to this particular phenomenon.

The global government lockdowns initiated in 2020 have provided climate scientists with a natural experiment of sorts with which to test the robustness of their claims on the link between CO_2 emissions and atmospheric concentrations of CO_2, and between emissions and climate phenomena. As the world economy went into a debilitating shutdown starting in March 2020, there was a very significant reduction in aviation and car driving, two major sources of CO_2 emissions. The shutdowns were devastating for the livelihoods of billions worldwide who lost their jobs and their earnings and is an extreme example of the kind of economic reform that environmentalists propose to alleviate climate change. What was the impact of these shutdowns on the atmosphere and climate? One year later, we are beginning to see studies estimate this.

The results so far are a complete slap in the face for the delusion that humans control the climate through our emissions of an essential trace gas. Most fascinating is the discovery that all of these lockdowns had no discernible impact on the trend in CO_2 atmospheric concentration growth, which continued with no perceptible change.

Another study[76] examined the impact of lockdowns on temperature and rainfall and found no discernible effect. To the best of my knowledge, there has not been a single study to find evidence that the global shutdown had any

76 Jones, Chris D., et al. "The Climate Response To Emissions Reductions Due To COVID-19: Initial Results From CovidMIP." *Geophysical Research Letters*, vol. 48, no. 8, Apr. 2021. Print. Crossref, doi:10.1029/2020GL091883.

discernible impact on any aspect of the earth's climate or atmosphere. If locking billions of people at home, with their cars parked and global aviation coming to a near-complete halt, had no detectable effect on climate, there is no good reason to believe any of the dire predictions of fiat climatologists. Nor, for that matter, is there any good reason to countenance the hubristic notion that central governments have the power to control the very air of earth.

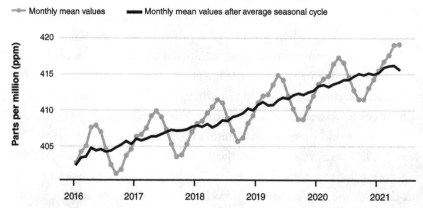

Figure 11. Recent monthly mean CO_2 at Mauna Loa Observatory.
Source: "Trends in Atmospheric Carbon Dioxide." *Global Monitoring Laboratory*,
National Oceanic and Atmospheric Administration. Web. 3 Oct. 2021.

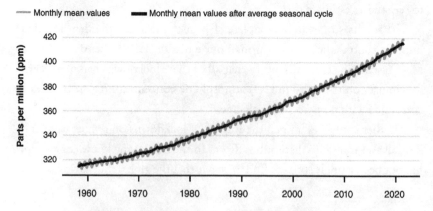

Figure 12. Atmospheric CO_2 at Mauna Loa Observatory.
Source: "Trends in Atmospheric Carbon Dioxide." *Global Monitoring Laboratory*,
National Oceanic and Atmospheric Administration. Web. 3 Oct. 2021.

Similarly, there is no good reason to think that the greenhouse gas effect as studied in laboratory settings will translate to the world at large, where the environment is far more complex than any lab could ever be. One cannot dismiss the hypothesis that humans are having an impact on atmospheric CO_2 concentrations and the climate, but the burden of proof is on the people making these extraordinary claims to present convincing evidence that illustrates the causal mechanisms involved, the likely impacts, the value of the mitigation measures they propose, and their true cost. Without testable hypotheses, the entirety of modern climate science is at best conjecture but more likely motivated reasoning in search of a predetermined conclusion to secure more funding. Without testable hypotheses, climate scientists ought to be far humbler and more modest about whatever conclusions they arrive at.

It is debatable whether the findings of the modern field of climatology would exist in a free market for research without fiat funding, but it is pretty clear that a society running on hard money, which would force everyone to constantly think about the opportunity costs of action, would come nowhere near contemplating the precautions and measures called for by carbon hysterics. The threats of climate change are an ever-shifting set of vague hypothetical threats of doom, while the threat from the transitioning of energy sources from reliable hydrocarbons to unreliable "renewables" is a matter of life and death for billions on the planet, as discussed below.

As time has gone by and the many calamitous predictions of the climate hysteria industry have failed to materialize, a more sober and reasonable assessment of the dangers of CO_2 emissions is becoming possible. The last year has witnessed the publication of two extremely important books on the topic of climate, whose authors come with impeccable scientific and environmentalist credentials. Physicist Steven Koonin, a former chief scientist for the Obama Administration, has just published Unsettled: What Climate Science Tells Us, What It Doesn't, and Why It Matters,[77] the culmination of many years of examining the scientific studies published on climate

77   Koonin, Steven. *Unsettled: What Climate Science Tells Us, What It Doesn't, and Why It Matters*. Dallas: BenBella Books, Inc., 2021. Print.

change, the supposed consensus around it, and the real-world evidence for it. Koonin's conclusion is unabashedly nonpanicky. One by one, he takes apart the major tenets of the climate hysteria religion and shows how little evidence there is to support them. Most importantly, Koonin absolutely destroys the antiscientific and totalitarian claim that "the science is settled" and not up for debate.

In *Apocalypse Never: Why Environmental Alarmism Hurts Us All*, lifelong environmental activist Michael Shellenberger takes a very sober look at similar topics and shows why the popular alarm and hysteria around climate change is very misplaced.[78] Beyond just dispelling the fears of climate alarmists, Shellenberger provides a very thoughtful and eye-opening treatment of the social and psychological impacts of the growing number of people who have been conditioned by fiat scientists into a state of despair, panic, and constant fear over the weather. Moreover, he illustrates how the obsession with CO_2 has overshadowed and displaced the interest in other pressing environmental phenomena.

Reading these two books is a massively relieving let-off for anyone still suffering under the delusion that driving a car or taking a flight is causing irreparable damage to the planet and our environment. There is little reason to believe whatever changes in temperature we've witnessed over the last century are in any way out of the ordinary for our planet, which has witnessed far greater variation in the past without our CO_2 emissions affecting it. There is also no reason to suspect changes in CO_2 concentration in the atmosphere will cause catastrophic ocean acidification. Beyond these two headline threats, what remains is an ever-shifting endless list of supposed threats, each with a very tenuous link to CO_2 emissions.

But more important than the hallucinations of fiat scientists looking to get published is the state of the planet and the livability of the climate, for which we have very reliable data. If CO_2 emissions were in fact causing dangerous damage to the climate, we would expect to see this reflected in

---

78   Shellenberger, Michael. *Apocalypse Never: Why Environmental Alarmism Hurts Us All*. New York: HarperCollins, 2020. Print.

an increasing number of deaths caused by climate and natural disasters. Yet reality shows us the exact opposite: deaths from hydrological, climatological, and meteorological disasters have declined drastically throughout the past century, thanks to the amazing technological advancements of the past century, which have made survival into old age far less uncertain than it was at any point in history. As humans have mastered our natural environment, we have steadily tamed the harms of nature and protected ourselves from them. Perhaps the most significant factor in the mastery of our climate has been the use of high-power energy sources to meet our needs. It gave us modern sanitation and indoor plumbing, modern wastewater treatment, ubiquitous cheap steel to fortify our houses and protect them from the elements, drained swamps that stopped breeding insects and diseases, warm homes at little cost, hospitals full of modern equipment, and pharmaceuticals that save our lives. The irony completely lost on the climate alarmists is that the materials they want to ban are our best weapon to survive the natural dangers of climate.

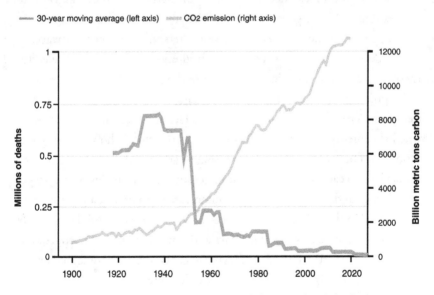

Figure 13. Global CO_2 emission and climate-related deaths.
Source: Epstein, Alex. *The Moral Case for Fossil Fuels.* New York: Portfolio / Penguin, 2014. eBook.

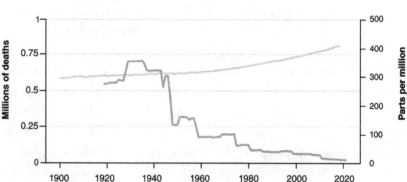

Figure 14. Atmospheric CO$_2$ and climate-related deaths.

Source: Epstein, Alex. *The Moral Case for Fossil Fuels.* New York: Portfolio / Penguin, 2014. eBook.

Fiat Thermodynamics

Fiat society thinks it can decree new laws for thermodynamics and override engineering reality by government fiat. The eternal adolescents of fiat want to live in modern homes, easily survive winters, travel faster than walking, use modern electronic devices and medical equipment, and have electricity on demand, but they don't want to use the substance that makes all of these possible. Any person with a familiarity with the engineering realities of modern life will realize that the policies and demands of fiat people when it comes to energy are as reasonable as the child who wants to go to Disneyland but throws tantrums refusing to get into the car taking him to Disneyland because he doesn't want to get into the car; he just wants to get into Disneyland. It is difficult to communicate to a child in a tantrum that the car is his only realistic option for getting to Disneyland and that the only possible alternative is walking for days and not some magical teleportation device. This is exactly the plight of trying to explain to fiat people that hydrocarbons are the only reason most of our modern life is possible, that working alternatives cannot be conjured by fiat, and that the only realistic alternative is grinding poverty and a precarious existence, not some absurd Star Trek world where all that we want materializes with the flick of a switch without any combustion taking place. Just like the child who wants to be teleported to Disneyland should present their teleportation device before throwing a tantrum, it is time for fiat fuel enthusiasts to first show the rest of us how they can survive on fiat fuels before demanding we give up the hydrocarbons that are essential for our survival.

No evil conspiracy of oil companies and oil-producing nations is forcing fiat fuel enthusiasts to consume oil. They consume it because their actions are grounded in the real world, unlike their ideas. The intellectual brain, being largely used for insignificant entertainment purposes for most people, can contemplate insane and meaningless ideas like a modern world free of hydrocarbons, but the acting human looking to survive and thrive cannot. Even as they virtue-signal about wanting to get rid of hydrocarbons, they do so from the safety of a house built with hydrocarbons, lit with hydro-carbons, powered by hydrocarbons, using electronic devices impossible to make without hydrocarbons.

Beyond very small-scale noncommercial applications employing wind-mills and solar energy sources, the vast majority of humans' actions (and not their empty virtue-signaling) clearly show that humans prefer and require hydrocarbons. The growth of the renewable energy industry is almost entirely a function of growing government subsidies. As Warren Buffet put it, "we get a tax credit if we build a lot of wind farms. That's the only reason to build them. They don't make sense without the tax credit." This was the case in the 1970s, and that left behind a large number of white elephant projects. Today, easy money is creating a similar misallocation of resources in these industries.

Initially, you might expect that solar energy, being so plentiful and abun-dant, would be far cheaper than hydrocarbon energy, which needs extensive prospecting, drilling, extraction, and transporting to use. The sun shines down on every inch of the earth for significant parts of the year, and its rays bring large quantities of energy. It is estimated that the solar energy that falls on the earth in one hour is larger than the energy that all humans consume in a full year. Why would solar energy then not be cheaper than hydrocarbon energy?

The answer is that in its raw form, solar power is cheaper than hydrocarbons, but in its raw form, solar power can only satisfy the human needs
for skin exposure to sunlight and for growing plants. Solar energy in its raw
form cannot satisfy the majority of our modern energy needs, since humans
do not need large quantities of energy in the aggregate; we require high
amounts of energy at the margin, in large quantities over short periods of
time in order to produce power (defined as unit of energy per unit of time).
High power is the driving force of modern technologies that makes modern
construction, industry, transportation, electronics, and many more modern
accomplishments possible. One cannot use the rays of sunlight directly to
move a car or power a factory, and their absolute quantities are irrelevant.
Whereas solar energy is plentiful, being able to concentrate it into high
power is a very complex operation that requires significant investment in
capital infrastructure through solar panels and batteries. As a form of energy
in the abstract, solar is infinitely cheap. But as an economic good that meets
our need for power, solar energy requires highly sophisticated and expensive
equipment to become usable, and that is why it remains far more expensive
as a source of energy than hydrocarbons and continues to require subsidies,
mandates, and subsidized fiat credit. It is not the aggregate quantity of the
good that matters but its ability to satisfy our particular needs at the time
and place where we need them. The best technology for channeling solar
power to meet our needs turns out to be the batteries of nature: hydrocarbon
fuels which have concentrated solar power over billions of years under the
earth's crust for us, abundant, packing a powerful punch, and incomparably
cheaper than modern man-made batteries.

The term "alternative" is a misnomer when used to refer to fiat fuels, as
no "alternative" energy source constitutes a satisfactory alternative to hydrocarbons. None of these energy sources could be used exclusively for building
and transporting the equipment that makes their own production possible.
There are no windmill factories operating purely on wind power or a solar
panel factory that operates purely on solar power. An attempt to collect these
energy sources into high power applications would require extremely expensive equipment, the production of which is also highly energy-intensive.

And even if someone had managed, against all common sense, to build a windmill factory running on windmills, it would be far more difficult to transport these enormous wind turbines to the locations where they need to be installed using wind energy. The technology needed to transform wind energy into electric energy, and then store it into a battery is far more expensive than just refining oil and putting it into a car engine. The more familiar one becomes with the industrial processes involved, the more you realize how utterly contingent they all are on the presence of hydrocarbon fuels.

The production of electric batteries and solar panels is extremely energy-intensive. The extraction of the rare earth metals that go into them is a highly sophisticated process, requiring large amounts of power to dig very deep holes into the earth. None of these processes would be practically possible without hydrocarbons, in a technical sense. In an economic sense, they are even less feasible when one remembers that in a world without hydrocarbons, we will have far more pressing and basic needs to invest our time and resources into. While engineers might in theory devise roundabout ways of producing batteries and windmills without hydrocarbons, in reality, without hydrocarbons, humans will have nowhere near the resources available to invest in such highly sophisticated methods of production, when survival in the winter is far from certain, and when basic transportation has become massively expensive. The entire division of labor on which our modern economy depends is impossible without hydrocarbons.

The only viable alternatives to hydrocarbons are hydroelectric power and nuclear power, but these are extremely limited in their scope for growth. Hydroelectric is only economical in areas near large sources of hydroelectric power, while nuclear faces very strong political and regulatory barriers to its expansion and is itself dependent on hydrocarbons for the industrial materials that make it possible. Even if all political and regulatory barriers to nuclear adoption were removed tomorrow, it would still take many decades before the infrastructure for nuclear energy could be built to match hydrocarbon fuels, it would still require hydrocarbons as inputs into the process, and it would not displace the use of hydrocarbons as fuels for mobile and remote requirements.

The Cost of Fiat Fuels

I studied these questions in depth when doing my PhD more than a decade ago and became disillusioned with the state of scholarship on these questions and the enormous and blatant theft these policies encourage. It appeared clear to me at that time that the renewable energy scam was fast becoming as entrenched as the corn subsidies that are a permanent fixture of U.S. politics. Powerful interests were making a significant income from these scams, and they set the terms of debate around these questions. Trying to discuss these issues with sanity was just an invitation for ostracism and abuse. Intellectually and professionally, there was little point in trying to confront these terrible ideas. Hydrocarbons would continue to provide the vast majority of energy in our world anyway, as people's market choices will inevitably triumph over their vacant virtue-signaling.

More recently, it has become evident to me these questions are far more significant than the economic inefficiency and theft they entail. As the use of unreliable and uneconomical energy sources has increased, the cost of power has begun to rise again, reversing the essential process of progress that is human civilization itself. In all of our history, humans have sought ways to increase the amount, and reduce the cost, of power. From lighting fire to domesticating horses, building waterwheels and windmills, burning coal, oil, gas, and utilizing nuclear energy, humans have constantly sought and found the technologies and raw materials that can bring them more and cheaper power to meet their daily needs. And with this growth came the constant improvements in the quality of life which most of us take for granted today. By mandating the use of primitive, low-power, unreliable energy sources, governments are raising the cost of all economic activity and making life more difficult. Through energy mandates and regulations, central governments are effectively rolling back human civilization.

All over the world, places that have aggressively mandated the use of fiat fuels for the grid are witnessing a steady rise in the cost of electricity. Germany has witnessed a 51% rise in the cost of electricity between 2006 and 2018, and a doubling in price between 2000 and 2020.[79] California,

---

79 "Germany." *Environmental Progress.* 22 Sep. 2011. Web.

the U.S. leader in mandating fiat fuels, has witnessed a 39% rise in the cost of electricity between 2011 and 2020.[80] The United Kingdom's electricity prices rose by 27% in the decade leading up to 2020.[81] Energy price increases seem to be normalized and accepted by many in these economies, but the implications are severe in the long term, in three particular ways.

First, higher energy prices badly impact the poorest in society, who usually spend a much higher percentage of their income on energy. Second, higher energy prices translate to rising prices in all goods and services, as energy is an input into every production process. Finally, rising energy prices are debilitating for energy-intensive industries, particularly manufacturing, which effectively means these societies are deindustrializing and destroying their high-productivity industries. It is astonishing to imagine that Germany, the industrial powerhouse whose efficiently engineered and manufactured goods have blanketed the planet, allowing the world to increase its productivity drastically, is now committing industrial suicide by making manufacturing prohibitively expensive in order to promote the engineering scam that is fiat fuels.

Energy prices rise with the deployment of fiat fuels due to their intermittent nature, which means that they produce energy according to the whims of nature and not the demands of consumers, resulting in expensive problems of underproduction and overproduction.[82] Since there are times in which renewable energy sources will produce no energy whatsoever, and these times can coincide with peak demand, all power grids must maintain reliable power plants able to provide them with peak demand when needed or else face brownouts or blackouts. As a result, the investment in fiat fuel plants is almost entirely an added cost to the grid, not a replacement. To ensure that electricity users have full power when they need it, there can be no reduction in the capacity of reliable power sources. Overproduction is

---

80 "California." *Environmental Progress*. 30 Aug. 2021. Web.

81 Bailey, Ronald. "Renewable Energy Mandates Are Making Poor People Poorer." *Reason*. Jun. 2018. Web. 3 Oct. 2021.

82 Constable, John. "The Brink of Darkness: Britain's Fragile Power Grid." *The Global Warming Policy Foundation*. 10 Jun. 2020. Web.

another major contribution to cost. When demand is low but fiat fuel plants are running at high capacity (such as windy nights for wind turbines, or cool sunny weekend days where there is little demand for heating, cooling, or industrial production), the grid must invest significantly to find ways to safely dispose of the excess energy, and this energy can cause damage to the grid, leading to blackouts.

Beyond the rise in the direct market price of electricity, the imposition of fiat fuels has also led to plummeting power grid reliability in much of the industrialized world, which entails significant indirect costs. The transformative power of hydrocarbons lies not just in the high power they deliver but also in their ability to deliver power on demand, when required, anywhere on earth, freeing humans from having to tailor their actions around the weather. Fiat energy is reversing this enormous leap forward for humans. It is astonishing to watch a place like California, which had managed to secure twenty-four-hour reliable electricity for its citizens many decades ago, reduced to having its governor call on its citizens to avoid doing activities requiring high power in the evening as the sun sets and solar power generation slows down.

Years of investment in unreliable energy sources, and underinvestment in gas and nuclear plants, have left the infrastructure of many advanced economies teetering at the brink, one natural disaster away from collapse. Shellenberger's *Apocalypse Never* provides a good overview of the extent of this malinvestment in California,[83] and as the rest of the world continues to head in the direction of California with fiat fuels, it is hard to escape the conclusion that these catastrophic grid failures will become far more common, leaving humans to fend for themselves against the challenges of the natural environment without the power technologies that have made survival progressively easier over the past few centuries.

Once one strips away the carefully crafted and expertly marketed romantic pseudoscientific halo around fiat fuels, there is no escaping the conclusion that they represent nothing less than the reversal of the process of civilization and the devastation of human progress achieved through centuries of hard

83   Shellenberger, *Apocalypse Never*.

toil, sacrifice, capital accumulation, and technological ingenuity. Providing twenty-four-hour electricity reliably, regardless of the weather or time of day, is an engineering problem that advanced industrial societies like California and Texas solved many decades ago. The failure to have this luxury in the twenty-first century cannot be explained through any technological or natural reasons; it is the work of fiat fuels.

But the disasters of fiat fuels are not limited to the developed industrial societies forsaking development and progress. Fiat fuels have arguably been more devastating for many undeveloped and predominantly preindustrial societies, countries with low levels of capital for which spending on these luxuries is an unconscionable waste. Poverty is the inevitable consequence and symptom of a lack of available power, and the only proven technologies for delivering high power on demand at low prices are based on hydrocarbon, nuclear, and hydroelectric energy. Yet the last three decades have witnessed a proliferation of development projects aimed at helping poor countries "transition" to renewable energies instead of investing in reliable energy. The track record of these projects has been dreadful. Western donors and "misery industry" bureaucrats get to write their virtue-signaling reports full of rosy language on the transformative potential of these energy sources, but the people who have to rely on them end up with unreliable low power available intermittently, and usually, they still have to pay enormous costs in debt servicing and maintenance. At a time when reliable power generation from hydrocarbons is becoming cheaper than ever, burdening the world's poor with the expensive, useless, virtue-signaling toys of the West is no less than criminal.

In his book *Where Is My Flying Car? A Memoir of Future Past*, J. Storrs Hall finds a steady trend, stretching for three centuries, of usable energy growing at about 7% per year, which can be approximated as a result of a 2% increase in energy efficiency, 3% population growth, and 2% growth in actual energy consumed per capita.[84] The growth in energy consumption per capita at 2% is a relationship that has held since the beginning of the

---

84   Hall, J. Storrs. *Where Is My Flying Car? A Memoir of Future Past*. Self-published, 2018. eBook.

nineteenth century, with the beginning of the utilization of fossil fuels, until the 1970s. The material of this chapter can go a long way toward explaining why the growth in per capita energy consumption stopped rising in the past fifty years. With inflation causing the prices of energy to rise, and increased interventions in energy markets, the growth in energy consumption has

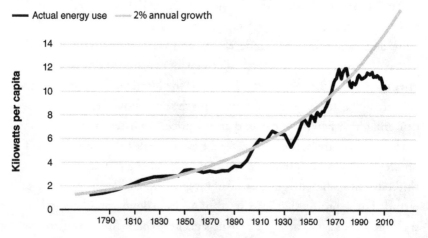

Figure 15. Energy Consumption Per Capita vs. 2% annual growth.

Source: Hall, J. Storrs. *Where Is My Flying Car? A Memoir of Future Past.* Self-published, 2018. eBook.

slowed.

An industry that best illustrates this trend is aviation, which I have written about before.[85] It is a remarkable feature of the modern world that airplanes today travel at slower speeds than they did in the 1970s. Commercial flight times have not only failed to get shorter; they actually take longer than they did in the 1960s, at least in the U.S. where I was able to obtain reliable data. Forty years after its introduction, supersonic flight is no longer available for civilians, neither in commercial nor private jets. Jet manufacturers continue

---

85   Ammous, Saifedean. "Slowdown: Aviation and Modernity's Lost Dynamism."
       SSRN Electronic Journal, Elsevier BV. 25 May 2017. Web. Crossref, doi:10.2139/
       ssrn.3036275.

to be conspicuously silent about any plans to reintroduce supersonic flight.

But perhaps most astonishing is the failure of anyone to come near challenging the world speed record for flight for four and a half decades. The world speed record for flight was constantly increasing from the Wright brothers' maiden flight in 1903 until July 28, 1976, when a U.S. Air Force SR-71 Blackbird registered the fastest speed for an air-breathing aircraft: 3,529.6 kmh, or Mach 3.3. On that same day, another SR-71 registered the highest airplane altitude record of 25,929 meters. Forty-five years later, both records still stand. The SR-71 was decommissioned in 1991, and none of the

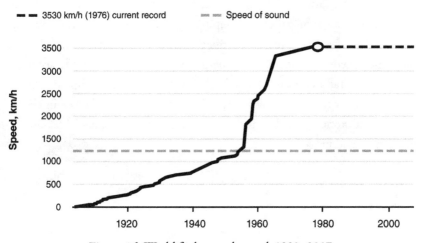

Figure 16. World flight speed record, 1993–2017.

Source: Ammous, Saifedean. "Slowdown: Aviation and Modernity's Lost Dynamism." *SSRN Electronic Journal*, Elsevier BV. 25 May 2017. Web. Crossref, doi: 10.2139/ssrn.3036275.

replacement aircraft has come close to achieving its speed or elevation.

The closing of the gold-exchange window in 1971 caused a rise in costs of all goods, including food and fuel. The rise in the price of energy was massively disruptive to a highly industrialized world economy reliant on modern high-power tech. Environmentalist ideologies that villainize consumption and human prosperity became widespread. As illustrated with aviation, innovation in many industries shifted from improving performance to reducing consumption. If human progress in the past two centuries had come through the steady exponential increase of energy consumption, one can only wonder what progress we have missed out on from the increasing costs of energy and the stunting of our consumption of it.

Whether in food, science, or energy, the introduction of government fiat to a market disfigures it completely. We have no idea what the world would look like if we had continued to have a free market in energy and inflation hadn't spiked prices and made them so volatile. There are advantages and drawbacks to each source of energy, and a free market would have allowed individuals to make the choices that maximize the benefits while reducing the costs. The enormous resources wasted on fiat fuel fictions would probably have been spent on gas plants, helping more of the world transition from dirty coal to clean gas. Nuclear energy might have advanced enough to displace most hydrocarbons used in energy generation. With steady accumulation of capital guided by rational calculation on an uncorrupted money, energy prices would likely be a fraction of where they are today. In short, corrupt fiat money has robbed countless generations of incalculable human flourishing and prosperity.

Chapter 11

Fiat States

In Chapter 2, we saw how the development of the global monetary system after World War I, the gold-exchange standard, largely mirrored the arrangement the British empire had with some of its colonies before the war. As the victors of the war, and the main financial heavyweights of the world economy, Great Britain and the U.S. used the 1922 Genoa Conference to institute the gold-exchange standard, a new global monetary system in which their client states had to rely on the dollar or the pound sterling.

In theory, if the U.S. and Great Britain had been on a strict gold standard, then the gold-exchange standard would have been no different from the gold standard. But because thirty-two foreign central banks needed to leave their gold with the two major central banks in order to give it salability across the planet, these two countries had significant leeway in inflating their currencies beyond their gold reserves, effectively exporting their inflation abroad. This alleviated the pressure on their currencies, particularly the overvalued pound sterling. The Genoa Conference was the prototype for the monetary arrangements that prevailed between the leading economies with reserve currencies and the neocolonies.

Bank of France Governor Emile Moreau astutely described this arrange-ment as "veritable financial domination" and a separation of currencies into two classes:

> England having been the first European country to reestablish a stable and secure money has used that advantage to establish a basis for putting Europe under a veritable financial domination. The Financial Committee [of the League of Nations] at Geneva has been the instrument of that pol-icy. The method consists of forcing every country in monetary difficulty to subject itself to the Committee at Geneva, which the British control. The remedies prescribed always involve the installation in the central bank of a foreign supervisor who is British or designated by the Bank of England, and the deposit of a part of the reserve of the central bank at the Bank of England, which serves both to support the pound and to fortify British influence. To guarantee against possible failure they are careful to secure the cooperation of the Federal Reserve Bank of New York. Moreover, they pass on to America the task of making some of the foreign loans if they seem too heavy, always retaining the political advantage of these operations.
>
> England is thus completely or partially entrenched in Austria, Hungary, Belgium, Norway, and Italy. She is in the process of entrench-ing herself in Greece and Portugal.... The currencies [of Europe] will be divided into two classes. Those of the first class, the dollar and the pound sterling, based on gold, and those of the second class based on the pound and dollar—with a part of their gold reserves being held by the Bank of England and the Federal Reserve Bank of New York. The latter moneys will have lost their independence.[86]

The larger the liquidity pool of a currency, the smaller the domestic impact of any inflationary credit creation by the respective monetary author-ity. In an economy in which the total demand for monetary cash balances

---

86   Rothbard, Murray. *America's Great Depression*. 5th ed., Auburn, AL, Ludwig von Mises
     Institute, 2000, p. 152.

is $10 billion, the money supply increasing by $1 billion would cause a far bigger impact on prices and economic calculation than if the same increase had happened in an economy in which the total demand for monetary cash balances was $100 billion. The larger the pool of liquidity using the Bank of England and the Federal Reserve payment and clearance networks, the less U.S. and British inflation would be felt at home.

After Genoa, the U.S. and the British governments' prime imperative was to get as many central banks to hold as much of their currencies as possible. This was unprecedented money printing and inflationism on a global scale. As other governments, institutions, and private actors began settling trade in dollars and pounds, they needed larger quantities of these reserves. World politics has since been largely motivated by major governments' desire to get their inflationary currencies adopted as international reserves to allow them to engage in more politically expedient inflation.

National central banks were the nodes of the fiat network. The more nodes that could be set up worldwide, the more gold would pour into the British and American central banks. The more liquidity that existed on the network, the more inflation America and Britain could get away with. The dynamic created by the gold-exchange standard might lead an observer to wonder whether British and American support for national liberation movements was not purely altruistic but rather a self-interested move to create more fiat nodes in nascent countries.

The new global monetary system was termed a system of monetary nationalism by Friedrich Hayek:

> By Monetary Nationalism I mean the doctrine that a country's share in the world's supply of money should not be left to be determined by the same principles and the same mechanism as those which determine the relative amounts of money in its different regions or localities. A truly International Monetary System would be one where the whole world possessed a homogeneous currency such as obtains within separate countries and where its flow between regions was left to be determined by the results of the action of all individuals.

It was only with the growth of centralized national banking systems that all the inhabitants of a country came in this sense to be dependent on the same amount of more liquid assets held for them collectively as a national reserve.[87]

For a time the ascendancy of the gold standard and the consequent belief that to maintain it was an important matter of prestige, and to be driven off it a national disgrace, put an effective restraint on this power. It gave the world the one long period—200 years or more—of relative stability during which modern industrialism could develop, albeit suffering from periodic crises. But as soon as it was widely understood some 50 years ago that the convertibility into gold was merely a method of controlling the amount of a currency, which was the real factor determining its value, governments became only too anxious to escape that discipline, and money became more than ever before the plaything of politics. Only a few of the great powers preserved for a time tolerable monetary stability, and they brought it also their colonial empires. But Eastern Europe and South America never knew a prolonged period of monetary stability.[88]

What came to be known as the "developing world" consists of countries that had not yet adopted modern industrial technologies by the time an inflationary global monetary system began replacing a relatively sound one in 1914. This dysfunctional global monetary system continuously compromised these countries' development by enabling local and foreign governments to expropriate the wealth produced by their people.

By 1914, the only nations that had achieved a considerable degree of industrialization and capital accumulation were those of Western Europe, as well as the U.S. and Canada. At the time, modern industrialization was

---

87   Hayek, Friedrich. *Monetary Nationalism and International Stability*. London: Longmans, Green, and Company, 1937: 4+. Print.

88   Hayek, Friedrich. *Denationalisation of Money—The Argument Refined: An Analysis of the Theory and Practice of Concurrent Currencies*. London: Institute of Economic Affairs, 1976: 35. Print.

beginning to spread into Eastern Europe, the north and south of Africa, and many parts of Asia and South America. The more a country engaged in trade with industrialized economies, the more it imported the revolutionary technologies of the nineteenth century, chief among them the steam and internal combustion engines. The more technologically advanced a developing nation became, the more it accumulated capital, the more productive its workforce became, and the higher its living standards were. World War I stunted this progress, and the global monetary system that emerged after (and consequently the Great Depression) undermined global economic development even further.

As central banks inflated away the value of their currencies, international trade and finance became the release valve through which national inflationary economic distortions would correct themselves. A devaluing currency encouraged citizens to unload their local currency for foreign currencies or for foreign goods. This in turn further reduced demand for the local currency and further decreased its value. This dynamic undermined the ability of developing nation governments to finance themselves through inflation, necessitating even more inflation and taxation to finance spending. Governments could have tried reversing that trend by reducing inflation, but the statist economists of the time sought to fix it by limiting the free movement of capital and goods. Trade barriers proliferated during the Great Depression, resulting in heightened international hostilities around trade.

The imposition of trade barriers in turn resulted in a further deterioration of economic conditions in the countries imposing them, even as their own citizens suffered from these very policies. The governments imposing such barriers, and the economists advocating them, would of course never admit that inflation, increasing centralization, and protectionist policies caused the progressively worsening depression. Instead, political leaders blamed other countries and local ethnic minorities. Years of scapegoating and growing hostility toward foreigners and minorities came to a head in 1939. The world's totalitarian fiat regimes began to turn on each other and on their ethnic minorities. Hayek had identified this threat to global peace in his "Monetary Nationalism and International Stability" lectures in 1937.

Alas, his warnings fell on deaf ears. The monetary standard was no longer a homogeneous money freely moving around the world wherever its owners found the best use for it. Instead, state-controlled money became a tool for increasingly omnipotent governments to finance war and totalitarianism.

Government-approved history and economics textbooks are completely silent on the monetary origins of the Great Depression and World War II. The promoters of increased government centralization and control claimed this new alchemy allowed governments to build a bright future. In reality, government-controlled money destroyed the world's economies by the late 1930s, crippled global free trade, created omnipotent, totalitarian governments with many reasons to be hostile to one another, and increasingly turned previously prosperous and civilized populations into government dependents and cannon fodder.

Government-controlled money allowed economies to be centrally planned in a way that was probably last seen in the Western world during the last gasps of the Roman Empire. To fight the growing unemployment and inflation caused by their inflationist monetary policies, politicians imposed price controls, minimum wage laws, work-sharing laws, and various others brands of destructive statist economic policies. As the economy shrank further and people's lives suffered, they became more and more dependent on increasingly centralized governments that could conjure money from thin air. Such dependency upon the state served only to reinforce governments' power.

By controlling the money, governments could also extend their reach into the education system. Universities had been places where citizens could learn and train, but in a matter of decades, they were transformed into propaganda machines, bent on the indoctrination of young people. Toeing the statist line became more important than free inquiry, rational debate, and the exchange of ideas. Tenured statists have shaped the understanding of economics and politics for generations of leaders and economists in developing countries. This intellectual and historical context is essential to understanding the economic catastrophes of the developing world in the latter half of the twentieth century.

The number and influence of third-world leaders who were educated in

British and American universities from the 1930s onward is staggering.[89] I have seen no systematic study or data on the topic, but anyone familiar with the economic history of developing countries, or with the rhetoric of any development agency or ministry in a developing country, will see this influence in the distinct stench of Marxist and Keynesian notions of central planning. The entire framing of the notion of economic development is driven ultimately by a highly socialist view of how an economy works. The alert reader will not miss the economic development literature's fascination with macroeconomic aggregates and the way in which the government and the development sector are viewed as the omniscient, omnipotent forces of justice working to achieve the holy goals of development.

The Misery Industry

As outlined in *The Bitcoin Standard*, the International Monetary Fund (IMF), World Bank, and World Trade Organization (WTO) were the brainchildren of the communist activist Harry Dexter White. This fact does not feature heavily in these organizations' voluminous and slick marketing material, but it nonetheless makes a lot of sense when one examines what these institutions actually do. The function of central banking itself is the essence of communist and socialist thought. Back in 1844 when Karl Marx and Friedrich Engels penned their *Communist Manifesto,* a central bank was one of the ten main pillars of the communist program they sought to implement.

The IMF's main role is as a global lender of last resort. Since individual governments can suffer from foreign reserve payment problems, and since this monetary system runs on an easy currency, it was almost inevitable that expansionary monetary policy would be used to keep this system functioning. Thanks to its financing from the U.S. Federal Reserve, the IMF is able to issue large amounts of U.S. dollar-denominated credit to central banks around the world and has performed this function continuously over the past seven decades. Its existence is essential for the U.S. dollar to maintain

89   Bartholomew, James. "Degrees in Disaster." *The Spectator*. 25 July 2015. Web.

its role as the global reserve currency. Without a global lender of last resort, every third-world country would have run out of its dollar reserves, and their central banks would have gone bankrupt. Banks and individuals in these countries would then use other currencies, or gold, to engage in global trade. It is no coincidence that the IMF strictly forbids its members from tying their currencies to gold, because this would prevent the U.S. dollar from continuing to function as the global reserve currency, even though a global gold standard would achieve all of the IMF's stated goals of international stability, as it did in the nineteenth century.

The problem with the IMF serving as the lender of last resort is the same that exists with a monopoly central bank. Its ability to bail out individual banks is a huge moral hazard that incentivizes banks to take on more risk, as they can rely on being bailed out. As the IMF looks to maintain the role of the dollar as the global reserve currency, it encourages all governments to use it and lends to them when they run out of it. Under the gold standard, countries that ran out of gold and went bankrupt were effectively taken over by their creditors. Kings would abdicate if they were bankrupted, and entire lands would be taken over by other countries. There were very serious consequences to government defaults and bankruptcies, which taught fiscal and monetary responsibility. But with the IMF able to bail out countries, the consequences for government incompetence and mismanagement are far less serious, as political leaders can always borrow from the IMF to foist the cost of insolvency onto future citizens.

The initial purpose of the International Bank for Reconstruction and Development, later to be renamed the World Bank, was to finance the reconstruction of Europe and the development of the world's poorest countries. Inspired by the terrible Keynesian and socialist ideas infesting British and American universities, the Americans decided that what was needed for the world's poor countries to develop was funding for massive government development efforts. From the perspective of the average U.S. or U.K. bureaucrat and academic at the time, the Soviet Union was the exemplar of economic success. The Soviet brand of central planning would provide, they believed, substantial economic growth and development for poor countries. In order for the U.S. to prevent countries from allying with the Soviets, they reasoned, all centrally planned global development efforts should be American-led.

The World Bank was also financed with a line of credit from the U.S. Federal Reserve, and it was the main driver of development planning in the third world from the 1950s on. The bank's main business model is to issue development loans to poor countries and help them plan their development. The 'scholarship' of development economics in the past seventy years can best be understood as elaborate marketing material for these loans. When World Bank planning inevitably fails and the debts cannot be repaid, the IMF comes in to shake down the deadbeat countries, pillage their resources, and take control of political institutions. It is a symbiotic relationship between the two parasitic organizations that generates a lot of work, income, and travel for the misery industry's workers—at the expense of the poor countries that have to pay for it all in loans.

The General Agreement on Trade and Tariffs (GATT), later to evolve into the WTO, has been the forum in which governments seek to reach agreements on trade. After the value of currencies became arbitrary and unconnected to a neutral free-market commodity, and as capital controls limited the free movement of capital, trade became a significant pressure release valve for monetary distortions. The GATT/WTO was built on the insane premise that a central global authority could somehow regulate the flow of trade to prevent imbalances, as if the trade flows were the cause of the imbalances rather than a symptom of monetary manipulation. The GATT/WTO severely undermined the free movement of goods and services in the twentieth century, even though technological advancements allowed for faster and cheaper movement of goods than ever before. One of the most important functions of the WTO today is to stifle the free movement of technological innovations worldwide by forcing countries to accept U.S. patent and copyright law.[90] Forcing countries to apply U.S. intellectual property

---

90   For the case against intellectual property laws, see Kinsella, Stephan. "Against Intellectual Property." *Journal of Libertarian Studies*, vol. 15, no. 2, 2001, pp. 1–53. Web.

laws domestically makes it much harder for developing country industries to build on new technologies and slows the speed and spread of innovation. But it does benefit the large corporations that have enormous influence over the WTO.

In addition to these three main institutions, commonly referred to as the international financial institutions (IFIs), there has been a large growth in international and national development organizations globally. These organizations are involved with all aspects of life in the average third-world country and have grown into monopoly central planners with control over many sectors of developing economies.

The final component of the misery industry is its academic wing. This wing comprises thousands of academics who study development and plan, execute, and assess development projects and strategies worldwide. "Development economics" makes no sense whatsoever as an independent discipline of economics since the realities of economics are equally true in developing and developed countries. Nothing is gained from isolating developing countries' economies and studying them as if they were different. No intellectual reason exists for this separation, nor is there market demand for this ridiculous field of study. The demand is purely manufactured by the misery industry and its many intellectual tentacles.

Readers who are unfamiliar with development economics literature should consider themselves lucky. In seven decades, thousands of scholars have produced endless heaps of reports, papers, studies, and books on development economics, all of which essentially conclude nothing. These academics' only real achievement is the creation of very rich case studies on central planning's myriad failures, in an endless tale of self-reinvention with ever more ridiculous feel-good buzzwords and corporate boilerplate that never questions one universally important tenet: development requires debt and financing, which require growing amounts of bureaucracy and more funding. No matter what the latest global menace is, operationally, the solution is to convert a Federal Reserve line of easy money into third-world debt to produce more jobs for misery industry bureaucrats and their foot soldiers.

Freedom from Accountability

The misery industry's fiat foundations make it so far removed from the free market that it operates in a complete vacuum of accountability and responsibility. As explained by William Easterly,[91] these organizations have a fundamental and intractable principal agent problem. The supposed beneficiaries of their services are not the ones paying for them, so the providers will never be accountable to them. They are instead accountable to their donors and funders in the rich countries. As such, their actions are always driven to satisfy the demands and interests of their employees first, their donors second, and their beneficiaries last. The misery industry is full of stories of projects that sound great to the donors but are terrible for the recipients.

Since the donors do not benefit from the project, they will never have more than a passing interest in its outcomes, as opposed to the beneficiaries whose lives are dependent on it, despite not having the power to control the project. This asymmetry creates highly skewed incentives for the project's providers and ensures they do not face real accountability for their actions. The World Bank has for decades been the butt of many jokes because it alone is responsible for assessing the success of its own projects. Whereas in a free market, the consumer is the beneficiary who decides which companies to "finance," and governments have at least a pretense of political accountability to democratic institutions, in the misery industry, the only kind of accountability is self-accountability.

The World Bank itself decides on which projects to undertake and how much to fund them. Afterward, bureaucrats drawing a salary from the bank conduct internal reviews and issue assessments. As you would expect from any bureaucracy, it is not really possible for any real critical self-assessment to emerge because it does not have to. The World Bank's funding is practically limitless. So long as the Federal Reserve's fiat credit

---

91   This chapter draws on William Easterly's work, in particular, *The White Man's Burden*, *The Elusive Quest for Growth*, *The Tyranny of Experts*, and "The Cartel of Good Intentions."

is accessible, there is no market pressure to deliver goods and services. The Fed ensures that the World Bank can never go out of business regardless of whether its projects fail miserably. Without real consequences, there cannot be real accountability.

The misery industry is also notorious for retaining and rewarding the most incompetent of its staff members, an ideal and lucrative gig for anyone seeking to avoid accountability and responsibility. In free markets, any job entails significant responsibilities and accountability, but working in development organizations comes with even less accountability than working in government. At least in the so-called public sector, the beneficiaries, or citizens, are also the ones funding the projects (albeit involuntarily), and the government at least pretends to want to serve them. In the misery industry, the payers are not the beneficiaries, and they rely on the misery industry for the assessment of its own work.

Projects in the misery industry pay lip service to serving the population of poor countries, but their underlying motivations can be best summed up in one phrase: self-preservation. Like any bureaucracy isolated from the healthy feedback of the free market, these organizations do not exist to serve their customers but rather their insiders. Failed policies can continue for decades as long as they are financed. The IFI's access to a line of credit from the Federal Reserve grants them immunity from market failure. After seven decades, their budgets and staff continue to grow each year, irrespective of performance, and this growth shows no sign of abating.

The more one reads about it, the more one realizes how catastrophic it has been to hand this class of powerful yet unaccountable bureaucrats an endless line of fiat credit and unleash them on the world's poor. This arrangement allows unelected foreigners with nothing at stake to control and centrally plan entire nations' economies. These organizations can easily override domestic property rights and institutions under the guise of development. The World Bank can decide on a development project and have the local government work on implementing it regardless of the domestic impact. Indigenous populations are removed from their lands, private businesses are closed to protect monopoly rights, taxes are raised, and property is confiscated to make the projects happen for the sake of development. Tax-free deals are provided to international corporations under the auspices of the IFIs, while local producers pay ever-higher taxes and suffer from inflation to accommodate their governments' fiscal incontinence.

The utilitarian and totalitarian impulses of the socialist and Keynesian textbooks taught to these development planners come to the fore in their dealing with poor populations. These textbooks teach that welfare and human well-being can be judged through statistical aggregates which central planners need to manage and through measuring the impact of policies on society. The fact that economics is fundamentally subjective, as Austrian economists teach, and that welfare metrics cannot be meaningfully measured any more than feelings can be measured, is not something that has occurred to the many economists of the misery industry.

The misery industry never lets methodology or logic get in the way of a good third-world loan, and so they have devised astonishingly ridiculous, and potentially criminal, ways of measuring the impact of their policies and loans on local welfare. Since the goals of development pertain to things like health, education, and general well-being, development planners will put prices on all these things and attempt to make economic plans to maximize national welfare, which would be a measure that includes gross domestic product (GDP), years of schooling, life expectancy, and similar development metrics. This might sound innocuous at first, but its application is the best argument against the mathematization fetish in economics. By putting a price on human lives, projects that destroy them can go ahead as long as the financial return outweighs the "cost" of these destroyed lives. As all aspects of human life are priced on the central planners' spreadsheets, everything and everyone is within the purchasing power of bureaucrats with a limitless credit line; entire countries become computer games for them. And since the numerical values placed on human lives, health, and education are a product of the fictions of these economists, they can always be manipulated in whichever way makes the project sound good. World Bank projections always look great on paper but almost always fail in their implementation. These failures are an inevitable outcome of planning based on fictitious numbers with no measurement units.[92]

Take, for example, an industrial plant, the construction of which would require displacing an entire village of indigenous people, producing enough pollution to ruin the lives of thousands who live on a river downstream. Such a plant would look great according to the World Bank's projections because they will find that the extra benefits it would produce, in the form of tax revenue for the government and jobs created, would be more valuable than the lives the factory would ruin. This is simply the inevitable outcome of using the collectivist mathematics fetish of twentieth-century economists as the guiding light for planning people's lives. In a free market where individuals could make their own choices, no industrial plant would be able to displace locals without compensating them enough to willingly sell their property. But with World Bank loans, greedy governments can run roughshod over their people in the pursuit of self-serving ends.

Proper economic analysis is methodologically individualistic because it recognizes there can be no rational or moral basis for centrally calculated collective decisions. Welfare is not comparable between individuals, and it cannot be added or subtracted across people. No collectivist central planner calculations have any coherent basis in fact. The economists who engage in them are no more legitimate than actors being paid by IFIs to appear as economists in front of third-world governments to entice them to draw on their infinite zero opportunity cost credit line.

Development's Ugly History

The main ideas driving international development in the early years were Walt Rostow's theories on the linear stages of economic growth and modernization, the Harrod-Domar model[93] on capital accumulation driving

---

92   For more on this, see my textbook *Principles of Economics*, https://www.saifedean.com/
     principles-of-economics.
93   The Harrod-Domar model is comprised of two papers: Harrod, R. F. "An Essay in...

economic growth, and Rosenstein-Rodan's "big push" model.[94] The Harrod-Domar model assumes and concludes (all of these models basically assume the conclusions they want) that growth is a direct function of the savings rate. The growth rate in an economy in this model is simply the savings rate multiplied by a made-up constant. The model argues that the reason developing countries do not have the desired economic growth is that they do not have enough savings. To have higher growth, they need more savings. But since developing countries cannot save because they are poor, the model assures us, it is incumbent upon their governments to borrow to fill "the savings gap." In other words, debt must be acquired to ameliorate the savings deficiency and thus achieve the desired growth. According to Rosenstein-Rodan, the government's central planners would spend capital on a big push to build out critical infrastructure and transform the economy from agrarian, rural, and isolated to educated, modern, urban, and industrial.

While any sane economist would agree that capital accumulation is key to growth, it does not follow that governments borrowing capital would have the same effect as if they were to accumulate it. Borrowing is the exact opposite of saving, and investments financed by loans will incur extra interest costs, whereas investments financed with capital will incur no interest. But more importantly, when governments borrow to spend, they are centrally planning their economies and thereby gaining power over the productive members of their society who have to foot the bill. Diabolically, billions of people worldwide have been thrown into generations of debt slavery in order to finance their governments' megalomaniac economic plans.

One of the key insights from Austrian economics concerns the role of government in allocating capital. If the government owns capital goods, a market is not possible in these goods, so there will be no prices to determine

...Dynamic Theory." *The Economic Journal*, vol. 49, no. 193, Mar. 1939, pp. 14–33. Print. Crossref, doi:10.2307/2225181.

94   Rosenstein-Rodan, P. N. "Problems of Industrialisation of Eastern and South-Eastern Europe." *The Economic Journal*, vol. 53, no. 210/211, 1943, pp. 202–11. Print. Crossref, doi:10.2307/2226317.

the most productive uses of capital, and government will fail to allocate them in a way that meets the needs of the beneficiaries. As governments are handed large amounts of funds to spend, they are able to engage in all kinds of politically popular projects with little regard for the opportunity cost, alternatives, or long-term consequences. Whereas in a free market, capital is allocated by people who have generated it and is lost by those who do not use it productively, in a government-planned economy, politicians who did not earn the money are able to do with it as they please without facing the consequences of their folly. Government can continue to tax and borrow to finance itself as it makes bad economic decisions, while private actors are not afforded such a luxury.

Capital allocation by governments cannot be compared to capital allocation by individuals. It makes little sense to think of the money that governments spend as capital investment, as it really resembles consumption more than investment. Governments and politicians spend money more on buying votes and loyalty than on investing in the future. The profligacy of government development projects and the conspicuous consumption by everyone involved only highlights this point.

Having been miseducated at Keynesian and socialist fiat universities, development economists blamed the failures of their plan on everything and everyone except international lending and the World Bank. A new round of models, buzzwords, and development strategies were announced, and lending and central planning resumed under their banner. This ritual would continue for seven decades of insanity and has proven highly rewarding for those who work in the misery industry yet highly destructive to the powerless victims of their relentless help. The misery industry constantly judges its failures and concludes the problems lie in some of the meaningless cosmetic terms they use to impress each other ("more participatory planning is needed," "stakeholder engagement needs to be improved," etc.). The solution is inevitably bigger budgets, more debt, and more central planning.

After the failure of the initial generation of development planners, development economists moved on to more convoluted models that viewed development as a more complex transformation of society. With lots of meaningless mathematical models, the misery industry started moving toward a more hands-on approach to central planning, getting into smaller projects, managing critical infrastructure, and targeting poverty alleviation directly. The results were not much better than before. By the 1970s, the development failures piled high, and a lot of soul-searching within the misery industry would lead to more government control and more centralized economic planning. As the "dependency school" approach became more popular, government central planning became far more pervasive. The combination of global easy money, following the U.S. government's decision to suspend gold redeemability, and governments and international bureaucracies staffed with Keynesians and Marxists proved disastrous.

Global banks were flooded with liquidity they wanted to lend, and governments had an insatiable demand for more money to run their catastrophic schemes. The misery industry was more than happy to be the matchmaker. More and more developing countries became saddled with massive debt in the 1970s as interest rates continued to drop.

Toward the end of the 1970s, the inflationary pressures unleashed by the Keynesians at the U.S. Federal Reserve had escalated wildly, leading to increasingly high prices and speculative bubbles. Wealth holders worldwide started to dump their highly inflationary government monies in favor of gold. The price of gold had risen from $38 an ounce in 1971 to $800 in 1980, and there were serious concerns in Washington over the dollar's survival.

As things got perilous for the dollar, U.S. President Jimmy Carter, sagging in popularity thanks to a broad economic malaise, nominated economist Paul Volcker to serve as the twelfth chairman of the Board of Governors of the Federal Reserve System in July of 1979. Volcker immediately set to work saving the dollar from destruction by reining in monetary policy and raising interest rates, which had enormous repercussions globally. Suddenly, every government with an unsustainable but manageable debt burden under low interest rates was now unable to make their increasingly larger interest rate payments. The 1980s would be the decade of third-world debt crises.

As a third-world country's central bank's foreign reserves become insufficient to cover its government's debt obligations, the problem of the balance of payment functions described above turns the government's own insolvency into a national catastrophe. Under the classical gold standard, life could continue relatively normally for citizens of a country whose government went bankrupt. The king or government would be considered personally liable for the debts, and they would have to sell lands or property or abdicate their rule to their creditors. But under monetary nationalism, the first thing sovereigns can do when facing repayment problems is to lean on the central bank to use its monopoly control over virtually all of a country's capital to finance the government. This can take many forms, of course, all of which have been tried by your favorite kleptocratic regimes of the twentieth century. The simplest is for the government to issue more local debt and have the central bank buy it, which in turn increases the local currency supply, reducing its value. Inflation is just the first and most inevitable outcome of the debt burden and central planning foisted on poor countries. Far more terrible consequences follow as governments attempt to fight this inflation.

Should the government try to prevent the exchange rate from declining by setting a fixed rate, its reserves would collapse as people redeem their local currency for global reserve currencies. As it seeks to stem the bleeding of reserves, it will start to compromise the other functions of the central bank, with devastating consequences. It could begin to restrict trade to prevent people from sending their foreign exchange abroad. It could forcefully prevent capital from exiting the country. It could confiscate bank accounts. Each of these interventions would result in the exact opposite of their intended consequences. As capital controls proliferate, the government may maintain the foreign reserves already in its possession, but it would scare away any new foreign capital from entering the country for a very long time. This would snowball into an even bigger problem for the balance of payment accounts. Trade protectionism can prevent the loss of foreign reserves in the short run, but its second and third-order effects are highly destructive to the economy. Protectionist policies lead to a large increase in the cost of crucial goods and put more downward pressure on the currency, driving people to hold more foreign reserve currencies instead. Such policies also lead to an increase in the costs of imported inputs for domestic industries, which are usually fairly significant for developing countries reliant on developed countries for their most advanced capital goods. As the cost of importing capital goods increases for local producers, the competitiveness of local industries in global markets is severely compromised and exports decline, which in turn hurts the balance of payments further. While confiscating bank accounts can provide a quick short-term fix, it destroys the trust people have in their banking system and makes them far less likely to save for the future, reducing the amount of capital accumulating in banks.

As governments fell into debt servicing problems, their entire economic systems collapsed because their central banks allowed them to pillage productive capital to keep financing themselves and to keep paying off the misery industry loan sharks. As the misery industry's raison d'être is to lend and create more development programs, it also had a vested interest in maintaining the status quo, so it took steps to help governments avoid defaulting on their debts. Propping up states at risk of insolvency by having them borrow ever-larger amounts was the only way the circus of "economic development financing" could continue.

The IMF shined in its role as global lender of last resort in the 1980s, with its famous stabilization policies and structural adjustment programs. As countries were close to default, the IMF would provide them emergency financing conditional on their compliance with its package of stabilization policies and policy reforms. These policies were marketed around the world as free-market reforms, but in reality, they were largely a continuation of debt-financed government central planning.

The IMF's privatization programs replaced government monopolies with private monopolies, usually owned by the same people. As part of the debt relief deals signed with the misery industry, governments were asked to sell off some of their most prized assets. This included government enterprises, but also natural resources and entire swaths of land. The IMF would usually auction these to multinational corporations and negotiate with governments for them to be exempt from local taxes and laws. After decades of saturating the world with easy credit, the IFIs spent the 1980s acting as repo men. They went through the wreckage of third-world countries devastated by their policies and sold whatever was valuable to multinational corporations, giving them protection from the law in the scrap heaps in which they operated. This reverse Robin Hood redistribution was the inevitable consequence of the dynamics created when these organizations were endowed with easy money.

As part of these "free-market reforms," the IMF would recommend imposing more taxes to close the budget gaps, using "free markets" as a cover to pass off its global fiat mining enterprise. The role of the IFIs as enablers for multinational corporations is something that has been repeated often by its leftist critics, such as John Perkins in his *Confessions of An Economic Hitman*.[95] While there is some kernel of truth to Perkins's sensationalist stories, there is of course much that is missing. Having worked for these organizations for decades, Perkins's critique is typical of the lefty fiat insiders who criticize these institutions while living off of their paychecks, concluding that the problem is that they are free-market institutions and the solution is more central planning. In my estimation, approximately 90% of the people who work for international financial institutions can be classified as "leftist critics" of these institutions. American actor Joseph Stiglitz has made a lucrative career from these organizations by playing the role of an economist who criticizes them, demanding they shift toward more central planning and debt financing, even as he collects paychecks from them.

The work of Perkins and many others clearly exposes how much large multinational corporations benefit from the special arrangements that the IFIs negotiate for them with developing countries. However, that cannot be understood as the root problem but rather as a symptom of it. The enormous power of a credit line from the U.S. Federal Reserve that gives these organizations power over developing countries also makes them ripe for capture by multinational companies looking to do business in the developing world.

Fiat economists lash out at multinational corporations as if Nike and McDonald's are the most serious problems facing the third world, completely

---

95   Perkins, John. *Confessions of An Economic Hitman*. New York: Plume, 2004. Print.

oblivious to the far more mendacious horror unleashed by the fiat debt that pays their salaries. This superficial ritual prevents them from coming to terms with harder questions: Why is there a global lender of last resort in the first place? Why do all the world's governments have to get into debt? Why should the IFIs get to plan economic development when the history of central planning is the history of comprehensive failure? Contrary to Perkins's vision, the problem is not that the IFIs allow free trade or free capital movement. The problem is that they control and centrally plan trade and investment and that their loans are impossible to repay. These problems do not start when the country defaults and needs a bailout; they start the moment that the first misery industry plutocrat sets foot in a country and begins to centrally plan its economy.

What happened in the 1970s and 1980s with third-world debt is no different from standard business cycles as explained by Austrian business cycle theory: the manipulation of interest rates downward causes an unsustainable increase in credit, which can only then be sustained with even lower interest rates and will implode as soon as these artificial rates normalize. This phenomenon was observed in stocks in the 1920s, dot-coms in the 1990s, and housing in the 2000s.

To get an idea of how utterly destructive the misery industry is, one need only pick up a development economics textbook and read the laughable explanations of this third- world debt crisis. It is astonishing to see the mental gymnastics required in order to pretend that the problem has nothing to do with the monetary policy that bankrolls the misery industry, or with flooding the third world with debt, or with their centrally planned economies. In the misery industry, the reason developing countries took on a lot of debt is that Arab countries raised oil prices in the aftermath of the 1973 Arab-Israeli War, which led to them having excess capital stored at banks, which banks then had to lend out. The inflationary monetary policy of lowered interest rates is completely ignored. To the extent that the U.S. Federal Reserve is ever blamed for this, it is only blamed for raising interest rates in 1980, not for the decade of low interest rates that had ensnared these countries in debt. The masochistic reader is invited to read chapter 13 of Michael

P. Todaro and Stephen C. Smith's *Economic Development*[96] and see for themselves a fine sample of these rationalizations.

The misery industry grew enormously while destroying the economies of the third world and bringing them to bankruptcy, and it also thrived while "rescuing" them from their debt crises. The staff and budgets of these organizations have continued to rise, before and after debt crises, irrespective of any success or failure metrics. IFI internal reports will forever bemoan their failures to achieve their macro goals and the individual failure of their projects. The only way to understand their continued survival is to realize that the feel-good buzzwords of their stated objectives (development, growth, sustainability, children's education, disease elimination, etc.) are not their actual objectives. Their survival can only be understood as the result of their success in meeting their real objectives: (1) providing lucrative careers for the insiders in these organizations, (2) maintaining the dollar's role as the global reserve currency, and (3) allowing the U.S. government an unprecedented degree of control over the economies of the world. On all three counts, the IFIs have succeeded remarkably. Any goal these organizations might have outside these three is rhetorical.

A Real Impact Assessment

The impact of the misery industry has been to pillage the citizens of the world's poorest countries to the benefit of their governments and the U.S. government that issues the reserve currency they use. By ensuring the whole world stays on the U.S. dollar standard, the IMF guarantees the U.S. can continue to operate its inflationary monetary policy and export its inflation globally. Only when one understands the grand larceny at the heart of the global monetary system can one understand the plight of developing countries. Fiat economists are completely silent on this since their paycheck and third-world raj status are dependent on them not understanding it.

---

96   Todaro, Michael, and Stephen Smith. *Economic Development*. London: Pearson, 2014. Print.

Domestically, the main impacts of the misery industry have been to allow governments to take on larger amounts of debt and to disrupt the flow of financial and human capital. Instead of allowing entrepreneurs and individuals to reap the rewards of their productive work and have the successful among them in charge of more capital allocation decisions, thus shaping the decisions of other producers in meeting their demands, the average third-world government confiscates the wealth of its productive citizens and puts capital in the hands of clueless, unaccountable misery industry central planners and their subordinates in local governments.

In the absence of a free market (thanks to the misery industry's central planning), the misery industry itself ends up being the most lucrative employer in developing countries. Instead of the brightest talents of developing countries seeking to work in a productive capacity and serve their fellow citizens, they are attracted to jobs in the misery industry and end up shuffling papers, writing reports, and conducting the studies nobody reads but that are necessary to keep the funding flowing.

On top of destroying the market economies of poor countries and turning them into centrally planned failures, the large amounts of debt enable them to persist longer in failed policies, which conveniently gives the donor governments a great excuse to control them politically. The net result is that the third world is not just centrally planned; it is also accountable to foreigners instead of locals. Without the misery industry to bail out every kleptocrat in the third world, there would not be constant inflation and recession. On the contrary, it would only take one of these crises to completely destroy any government that engaged in it, thus allowing for a new start. Had kleptocrats not constantly had recourse to the IFI's endless credit lines, they would quickly bankrupt themselves until they were replaced by governments that behaved responsibly and only spent less than they taxed. A single hyperinflationary episode that destroys a government and replaces it with a monetarily disciplined one is a far better outcome than the eternal purgatory of constantly high inflation, fiscal crises, capital controls, protectionism, and central planning that the IMF promotes.

If you live in a poor country, you are witnessing the collapse of your money's value through your government's own inflation and the inflation of the U.S. dollar backing it. You are suffering from monetary central planning on a local and global level. You are witnessing the distortion of your local markets through the intervention of foreign central planners. The brightest minds in your country will be tempted to enter into careers in the misery industry rather than produce something of value. The argument of this book is not that the misery industry is responsible for making poor countries poor. Rather, in light of all the ways in which the misery industry disrupts and destroys the economic and political institutions of a poor country, it is very hard to argue that it has not hampered developing countries from developing, growing, and eliminating poverty. In sum, the sprawling bureaucracy that is the misery industry has achieved precisely the opposite of its stated goal.

Development Successes

Within the development industry, there is an almost mystical air to the question of how development can happen. The time of simple answers is well past us at this point, and the gibberish reports produced by today's international organizations offer nothing concrete in their meaning-free but grammatically and politically correct platitudes. These organizations cannot in any meaningful way claim to have succeeded in their original missions. Nevertheless, the world has witnessed significant improvements in standards of living, along with the steady elimination of poverty, absolute poverty, illiteracy, and many diseases.

The idea that these organizations are in any way to thank for this progress is a fiction that not even their own economists entertain too seriously. An examination of the history of economic development over the past seven decades shows very clearly how there is no mystery to it and that development conforms to the fundamental tenets of economics. All over the world, and not just in developing countries, societies that have secure property rights, free markets, and relatively open international trade have prospered and eliminated poverty the most effectively. As nineteenth-century industrial technology has spread to the rest of the world in the twentieth century, despite government restrictions and controls, it has brought the living standard improvements that it always brings. As modern telecommunications technology has also spread worldwide, it has helped people integrate into markets, learn skills, and make massive productivity gains.

The most important stories of growth and transformation have been in countries that have escaped socialist regimes and transitioned to more market-friendly political institutions. China is the most important example. In the 1970s, China had little private property and an almost completely centrally planned economy. After the death of Mao Zedong, the founding father of the Chinese Communist Party, the country shifted gradually toward a market economy, and living standards improved drastically. Extreme poverty has been almost entirely eliminated in just four decades. India's move away from the rule of British-educated Fabian socialists started in the 1980s, and with it has come a huge change in the living standards of many of the world's poorest. Neither of these countries had significant amounts of World Bank or IMF lending. Nor did they have anywhere near as many projects driving their development as the African and Latin American countries still languishing in poverty today.

Within Africa and Latin America, the only two examples of undeveloped countries that have successfully maintained economic growth for any appreciable period are Botswana and Chile, both of which are the freest market economies in their continents. Regimes that borrowed heavily and centrally planned their economies invariably ended up with economic disaster and hyperinflation.

Among development economists who subsist on "jobs" from the misery industry, the success of India and China is viewed as a testament to the good plans followed by their governments, and proof that active government management of the economy is necessary and good. But anyone without a paycheck from the misery industry can clearly see that the real driver of growth is the massive reduction of government intervention in their economies. It is also clear that further limiting the state and the misery industry will result in even faster growth and development. The policies of Chinese and Indian bureaucrats and politicians are not driving their economies forward because they are good policies but because they are far less horrible than the much more statist policies of the past.

Achieving economic development is no mystery. It merely requires peace, sound money, and the freedom of citizens to work, own property, accumulate capital, and trade freely. The mystery is how to centrally plan economic development while taking on large amounts of loans from international financial institutions. This is why development economists are ultimately mystified. Their job is not to end poverty or bring about development, but to further their careers and sustain the fiat international monetary system that makes their jobs possible, which forestalls economic growth in numerous ways.

Chapter 12

Fiat Cost-Benefit Analysis

T he previous eleven chapters offered an overview of the mechanisms and consequences of the deployment of fiat money as a global monetary operating system. This chapter attempts to account for the benefits and costs of this technology.

With bitcoin, the cost for securing the network is incurred up front by miners. But the cost of operating and securing fiat, like the cost of sniffing glue, lies not in the small direct cost paid up front, but in the expensive long-term consequences. The physical infrastructure and energy needed to run the fiat monetary system are insignificant compared to the economic, political, social, nutritional, and civilizational consequences of deploying fiat monetary technology. Most of these costs are invaluable and incalculable. But when some of them are approximated, they convey the extent of the damage caused by fiat.

The benefit fiat offers to humanity is that it allows for savings on moving gold for payments. The costs are incalculable. We can classify the costs of fiat into four broad categories: (1) the destruction of holders' wealth through inflation, (2) the destruction of the role of money in economic calculation,

(3) the increased power of government to shape economy and society, and (4) the increased likelihood and cost of conflict.

Fiat Benefits

The benefits from fiat are primarily in the cost saving associated with moving physical gold around. The clearance, settlement, and verification of physical gold would cost somewhere in the range of 0.05–0.5% of face value, as discussed in Chapter 6. It is difficult to estimate how many transactions and at what face value they would be conducted had we lived in a world based on a gold standard today. We have no idea how much final settlement would take place compared to "second-layer" transactions which involve no physical gold movement. An absolute higher bound estimate would be that the face value of the gold final settlement transactions is equal to 10% of total world wealth. By this estimate, the maximum cost of gold settlement would be 0.5% of that, which is 0.05% of world wealth. While it is very hard to estimate the true cost of a modern economy running on a gold standard, we can think of this as an absolute upper bound. Fiat does not entirely eliminate this cost, as gold trading continues, but it reduces it significantly. Fiat's costs, however, are numerous and far more substantive.

Inflation

The first and most obvious cost is the wealth destroyed by the devaluation of national currencies. Every national fiat currency has devalued in real terms almost every year since its creation. This has continuously eroded the wealth of their holders. As bitcoin amply proves, there are no good reasons for the increase in the size of economic activity or user base to require an increase in the supply of tokens used in a monetary system. But government credit money is constantly expanding in supply, and as a result, it is constantly declining in value.

Measuring consumer price inflation is inadequate for measuring the waste of fiat, for reasons discussed in Chapters 4 and 8. Reliance on government statistics has more than just the obvious and severe problems. Governments have an extraordinarily strong incentive to influence the numbers, and government bureaucrats have proved pathologically dishonest when it comes to generating statistics. Further, changes in consumer prices are a complex product of a decrease in the value of fiat money and the increase in productivity causing a decline in goods' value. Without any monetary inflation, productivity increases would translate to price decreases. With monetary inflation, rising prices indicate an increase in money supply larger than the increase in productivity. This means consumer price inflation does not allow us to estimate the wastefulness caused by using fiat money. The increase in the supply of the monetary unit is a much better proxy for it since it is unnecessary and purely a dilution of the value held by the holders.

The average US house price in 1915 was $3,500. In 2021 it was $269,039. That is compound annual growth in the price of the house at a rate of 4.18% over 107 years. Had the fiat standard adopted a fixed supply in 1914, and prices declined by 2% per year instead, the average American house would today cost $411. With a much smaller supply of the dollar, prices would be far lower than what they are today. Incomes would of course also be much lower, but the decreasing price of goods means that they become more affordable over time, and that saved money buys more goods every year. $411 in 1915 could have bought your great grandfather 12% of a house. But if he had saved it and passed it on to you, it would buy you an entire house today. Your great grandfather's pocket change would be enough for you to live off today. A world of decreasing prices would provide people with a strong reason to save for the future, and one can only imagine how much better living standards would be today had humanity not been afflicted by inflationary fiat.

Based on World Bank data, the average annual supply inflation for the major national currencies between 1965 and 2020 is 6.67% for Switzerland, 7.44% for the U.S., 9.76% for Japan, 10.87% for the United Kingdom, and 20.33% for China. The euro area data is not available from the World Bank data, but it is found at the OECD, and averages 7.79%. The simple average for all the remaining countries in the World Bank dataset is 30.10%. The overwhelming majority of economic value exists in the major currencies; a weighted average inflation rate should reflect this, and when calculated, we can estimate that the average fiat user has suffered a 13.72% inflation in their money supply per year.[97] When compared to holding hard money with a fixed supply, the average fiat user is witnessing a devaluation of the wealth stored in their savings by around 14% per year.

In 2019, the total global broad money supply stood at around $95 trillion, while total global wealth was around $360 trillion. This means that fiat money made up around 26.3% of humanity's wealth. As that money is being devalued at 13.72%, humanity is losing around 3.6% of its wealth on average, every year, to fiat inflation depleting the value of its money. If the average trend holds over the coming year, we could expect fiat inflation to destroy around $15 trillion of value in the next year.

It is important here to stress the supremely regressive impact of the fiat tax on humanity. The world's poor are predominantly distributed in countries experiencing higher inflation than that of the world reserve currencies. Further, the world's poor have most of their wealth in money, not in financial assets. The world's rich are the ones who hold the vast majority of the 75% of the world's wealth that is not in fiat but in hard assets like stocks and bonds. The rich will own more liquid wealth than the poor, but their liquid wealth is a small fraction of their wealth, a fraction that declines as wealth increases. By having much of their wealth concentrated in the little liquid fiat they can own, the poor are constantly paying a heavy price for inflation.

A lot of ink is spilled over the evils of inequality, but very few will point to this very obvious and devastatingly cruel form of economic punishment inflicted on the world's poor. Central governments are constantly devaluing and degrading what little hope the poorest among us have for achieving a better life. At the same time, this regressive inflation tax rewards the rich

---

97   Major currencies are collectively given a weight of 80%, while the remaining countries'
     inflation rate is given a 20% weight. A simple numerical average is calculated for the
     163 countries, while a weighted average of the major currencies is obtained by weighing
     each currency by its M2 share of the total group's M2, based on data from the year
     2000, obtained from the St. Louis Fed: fred.stlouisfed.org.

who can borrow large quantities of devaluing fiat, and who can protect themselves by holding hard assets. Predictably enough, the economists, academics, activists, and politicians obsessed with inequality tend to be highly concentrated in fiat institutions, supported by government fiat subsidies, and understandably unable to draw the obvious connection between the inflation that pays their salaries and the poor who foot the bill. Bitcoin is far more efficient than fiat because it does not impose this form of wealth confiscation through inflation. Holders of bitcoin can verify the supply for themselves, and the supply is devaluing at a current rate lower than 2% per year, which is halving every four years on its way to zero, eventually.

Economic Distortions

The second cost of fiat money can be understood as the second-order economic effects of an inflationary global system of partial barter around government currencies, and the enormously costly distortions it causes for the world economy. Chapter 5 in *The Bitcoin Standard* and Chapter 7 of this book discuss the connection between money and time preference, and how devaluing currency disincentivizes long-term thinking and encourages short-term focus in decision-making. The result is a reduction in saving and an increase in indebtedness. Quantifying the enormous impact on humanity of a century of government manipulation of time preference is nearly impossible. The same goes for the centrally planned distortion of the most important economic calculations each human performs: their trades with their future selves. We have no idea what the world would have looked like had everyone continued to have a safe store of value to provide for their future selves. We likely would have seen more long-term thinking and less short-termism and impulsiveness. The impact on technological advancement, capital accumulation, and many societal problems can only be imagined. Chapter 6 in *The Bitcoin Standard* discusses in depth how business cycles are the inevitable result of the manipulation of the money distorting the price of capital, causing malinvestments, liquidations, recessions, and enormous amounts of capital destruction. The financial crisis of 2008 is estimated to cost every

American $70,000 in lost lifetime earnings, or roughly a total of $21 trillion for the nation overall.[98]

Another second-order effect of inflationary money is that it causes losing investments to appear profitable to investors and thus attract their capital. A business expecting a nominal profit will appear like a good investment to an investor, but in real terms, with the devaluation of the currency between the period of investment and the period of revenue accrual, the investment could actually turn out to be a losing investment. With money expected to debase at X%, any business that offers a positive nominal return smaller than X%, will appear profitable while being a net drain of society's capital. Inflation turns money into a melting ice cube, strongly encouraging individuals to spend or invest, even if they cannot find a worthwhile purchase or investment. Wasteful spending and wasteful investments are an inevitable outcome of a monetary system in which the money cannot be expected to hold its value. The cost of the capital wasted in this way is incalculable, as we will never know how much more capital we could have accumulated, and innovations we could have discovered, had capital owners not had to dispense with it like a hot potato.

Also discussed in chapter 6 in *The Bitcoin Standard* is the balkanization of the world's money from one universal medium of exchange, gold, into hundreds of government tokens with limited salability across time and space. This was a huge step backward for humanity's monetary technology. It resulted in what Hoppe called a global system of partial barter. The foreign exchange market is not only an excessive cost in terms of transaction fees incurred by people engaging in cross-border barter. It is a much bigger expense in terms of the problems of calculation it creates for entrepreneurs. They must become part-time macroeconomic and monetary policy analysts to simply figure out the prices of their inputs and outputs. That cost, too, is incalculable.

---

98   Barnichon, Regis, Christian Matthes, and Alexander Ziegenbein. "The Financial Crisis at 10: Will We Ever Recover?" *Federal Reserve Bank of San Francisco.* 13 Aug. 2018. Web.

Fiat Governments

Fiat enthusiasts might argue that the cost of debasement discussed above is not entirely a cost. They claim devaluation has allowed the government and its Cantillon-favored partners to spend, which is not entirely wasted. I would argue the opposite. Government spending, unlike private spending, is by its nature distortionary and wasteful, causing a misallocation of resources. The spending is a cost by itself. It is independent of the devaluation of the currency because it enables the kind of catastrophes outlined in the second section of this book. It is difficult to imagine the degree of government intervention in food production and diet discussed in Chapter 8 under a hard monetary system. The scientific process could not have degenerated into the current corrupt cartel for the mass production of content-free papers. This has been made possible due to government spending distorting the entire structure of the market and its incentives, as discussed in Chapter 9. Without inflation and government intervention in the energy market, it is difficult to imagine a free market causing the recent rises in energy prices and the decreasing reliability of grids in places that had mastered reliable grids many decades earlier.

Conflict

The biggest and most devastating cost of fiat lies in the mechanism it uses to achieve consensus on a global ledger: violence. Whereas gold's monetary role was guaranteed by its physical and chemical properties, and verification of its authenticity is possible, fiat's monetary role is entirely predicated on the authority of the issuing central bank and government. By establishing a monopoly on the issuance and clearance of monetary tokens, Fiat converts all underlying monetary assets into virtual tokens arbitrarily assigned or removed by the central fiat node. Any transaction can be reversed, and any balance can be confiscated. Enormous amounts of these tokens can be conjured out of thin air into any balance, by pure fiat. All value and truth in the banking system can be decided politically. Fiat makes all domestic and international politics an extremely high-stakes game because the prize is virtual control over all economic value, domestically or globally. Further, and as discussed in chapter 8 of *The Bitcoin Standard*, the ability of government to draw on the entire wealth of its population makes it more likely to engage in military conflict and more likely to prolong such conflict, as the costs can be easily placed on the population.

Under the gold standard, governments fought until they ran out of gold and could no longer tax the population. Governments can fight under the fiat standard until they have appropriated all the value held by their citizens' money. As former U.S. Representative Ron Paul explained, it is no coincidence that the century of central banking was the century of total war. R. J. Rummel estimates government regimes murdered 169 million people during the twentieth century. All these governments were able to carry out these atrocities thanks to fiat money's extreme killer app: unlimited government finance. The two world wars and dozens of other wars and genocides have brought about horrors the likes of which the world has never seen. The cost for the dead and their many loved ones cannot be estimated in tangible terms.

Fiat's proof of work relies on violence and the use of physical power to subjugate opponents in the case of disagreement. Fiat is all about "might makes right." It rewards might with the biggest prize of them all: the accounting system for all of society, increasingly rewarding the powerful, and incentivizing humans to engage in power contests rather than economic production. The benefit of running a payment system that allows you to mint money is extremely high. People will spend resources they value close to that benefit to capture it. Fiat makes violence and power the method for incurring the cost. It takes an enormous human toll, almost entirely borne by people who stand to gain nothing from any authority capturing the printing press.

PART III

The Fiat Liquidator

Chapter 13

Why Bitcoin Fixes This

W hereas *The Bitcoin Standard* focused on examining bitcoin's salability across time, this chapter explains how bitcoin compares to fiat and gold in terms of its salability across space. As a present good whose value is not incumbent on credit obligations, bitcoin allows the world to escape from debt monetization and universal indebtedness. Unlike fiat, bitcoin is money without the need for the commands or regulations of any central authority. This allows for a separation of money and state. Bitcoin is, moreover, a neutral global currency that can obsolete the many geopolitical problems that have resulted from one country issuing a global reserve currency.

Salability Across Space

Consumer-facing payments based on any monetary medium can be instantly made between any two accounts with liquidity on the same proprietary network. Instant payments already exist with fiat applications. They could easily be adapted for gold, silver, bitcoin, or even seashells as the underlying asset. But comparing bitcoin to fiat-based money transfer systems is not very informative, and those who harp on such comparisons are likely misunderstanding the difference between consumer payments and final settlement. The correct comparison of salability across space can only be in terms of the *final settlement* of the asset.

Final settlement in fiat between financial institutions takes days domestically and weeks internationally. The mechanics of this process involve largely opaque shifts between central banks' nonpublic ledgers. Bitcoin, on the other hand, is currently proven to carry out half a million *final settlement* transactions every day in a way that is transparent, predictable, and public. Bitcoin offers a settlement whose finality increases every ten minutes and a system that has not reversed a single confirmed transaction once in its first twelve years of operation. This settlement can only be compared to the physical movement of gold, but the lack of material and physical form gives bitcoin a significant leap over gold in its salability across space.

Unlike gold transaction fees, as discussed at length in Chapter 6, bitcoin transaction fees are independent of the distance traveled and the size of the transaction. The implications of this for bitcoin's competitiveness against other monetary systems are enormous. Consider: sending one satoshi to your next-door neighbor costs exactly as much as sending 100,000 bitcoins, worth billions of dollars, from the U.S. to China. While transaction fees are currently under a dollar, it is probably safe to assume they will rise significantly in the future, but the fee will always be independent of the distance between transacting parties. Physical distance is irrelevant on internet-native money like bitcoin. The digital ownership of bitcoin on-chain is completely divorced from any physical location on earth. As the value of a gold transaction increases, the cost of moving it a certain distance increases. As the distance through which a gold payment needs to move increases, the cost of moving a certain amount of value also increases. Gold's salability across space declines with transaction value and distance, but bitcoin's salability is unaffected by these factors.

This can help us understand why bitcoin transactions continue to rise in value over time and will likely continue to do so. Bitcoin transaction fees can be a significant percentage of the value of a small transaction, but they are a very tiny percentage of large transactions. A bitcoin transaction fee of one dollar can be 100% of the price of your coffee, but it would be 0.0000001% of a billion-dollar transaction. Alternatives for buying a coffee are far more likely to be preferable to an on-chain bitcoin transaction than alternatives for the final transfer of $1 billion. This also suggests bitcoin on-chain transactions will likely be used increasingly for international money transfers rather than domestic money transfers. The domestic options for money transfer will likely be cheaper than international options. This is due to the increased costs of conducting transfers across central bank networks. As bitcoin block space becomes scarcer, domestic transactions will be gradually priced out in favor of international transactions whose parties will value the block space more.

As it currently stands, it costs around $3,000 to send a 400-oz good-delivery gold bar, worth around $750,000, across the Atlantic. A similar amount of economic value sent over the bitcoin network currently costs around $1. But as bitcoin continues to grow, you would expect this fee to rise significantly. Still, it has a long way to go before it matches the price of a cross-Atlantic gold transaction. Even a one-hundred-fold appreciation in bitcoin transaction fees would still leave the cost of the bitcoin transaction at around 3% of the cost of transporting the good-delivery gold bar. The comparison becomes even more favorable for bitcoin as the economic value transacted increases. This is because the transaction cost rises with the increasing physical weight of more gold but does not rise for bitcoin.

In terms of time, the gold transaction needs at least an entire day to be shipped to and from the two airports, fly over the Atlantic, and clear customs. The bitcoin transaction's clearance will take a few hours, depending on the number of confirmations the recipient wants. But perhaps the most important aspect of salability in which bitcoin improves over gold is in the ease of verification of transactions. Running a bitcoin full node costs around $100–$700 as a one-time setup cost. It can then verify the validity of all bitcoin payments at a marginal cost per transaction that is almost negligible, as it has a small daily running cost in terms of electricity, bandwidth, and hardware depreciation. By contrast, verifying the honesty of a gold transaction is significantly more expensive. Spectrometers exist that cost several thousand dollars and can verify the content of coins and bars. But for good-delivery 400-ounce bars, the thickness of the bar means that the only way to be 100% sure of the content is to melt the bar and make a new one. When the Bundesbank repatriated gold from the U.S. Federal Reserve in 2020, it melted them all into new bars to verify the purity.

The current global system of gold trading has at its base layer the London Bullion Market Association good-delivery bars. These are all marked and serialized. They must remain held by participating custodians and can only move between them. Should an owner of one of these bars choose to take physical delivery of it, the bar will no longer be part of the LBMA's network of bars. The owner will have a large brick that is expensive to send anywhere in the world, and expensive to break into smaller pieces.

Looking closely at how the gold market works is another useful way to understand the rise of fiat. Even gold trading is effectively done by fiat, with all participants having to trust a central organization to assay and guarantee gold bars that nobody else can verify and tamper with. With costly verification and difficulty of conversion into other monetary unit sizes, these LBMA bars become like digital tokens in an independent payment platform. This is not vastly different from bitcoin or fiat. The fact that the operation of this network depends on the authority of the LBMA makes it far more like fiat in its nature. The hardness of gold becomes less consequential to its operation when it increasingly resembles a fiat token on a proprietary payment network. It is precisely the absence of a cheap reliable free-market option for gold clearance that made its monetary role untenable in the twentieth century.

The higher the salability of a money across space, the more it can travel without needing third parties, the lower the cost of redeeming it out of a banking system, and the harder it is for the rail operators to tamper with the supply. The more expensive the cost of redeeming and verifying the underlying tokens, the more leeway the rail operators have with compromising the hardness of the money under their command. On a gold standard, the prohibitive costs of trading across significant distances reduce it to the equivalent of trading on a centralized scorecard managed by the operators of the rails. The premium gained from having a money placed with a centralized custodian declines the more salable the money is. The easier it is for a bank's clients to redeem their liabilities and spend them internationally, the harder it is for banks to increase their liabilities beyond their assets.

While bitcoin-based financial intermediaries are likely to be developed, the asset's superior salability across space means we can have many thousands, or maybe even millions of banks perform cross-border final settlement on-chain daily. The equivalent in a gold standard was a few dozen central banks. Under fiat, it is under two hundred central banks in name, but in practice, there is only one full node able to validate and reject transactions. The larger the number of entities able to perform final settlement and validate the rules of the network, the more decentralized the network, and the less likely it is to be corrupted to benefit one party at the expense of the rest.

Separation of Money and Debt

Money is a present good that can be exchanged for other present goods in a final transaction which leaves the seller not reliant on the purchaser performing any future obligations. Credit, on the other hand, is a promise to deliver money in the future. Credit can be exchanged for a present good, but the seller of the good requires the buyer to make future payments to complete the purchase. This means credit can only be exchanged for a present good at a discount, reflecting the probability the recipient assigns to getting paid back from the purchaser. An exchange of a present good for credit can only happen among people who have some familial or institutional bond, where they expect future repeated interaction between one another, which would strongly encourage the borrower not to renege on their future payments.

Throughout the twentieth century, trade became more globalized, and as this process unfolded, governments strengthened their grips on gold-backed payment rails and centralized all banking through monopolies they controlled. The best way to understand the gold standard, and its failure, is that the basic monetary asset on which it is built is not just the physical gold, but also the payment infrastructure used by the banks and central banks. As gold banks became indispensable for gold performing its monetary role, their gold was only as good as their credit, making their credit as good as gold. The limited spatial salability of gold meant the monetization of debt issued by custodians and payment rail operators.

An economist or engineer who lived in the nineteenth century would view gold as the monetary asset and the payment infrastructure around it as a secondary layer independent of the gold. A good economist or engineer would view a 100% gold-backed payment system as the desirable and rational way to organize a gold monetary system. But after everything we learned in the twentieth century, the economist or engineer of the twenty-first century is better off understanding the payment infrastructure as part of the monetary system. A party that has monopoly control of the payment system will inevitably end up using this control to further its interests. It does so by issuing more liabilities than the gold it holds.

If you expect the fallible humans of banks, governments, and central banks to act according to what is in the interest of the larger population relying on them, then you think the monetary asset is gold. But if you expect these fallible humans to act based on what their monopoly position allows them to do, you will understand the control of the payment rails itself as a monetary asset, along with the gold. There is no difference between having an ounce of gold in your bank or having a promise from your bank to pay you the ounce of gold. The bank can equally renege on both promises.

The conflation of money and credit has become so entrenched that most modern fiat academics insist that the two things are the same, ignoring the very real differences between the two.

Bitcoin is the live lesson that will eradicate this confusion one block at a time. Every block mined establishes consensus on the present ownership of all coins on the network and establishes who is able to spend how many satoshis in the next block. All satoshis are present goods, ready for final settlement with the next block. Ownership of bitcoin is control of the private keys corresponding to a particular address at a certain block height. There can be no ambiguity about this, and no conflation between future promises of bitcoin with bitcoin. If you have the private keys, you have bitcoin. If you do not have the private keys corresponding to an address, you have a promise from someone else to deliver your bitcoin at a future block height. That promise cannot be used on the bitcoin network, and so it has lower salability than the present ownership of bitcoin and will inevitably be discounted to it. Bitcoin's superior salability across space also means it is relatively cheap for bitcoiners to liquidate bitcoin deposits to discover if they are actually held on demand, or if they are being rehypothecated. The distinction between future satoshis and present satoshis is very clear and made clearer every ten minutes a block clears, making it harder to issue unbacked liabilities. This enables a clear distinction between present and future goods, and between money and credit.

In the fiat standard, customers have no choice but to deal with their local central bank for banking and settlement of international payments. Thus, central banks can mismatch the maturity of their obligations and give customers fiduciary media instead of money. The monopoly command over the international transfer of wealth protects central banks' fiduciary media from facing the kind of market test possible with bitcoin-based institutions.

Bitcoin is the zero-maturity asset against which all liabilities and obligations can be placed and measured. With banks no longer able to pass off their maturity-mismatched debt as money, the control of the banking system is no longer a license to print money. Banking returns to being a normal business offering services to customers, rather than a monopoly money-printing operation. Control of banking will no longer offer governments carte blanche to erase all their debts and foist them on their citizens through inflation.

A sizable part of the demand for debt creation in the fiat system comes from the large demand for holding debt assets, such as bonds or other credit instruments, as a store of value. As fiat money itself cannot meet this demand, and as lending also creates new money, there is a strong financial incentive to create debt. Bitcoin is the astonishingly neat technological solution to this problem. It monetizes a hard asset and offers everyone a chance to hold an asset as a store of value that does not have liabilities attached to it. You no longer need others to be indebted for you to have savings. You can hold a hard asset as your savings, and the work that went into it would already have been performed in bitcoin's proof-of-work calculations. It does not require future production and repayment from the borrower to have market value.

Bitcoin is a global debt jubilee of sorts. This is because its continued growth will likely undermine the demand for the creation of more debt. It could reverse the enormous growth in debt over the past decades of fiat.

Antifiat Technology

Fiat money gives government the ability to spend without limit until the currency collapses. By constantly devaluing the existing money supply with the creation of credit, governments are constantly robbing their citizens' futures to finance their present-day spending. As long as citizens have any savings, governments can continue to devalue them in an attempt to finance their spending and jackhammer reality into the shape they like.

By demonetizing government credit, bitcoin defangs government fiat. It reinstates reason to a world wrecked with the insanity of reality by fiat. Without the government monetizing its credit, most horrors described in the second section of this book would be impossible. Without the ability to hand out trillions in subsidies and artificially cheap credit to manipulate markets, economic reality will return to shape humans' incentives, actions, and world.

No government dietary guidelines existed in the U.S., U.K., and likely in most of the world before World War I. Neither did governments attempt to impose the choice of fuels on individuals. The U.S. and U.K. had no public funding for science before World War I. This was the period in which these countries led the world's industrialization and technological development. The engine, the telephone, the car, the airplane, and countless of the most important technologies of the modern world were invented in the eighteenth and nineteenth centuries. They mostly came about by individual inventors, financed by their savings or the savings of others, and not from government departments. There was no war on drugs in the nineteenth century. The notion of government micromanaging individuals' lives and choices was quaint before fiat. Fiat's unlimited spending power makes all these ideas possible by separating the lunatics who pursue them from the costs and consequences.

Neutral Global Currency

The importance of bitcoin for the world's poor lies in its ability to obsolete the horrific political and economic arrangements discussed in Chapter 11. Those who think citizens of poor countries need a cheap mass payment network in order to thrive are missing the forest for the trees. What they really need is a politically neutral international monetary system that will finally permit economic development. If bitcoin succeeds as a base global settlement network, the benefits would be of far greater significance than a cheaper payment network.

Economic growth does not happen according to some secret, complicated, or elusive formula. It is a remarkably straightforward process that happens when people accumulate capital, trade, and adopt productive innovations. These are the three drivers of economic growth at any time and place, and today's poor countries are no different. They have had little capital accumulation in the past and little to no integration into sophisticated global markets, and they have failed to innovate or adopt the innovations of others.

The correct question, then, is not "How can poor countries grow?" but rather "What is stopping these countries from accumulating capital, integrating into world markets, and utilizing advanced technologies?" The answers are as obvious as they are impossible to ever find among the thousands of unintelligible reports published yearly by various development agencies.

Government policies and monopoly control over the currency and banking system have severely punished capital accumulation. Government spending, prompted by the all-powerful International Financial Institutions (IFIs), shackles the population with debt that lasts generations and requires endless taxes to repay. This reduces their ability to accumulate savings from their income. When these debts are used to finance government central planning, most of the population's productive capital is put in the hands of central planners. Meanwhile, government control of the balance of payment accounts and trade flows scares away a lot of potential foreign investment, free trade, and technological imports.

On a national level, the division of labor and the natural workings of a market economy are sabotaged through the central planning that IFIs impose on developing countries. This destroys the price mechanism and leads to misallocated resources. On a global level, mercantilist bureaucrats hamper free trade and fail to see how critical it is for people's lives. For them, free trade is a threat to the international cash balance that allows them to continue extracting seigniorage. To cap it all off, IFIs and puppet-master foreign governments impose trade restrictions and prevent technological transfer under the name of "free trade agreements" and patent protection.

The three IFIs are inherently set up to destroy the only three mechanisms for economic growth and prosperity. The World Bank's central planning destroys the division of labor. The IMF's monetary stipulations destroy the chance of having sound and hard money and thus accumulated capital. Finally, the WTO prevents technological advancement of poor countries through patents and trade restriction masquerading as free trade agreements.

Bitcoin promises to undo the twentieth century's uninvention of global money. Bitcoin could then save the world's poor from those who have been catastrophically "saving them" for decades. There was no World Bank, IMF, United Nations, or WTO under the gold standard, and that is likely to be the case in a bitcoin standard.

Without governments' national currencies, protectionist policies, and capital controls, the movement of talent, technology, and capital around the world would be far freer. Had the IMF never existed as an enabler of the worst inflationist impulses of the world's governments, one can only imagine what sort of prosperous world we would live in today. Will there be corrupt governments under hard money? Of course, but they will face the consequences of their corruption far faster, as they run out of money and can no longer afford to pay the henchmen that prop them up.

Poverty cannot be ended in absolute terms any more than ill health can be ended. This is because it is a consequence of individual actions, voluntary and otherwise, that cannot be ended. Humans who choose to spend more than they regularly earn will eventually be left destitute, just like those who consume junk food will be left unhealthy. Bitcoin cannot end poverty and it cannot save those who cannot save themselves. But what it does offer is far more valuable than anything fiat can buy: the economic freedom allowing those who can save themselves to do so. A world financial system built around bitcoin would replace IFIs with the normal workings of the free market. There can be no global lender of last resort in that world. There can be no global bureaucracy to centrally plan the world's economies' trade and capital movement.

Chapter 14

Bitcoin Scaling

According to the "World Payments Report 2020" by Capgemini and BNP Paribas, 708.5 billion noncash transactions took place around the world in 2019 (about 1.94 billion transactions per day).[99] The report further expects this trend to continue until there are 1.1 trillion annual noncash transactions by 2023, around 3 billion transactions per day. For comparison, the highest daily transaction volume that the bitcoin network has ever achieved is 490,459, which happened on December 14, 2017. In the three years up to May 2021, the average daily number of transactions was 297,476, with a standard deviation of 50,682. Assuming bitcoin can process half a million transactions a day, it effectively means it can process approximately 0.0167 percent of all noncash transactions expected to take place in 2023. Put differently, if bitcoin is to handle all global digital payments in 2023, it needs to increase its on-chain transaction capacity by around 6,000-fold in the next two years.

---

99 "World Payments Report 2020." *Capgemini*. Web. 3 Oct. 2021.

The current bitcoin transaction capacity is achieved at a block size of around one megabyte. The naive and obvious approach to scaling simply suggests an increase in the size of blocks until they are large enough to accommodate the number of transactions needed for bitcoin to take over the world. This was the scaling approach favored by the doomed hard fork attempts Bitcoin XT, Bitcoin Classic, Bitcoin Unlimited, and SegWit2x. It was also the driver of the doomed Bcash hard fork (as well as its own even more doomed hard fork, BcashSV). The sorry history of all these poorly thought-out attempts is well worth studying for understanding bitcoin.[100] The important conclusion from all these episodes is that increasing the block size is not a workable scaling solution because even relatively small increases would come at the expense of a significant increase in the cost of running a bitcoin full node, likely resulting in a reduction in the number of full nodes, which is ultimately the only guarantee of bitcoin's continued decentralization and lasting immutability.

Bitcoin's core value proposition of immutability is enforced by strong consensus rules which only full nodes enforce. This enforcement ensures its uncensorable nature and hard monetary policy. Increasing the block size to improve scaling has proven highly unpopular with bitcoiners because it compromises the network's decentralization and makes it harder for the average bitcoiner to run a node. Anyone who attempts it will likely end up with a pointless altcoin like the many thousands out there. Even if bitcoiners were to sacrifice decentralization and adopt much larger blocks, it would not provide the orders of magnitude increase in scalability needed for bitcoin to handle all global transactions.

To handle all global transactions, bitcoin would need to scale to blocks of around five gigabytes each. This means that every computer on the bitcoin network would need to download this much data roughly every ten minutes. Each computer must also have the disk space to store all these massive blocks,

---

100 See Torpey, Kyle. "The Failure of SegWit2x Shows Bitcoin is Digital Gold, Not Just a Better PayPal." *Forbes*. 9 Nov. 2017. Web; see also: Bier, Jonathan. *The Blocksize War: The Battle Over Who Controls Bitcoin's Protocol Rules*. Self-published, 2021. Print.

which would accumulate at a rate of almost 0.7 terabytes per day, indefinitely. This is roughly equivalent to the total hard disk space on today's average commercial computer, implying that no commercial computer owners would be able to download the bitcoin blockchain. Only people who can afford highly advanced computers would be capable of running a full node. Such a form of bitcoin would have few people running full nodes. As a result, it would be under serious threat of either capture or centralization. Having only a few dozen full nodes worldwide makes it relatively straightforward for them to collude to change the rules of consensus, as fiat nodes did in 1914.

Fortunately, other solutions exist that can increase on-chain transaction capacity while avoiding a blocksize increase. Many of the recent Bitcoin Improvement Proposals (BIPs) promise more efficient transaction handling. But even with all these improvements, there are hard limits to how many transactions bitcoin's ledger can record. No matter what optimizations are performed, the bare minimum needed for a single payment to take place is the data required for the transaction output, which is still thirty-four bytes of data per transaction. Assuming four megabyte blocks, even the most theoretically efficient use of block space would translate to around seventeen million daily transactions, still a far cry from what would be needed for handling all global transactions.

Hard Money Cannot Stay Niche

Since bitcoin's decentralization is the only thing that makes it valuable, its transaction capacity cannot possibly come at the expense of a reduced number of full nodes. Does this mean that bitcoin is doomed to never scale? Does it remain a niche network processing a few million transactions a day? Could bitcoin become the monetary equivalent of the Esperanto language? A fringe group of enthusiasts using a protocol that is unintelligible to most people?

Hard money is by its very nature a viral and all-conquering technology. It simply cannot be restrained from growing. Monetary history is repeatedly about harder money destroying and eventually replacing the value of easier money. Hard money cannot coexist peacefully with easier monies around it. That situation is an unstable equilibrium. When Europeans found West Africans using beads for money, they took advantage of the fact that the beads are cheap to produce in Europe but expensive to produce in Africa. They brought in enormous quantities of beads to purchase everything valuable in West Africa. There was no way for beads to remain as money in Africa, no matter what the feelings of their holders. Anybody who chose to continue using them as money completely lost their purchasing power; in effect, the beads ceased functioning as money.

The existence of a harder money and other human beings acting in their self-interest will very severely limit your choice as to the type of money you can use. This is not just about finding someone willing to accept the money you have. More significantly, it is about the consequences for the money you hold that results from people producing it at a cost lower than its market value. That harder money will keep value better than the easy money over time, as its supply increases by relatively smaller quantities.

As the relative value of the two forms of money begins to change in opposite directions, the harder money's pool of available liquidity increases compared to the easier money's pool. In other words, the probability of wanting to trade with someone willing to pay with or accept hard money increases. The appreciation in the value of a money results in an increase in its salability, or the likelihood that an individual will be able to sell it when they need to dispose of it.

Salability, as Carl Menger emphasized, is the key property of money. Hardness is key to salability because it constantly serves to increase the relative value of the pool of liquidity available for trade. This process is naturally accelerated when people understand it and rationally choose the hardest money. Over time, as increased wealth shifts toward harder money, more people would want to use it. Thus, the demand for it must increase. The demonetization of silver, discussed in *The Bitcoin Standard*, and the countless failures of inflationary national currencies are further illustrations of this inexorable trend.

This brings us back to the earlier comparison between bitcoin and the World Payments Report statistics. The 708.6 billion transactions mentioned above were specifically called "noncash transactions" for a reason: they involve intermediaries processing the payment. While these transactions are mostly digital today, that does not make them categorically similar to bitcoin transactions in economic terms. Even though it is digital, a bitcoin transaction is still a cash payment because the payment is not the liability of anyone. Bitcoin is a form of cash because only the bearer is able to dispose of it, and they can do so without the need for the consent or permission of a third-party intermediary. Bitcoin as digital cash is more comparable to the physical transfer of physical money, such as in-person cash payments, or final settlement transactions, or movements of gold between gold clearing banks or central banks. It is not really comparable to the noncash payments, even though the two might appear similar because they are both digital. Bitcoin's essential quality is not that it is digital but that its transactions are free of counterparty risk.

Those who expect bitcoin to grow by displacing intermediated noncash payments have completely misunderstood its fundamental nature. If bitcoin is to continue to grow, it will grow primarily through an increase in the value of the cash payments or the final settlements it performs. It will not grow through an increase in the number of transactions. Payment solutions are being built on top of bitcoin through secondary layers. The trend toward higher-value transactions is already underway and will likely accelerate as users increasingly adopt second-layer technologies for lower-value transactions, which will involve trade-offs in security and censorship resistance.

Bitcoin Block Space Supply

A look at the twelve years of bitcoin's existence clearly shows the trend toward higher-value transactions. As figure 17 shows, while the number of daily transactions has grown, it is far outpaced by the increase in the value of these transactions. Comparing the most recent year of data (May 2020 to May 2021) to the earliest year of data, we find that the yearly average value of a bitcoin transaction has increased 150-fold. Daily transaction numbers have practically stalled for the last five years, mid-2016 to mid-2021, in the range of 200,000 to 400,000 transactions, while the value of transactions has increased roughly fifteenfold over the same period.

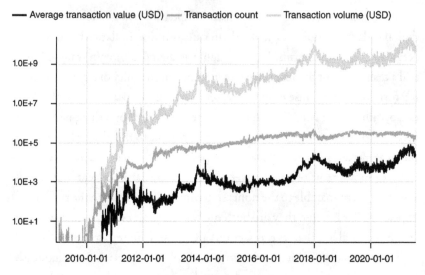

Figure 17. Bitcoin average transaction value, transaction
count, and transaction volume.
Source: Coinmetrics.io.

As demand for bitcoin has increased, bitcoin has not scaled through a
larger number of on-chain transactions but through on-chain transactions
having increasingly large value, both in bitcoin terms and U.S. dollar terms.
This trend should continue as demand increases. With a fixed block size,
there is a hard limit on how many transactions can be done on-chain. Even
assuming noncontentious forks can increase the block size, they will not be
adopted unless they avoid compromising average users' ability to run their
own nodes. This means that any block size increase will likely be slow and
gradual. Growth in demand for holding bitcoin, on the other hand, does
not have the same hard limit. Should bitcoin continue to live up to its core
value proposition as a hard money whose supply is perfectly predictable, the
growth rate of demand for it will far exceed its ability to handle individual
on-chain transactions.

The economics of bitcoin's block space beautifully illustrate market
dynamics at work. Its scarce nature necessarily means that a bidding war
will ensure only those who value block space the highest will get it. Over

time, this pressure has outpriced several types of transactions from being registered on-chain, and now most are settled off-chain, either through second-layer solutions or through custodial internal ledgers. Today, many bitcoin-based businesses conduct most of their transactions on their internal databases. They only use the bitcoin blockchain for final settlement to and from the business. Gambling websites, for instance, will record all bets and winnings on their internal ledgers and will only use the bitcoin blockchain when a user deposits or withdraws bitcoin from the website. The same is true for exchanges, where traders speculate on bitcoin and digital currencies. For each on-chain transaction, several thousands of bitcoin-denominated transactions can occur and settle on internal and private ledgers. This contrasts with the situation in the earlier days of bitcoin when betting services would record thousands of transactions daily on the bitcoin blockchain. As transaction fees on the network have risen, these models are no longer sustainable and have changed to rely on the bitcoin blockchain for final settlement only.

Should the demand for bitcoin increase significantly, many more small-value transactions will inevitably be priced out. Because there is no hard limit on its demand, its total daily transaction value can rise to many multiples of today's daily transaction value. If it does, the liquidity pool for bitcoin transactions will grow, allowing for more valuable purchases and sales to be conducted in bitcoin; this will inevitably outprice the transactions of smaller value, as they will not be able to match the transaction fees of these larger transactions.

When considering the types of transactions that will remain on the bitcoin ledger, it is instructive to think of the alternative avenues available for such transactions. By determining the opportunity cost of not using bitcoin on-chain for various use cases, we can see which ones can afford to bid the highest for block space. Assuming market participants want superior security and a harder monetary policy, they would be willing to use bitcoin even if transaction fees are significantly higher than alternative payment solutions that rely on trusted third parties and inferior security. Conversely, if users are not as concerned with superior security and a hard monetary policy for a given use case (e.g., involving smaller-value transactions), the opportunity cost of not using bitcoin is lowered.

Currently, individual consumer payments are processed with fees of 0–3% over various payment processors. Given that market participants are less concerned with bitcoin's value propositions for these use cases, it would only make sense to use bitcoin for these payments if a bitcoin transaction fee were in the cents or at most single-digit dollars. Similarly, for international remittances, transaction fees are usually tens of dollars, which suggests that range as a potential cost ceiling for bitcoin in this use case. If the use of bitcoin for these uses takes off, transaction fees will eventually rise past the cost ceiling, and it would no longer be economical for the users to conduct these transactions on-chain. This feedback mechanism will continue to price out all manner of uses of bitcoin's blockchain and will reserve block space only for transactions that need bitcoin's guarantees the most. As it stands, bitcoin on-chain transactions are a tiny fraction of total bitcoin-denominated transactions, if one were to count trades on exchanges and casinos, as well as all manners of second-layer transactions for companies conducting bitcoin financing.

As bitcoin transaction fees increase, one of the use cases likely to be the most willing to pay will be international final settlement payments between large financial institutions. These are by their nature the most valuable and most security-sensitive transactions today and the closest thing to a bitcoin transaction currently, in terms of their finality. International payments currently require days (or even weeks) to complete. Bitcoin is barely beginning to acquire the size and liquidity to allow it to conduct such payments with confidence and security. But as it grows, it will likely attract more of these transactions, which will crowd out many other use cases and push them off-chain. To accommodate smaller transactions whose parties will not be able to afford block space in this market, second-layer solutions are already emerging. These bitcoin-based transaction protocols hold the promise to preserve some of bitcoin's guarantees while relieving users of its on-chain fees.

Second-Layer Scaling

Silver coins coexisted with gold in order to accommodate the need for small transactions where gold was not feasible to use, but this arrangement was obviated by financial instruments based on gold. In the same way, second-layer bitcoin transactions are likely to displace transactions that currently take place with easier forms of money, especially as bitcoin adoption and liquidity grows. Bitcoin purists may complain that second-layer bitcoin transactions will never have the equivalent on-chain transaction security and certainty. They're right, but that misses the point. Second-layer bitcoin transactions do not compete with first-layer bitcoin transactions. Instead, they compete with second-layer transactions with inferior monies.

While the purists will complain that these kinds of transactions will never have the same level of security as real bitcoin transactions, the scaling limitations for bitcoin's on-chain volume discussed above make it clear bitcoin cannot scale to handle individual consumer payments.

Moreover, bitcoin transactions need about ten minutes to get a single confirmation on the network, which is highly unsuitable for individuals who expect their consumer payments to be complete much more quickly. The level of security and certainty bitcoin provides for a transaction after it has received a few confirmations is also wasteful overkill for small purchases, and the purists can do nothing to stop the economic reality of individuals preferring these second-layer payments with hard money to second-layer payments on easy money. The limitations that exist will also be present in second-layer payment solutions for other types of money. The main difference is that the payment solutions on hard money are likely to allow holders to preserve value better into the future. Given a choice between payment solutions on a hard money versus an easy money, salability across time dictates that the harder money will inevitably win.

The common mistake that many bitcoiners make when assessing second-layer solutions on top of bitcoin is to compare them to bitcoin transactions, but the more correct comparison is with consumer payment technologies that use fiat. Conceptually, bitcoin could scale to handle all the world's transactions by next week if central banks replaced all their reserves with bitcoin this week. If the bitcoin blockchain were only used to settle large transactions between central banks (while they issued currencies fully backed by bitcoin), then all the world's transactions would effectively be second-layer bitcoin transactions. Your government paper money, your checking account, your credit card, and your PayPal account would all become second-layer bitcoin payment solutions in that scenario.

As the number of bitcoin holders grows and more people demand payment solutions, there will be an incentive to supply them. These solutions will be optimized and tailored to work best with bitcoin as it is. This may lead to a reinvention of most of the mechanisms we use today for payment. Secondary layer transactions do not share the same level of security as on-chain transactions, but it is not clear why that level of security is needed at all for daily consumer transactions of small values. When a customer has an account with an exchange or online casino, they are already trusting that party on many different levels; allowing that party to record transactions on their own ledger after they have received the deposited customer funds adds no risk whatsoever. If they choose to abscond with client money, they could do so regardless of whether their internal transactions were recorded on-chain or off-chain. The funds are only truly under the control of the user after withdrawal from the third-party service.

As demand for bitcoin increases, these second-layer scaling solutions will only proliferate. Consequently, diverse levels of risk and safety will appear for different use cases. Opendimes are another good example. These physical USB keys are designed to be tamper-proof, and the bitcoin balance inside them can be verified very quickly. For small sums and transactions between people with a sense of familiarity and trust with one another, this is a particularly useful mechanism that allows for in-person transactions without needing to be registered on the bitcoin blockchain. While this could be unsafe for larger sums because an Opendime does not issue a backup seed phrase, bearer instrument-type technologies can nonetheless handle a remarkably high number of small transactions and allow for more liquidity in bitcoin transactions.

Multisignature custody solutions will likely also play a role in allowing for cheap second-layer payments. Holders could deposit their coins in multisig accounts, such that the coins can only be moved on-chain with both the private keys of the holder and the bank. That bank could then create a payment network for holders of such accounts on its internal databases to allow individuals to transfer ownership to each other, which would only be settled in batches with on-chain transactions at the end of the day, week, or month.

Lightning Network

Perhaps the most interesting and promising second-layer scaling proposal is the Lightning Network, which is a new emerging ecosystem of node implementations that allows for an automated, fast, and cheap implementation of a multisig, channel-based payment network. Lightning nodes open channels with one another by sending funds to a multisig address using an on-chain transaction. Each party keeps an individual balance on the multisig account, and the parties can pay each other by signing off-chain lightning transactions that reflect their updated respective balances. When either party chooses to close the channel, an on-chain transaction (reflecting the result of all the off-chain balance updates) is sent from the multisig channel address to the two parties with their respective outstanding balances.

But Lightning users do not necessarily need to build channels with everyone with whom they wish to transact, as payments can be routed through various other nodes and channels to link two parties who do not share a channel. As the number of channels and the liquidity they hold rise, the possibilities of routing payments between users increases. Individual nodes that route payments between nodes can charge routing fees to compensate them for providing liquidity.

The strength of this approach to scaling is that the setting up and closing of a channel requires just two on-chain transactions in total. This allows both parties to conduct an effectively infinite number of off-chain transactions at zero marginal cost. Additionally, the timing of the on-chain transactions is flexible since channels can be opened and closed when the demand for on-chain transactions is low. Users can observe publicly available information about the mempool to establish whether competition for blockspace is driving up fees and vice versa. People who establish a pattern of repeated transactions can settle transactions locally on their channel, or through other channels, without having to record every transaction on the bitcoin ledger.

Despite these benefits, it is important to remember that an off-chain transaction on Lightning is not as secure as an on-chain transaction. But the most important difference between the two lies in liquidity.

The real limitation of the Lightning Network is not in its security or number of transactions but in the depth of the liquidity pool in the network. The more people on the network and the more money sent to payment channels, the higher the chance that an individual can trade with someone else on the network. But the opposite is true as well, which means low liquidity may lead to higher fees and longer wait times. The provision of liquidity to the network is an overly complex web of individual economic decisions inextricably linked to people's valuation of time and the inescapable uncertainty of the future.

Ludwig von Mises discusses how uncertainty about the future is the key driver of demand for holding money.[101] With no uncertainty of the future, humans could know all their incomes and expenditures ahead of time and plan them optimally to avoid ever having to hold cash. But as uncertainty is an inevitable part of life, people must continue to hold money for future spending.

Committing a balance of bitcoin to a Lightning channel is not the equivalent of holding a cash balance. This is because the money on that channel is only useful for payment for the counterparty of the channel or others who are connected to them on the Lightning Network. It does not have the same liquidity of coins that can be spent immediately on the bitcoin network. Also, establishing channels involves nonnegligible costs in fees, time, and coordination, and a user's channel funds are only liquid to the extent the counterparties in their channel have liquidity. Since liquidity in a channel can generate a return in terms of routing fees, it is more accurate to understand channel balances as an investment to secure routing fees, as well as an option contract: having the right but not the obligation to instantaneously send value through that channel if it is open.

Since profits can be made from providing liquidity, the best liquidity decision for a particular node is not based on individual demand for liquid

101 von Mises, Ludwig. *Human Action: The Scholar's Edition*. Auburn, AL: Ludwig von Mises Institute, 1998, p. 250. Print.

cash balances but rather an investment decision based on expected returns from routing fees. If people managed their Lightning balances solely based on their need for cash balances, there would be no reason to expect sufficient liquidity to route the payments of others. But since there is a market demand for liquidity to make cheap transactions, the amount needed to meet that demand will be provided by investment in that liquidity for a return, which implies specialization. In other words, the dynamics of the Lightning Network strongly suggest that specialized node operators will emerge to earn profits in exchange for liquidity provision. The job of banks in processing payments can be understood as the provision of liquidity. In traditional finance, they are the ones able to put up cash for payments when needed. Similarly, Lightning Network growth depends on professional management and the provision of liquidity.

The management of the liquidity on channels to optimize for fees is more like a specialized commercial enterprise managing liquidity than individuals managing their expenditure between bank accounts, credit cards, and cash. It is unlikely that an extensive network of liquidity and routing could develop purely from individuals entering channels with one another. This is primarily because everyone will be bottlenecked by the liquidity held by their channel counterparties. When an individual opens more channels on the Lightning Network, they create more liquidity for it, but they will also incur higher costs involved in opening and closing many channels. In contrast, opening a channel with a single node specialized in providing liquidity (and with an extensive structure of channels open with many other nodes) will allow that person far more liquidity and reach. Specialized node operators will allow relatively new Lightning Network users to plug in to the network and immediately enjoy the benefits of bitcoin-based transactions that are quick and cheap.

The opportunity to profit from providing reliable liquidity and routing to users suggests that if the Lightning Network were to continue its growth, providing liquidity would likely grow into a profitable and highly sophisticated business. Economic efficiency suggests that the network would be far more robust if liquidity were to become a professional service provided by businesses to consumers. In such a scenario, one would expect a hub-and-spoke arrangement where a global network of specialized nodes with large liquidity all open channels with one another, while average users would have just a few channels open with these large liquidity nodes. A robust network of nodes each with large liquidity would allow individuals access to cheap and quick routing through deeper liquidity.

Further, if the above analysis on the need for custody is correct, then many people will prefer to avoid having to deal with many channels themselves. They will instead have their bitcoin held in custody by Lightning node operators who can also clear payments on-chain.

Trade-Offs and Risks

The move toward second-layer scaling entails risks not only for individual users but also a systemic risk for the network itself. The first and most obvious trade-off is in the network's censorship resistance. Bitcoin has produced the only reliable technology for transferring value without reliance on intermediaries, and it only manages to do a few hundred thousand of these transactions per day. As the demand for bitcoin transactions increases, and individuals resort to second-layer solutions that rely on third parties to clear their payments, these parties will be able to censor their transactions and possibly confiscate their coins. One of the main advantages of the bitcoin network is thus lost for individuals if they choose this type of second-layer scaling.

The second risk is more systemic to the whole network since it threatens the network's protocol and consensus parameters. If bitcoin transactions move to second-layer solutions where many individuals are trusting third parties to validate their transactions and enforce network consensus rules, bitcoin deviates from being a peer-to-peer system. Consequently, the risk of collusion between nodes processing transactions rises. One can think back to the SegWit2x attempted "upgrade" and imagine a world where far fewer individual users ran their own full nodes. Had users been reliant on bitcoin businesses to enforce consensus rules, businesses could have succeeded in changing bitcoin's consensus parameters. If the number of nodes declines, the remaining nodes become more influential and easier to co-opt by attackers or governments. A bitcoin network with a few hundred nodes is a far less immutable and secure network than one with tens of thousands of nodes.

The risk of losing censorship resistance is one that each individual needs to assess in contrast to the convenience and cost of other payment and custody options. The other risk is not directly the result of second-layer processing itself but rather a reduction in node count to the extent that it jeopardizes the decentralized nature of bitcoin. However, the Schelling point of bitcoin nodes agreeing on the main consensus parameters does not require every user to run their fully validating node. It requires enough independent full nodes to be active and enforcing consensus parameters to prevent any small group from changing these parameters in the direction that it chooses.

As Bitcoin scales, the challenge will be to introduce second-layer solutions that minimize both the trust in third parties and their ability to censor transactions. What is essential for bitcoin to survive is that the main consensus parameters, particularly the economic parameters, remain immutable. For that to happen, bitcoin needs many independent nodes that are unable to coordinate. The larger the number of nodes, the less likely it is that subgroups will collude. It is not strictly necessary for every individual to be able to verify each of their transactions on-chain for bitcoin to survive. If the growth of second-layer solutions results in a larger liquidity pool for bitcoin, and operating bitcoin full nodes becomes a profitable way to provide banking services, then it would financially incentivize the growth of independent nodes. This will make the bitcoin protocol more ossified and harder to change. Not only does the increase in the number of nodes make coordination more difficult, but the profit motive would likely make nodes conservative.

The good news is that Bitcoin does not need to be scaled globally on-chain. Bitcoin does not have any competitors for trustless, automated, and censorship-resistant global clearance. The only other asset that comes close to it is gold, whose movement is far more expensive and subject to confiscation. Bitcoin needs to be secure and decentralized enough to resist control and capture. It also needs a clear, broad, and immutable consensus around network rules and money supply considerations. It certainly does not need to accommodate your coffee transactions on-chain.

Chapter 15

Bitcoin Banking

B anking has two core functions: holding deposits and allocating investments. The need for these two specialized services is not the result of technical shortcomings of government money that bitcoin could improve upon. They are demanded in a free market for the same reason any good is demanded: consumers value these services, and providers specializing in them can offer them at a lower cost and higher quality than individuals could provide for themselves. There is a lot that is wrong with crony-capitalist modern banking, but this is primarily the result of government protection of banks that allows them to profit from unproductive practices and offload the downside risk of their activities to taxpayers. The demand for legitimate banking services will continue to exist under a bitcoin standard, just as it has existed under other forms of money. Bitcoin block space does not replace the two essential functions of banking.

Most people with appreciable liquid savings prefer to have most of their savings deposited with a specialized service that can ensure better security. The value of keeping large amounts of cash in a bank vault protected with firearms rather than under a mattress is obvious. Individuals do not want to always have physical possession of their entire life savings because of the risk of loss or theft, and the stress that comes with it. Homes are not designed to optimize for securing large amounts of physical money, but bank vaults are. It is an inevitable part of human trade and specialization that enterprising individuals would take the initiative and build a facility designed for securing stockpiles of money. Such a facility would employ the kind of security that is unsuitable for a residential home. Individuals would then benefit from paying a small cost to have their money secured at that facility.

Bitcoin allows people to send money globally without censorship, but it cannot possibly offer them safe and reliable self-custody. That is an inescapably real-world, flesh-and-blood problem. The same censorship-proof nature of bitcoin that allows the sender to irreversibly move money across the world can be misused by a thief to permanently steal someone's bitcoin. The nodes of the bitcoin network have no way of distinguishing between different people wielding a private key, and no notion of legitimate or illegitimate ownership of these keys. Even absent theft, hardware wallet passwords can be forgotten and backup codes lost. Expecting bitcoin to end humans' demand for custody solutions is entirely unreasonable.

It is also inaccurate to assume that the continued existence of banking under a bitcoin standard will necessarily result in censorship, inflation, and fractional reserve banking. Any industry functions well only when a free market exists that gives consumers a choice in their providers; this choice forces providers to either care for their clients or suffer the penalty of lost customers and potential failure. The evils many associate with banks may be more accurately understood as originating from centralized governments and the lack of free-market choice. The problem with banking, then, is not the nature of banking itself but government policies that create monopolies. In a free market, banking would continue to exist but would be subject to consumers' choice and satisfaction.

Many bitcoiners may want a world in which everyone gets to be their own bank, but most people do not want this any more than they want to be their own butcher, builder, car maker, or baker. To impose this model on everyone is impossible due to bitcoin's permissionless nature. There is nothing one bit-coiner can do to another bitcoiner who decides to sell custodial claims on the bitcoin they own.

That the benefits of bitcoin are lost to those who choose to deal with cus-todian services is also inaccurate. One may lose the censorship resistance and permissionless control of owning their own bitcoin private keys, but they would nonetheless benefit from holding an inflation-resistant hard asset. While there is demand for a permissionless way to send value worldwide, that use case is without a doubt dwarfed by the universal demand for the hardest money. Not everyone has a pressing need for making payments their gov-ernment does not approve of, but economic reality will inevitably compel everyone to converge on the hardest money in the market. As time goes by, and if current trends continue, we can expect demand for holding bitcoin as a hard money to increase even while more transactions are priced off-chain on internal ledgers held by bitcoin-based banks.

The second core function of banking is the allocation of capital into investments. The demand for this function is also not something bitcoin can eliminate. The development of banking institutions is an advancement in capital accumulation, allowing for a much more sophisticated division of labor and higher productivity. Because bankers specialize in the deployment of capital, they allow individuals to specialize in their respective fields and focus on being as productive as they can. The individual is freed from the labor of analyzing various investments and assessing their possible returns and risks. This task is delegated to professionals who specialize in match-ing individuals' investment goals and risk tolerance with suitable investment projects. The allocation of investment is an act that cannot benefit from the automation and immutability that bitcoin provides to financial transactions. These are activities that require a human judgment of factors outside of the bitcoin blockchain and would exist in any sufficiently advanced capitalist economy. This part of banking would also exist on a bitcoin standard.

Bitcoin cannot replace banks, but its monetary properties will lead to a banking system significantly different from one built around fiat. Here are seven ways in which we can expect bitcoin's monetary properties to influence a bitcoin-based banking system.

Savings Technology

Chapter 5 surveyed the historical evolution of the technologies used to fulfill the function of savings. Up until the nineteenth century, people would save in physical silver or gold coins. Then came the savings account, where the saver would hold government money that was backed by gold. Based on hard money, the saver could reliably expect these instruments to hold their value for the future. Everyone from a child to a pensioner could store their wealth in a medium they could hold for the future or carry anywhere in the world. But as governments eroded the gold backing of the money over the twentieth century, the ability of bank savings accounts to keep up with inflation disappeared.

To store value into the future, investors had to shift to buying government bonds. The demand for bonds as savings drove the enormous bubble in government debt worldwide, far beyond what governments' creditworthiness would support. This brought down the yields for savers, and as inflation continued, the returns on bonds could no longer keep up with it. Savers needed to take more risks with their capital to simply preserve their wealth. The stock index fund appeared as the saving vehicle of choice in the 2010s as bond yields continued to plummet and enter negative territory. After the coronavirus crisis of 2020 and the significant monetary intervention by governments and central banks worldwide, bond yields plummeted significantly, and investors have little choice but to take on more risk simply for capital preservation.

Ideally, one wants to save their cash balances in the instrument with the highest degree of salability across time and space. Fiat man faces a complicated problem here, as none of his potential choices has good salability across time and space. A dollar in a bank has great salability across space, allowing the owner to send it across the world in a few days, but it has terrible salability across time, making it unwise to hold large positions in it for the future. Fiat man thus must actively manage his cash balance between a part he uses for sending payments across space, and a part he saves for the future. This is an expensive balancing act that impedes individuals' ability to plan and reduces the utility of their cash balances in the present. The demand for saving is currently being met by a variety of suboptimal instruments: bonds, real estate, gold, art, and equities. To save and hold a cash balance, one needs to perform complex calculations to decide an allocation between forms of cash being held for spatial salability. Under the gold standard, the need for saving was met by the same money. But bitcoin offers a savings technology with superior salability across both time and space.

High Cash Reserves

The emergence of bitcoin as a hard asset, free from debt, supplies everyone in the world with a compelling alternative mechanism for saving. Unlike fiat money, whose supply is constantly expanding, bitcoin has a predetermined and constantly decreasing supply growth rate. Unlike stocks and bonds, bitcoin has no yield, which is more suitable for a monetary role. If stocks and bonds appreciate because of increased demand, their dividends and yields decline, making them less attractive to hold, and creating a bubble in their valuations. Either their valuations will decline nominally, or they will decline in real terms as devaluation continues.

By having no yield, bitcoin's appreciation does not make it less attractive as it grows. Bitcoin in this way is like gold but superior because of its higher salability across space. This makes it less likely to be captured and centralized by political authorities or corporate powers. As bitcoin is also starting from a small market capitalization, similar capital inflows will cause a much higher rate of price appreciation in bitcoin than gold. This makes it a more attractive proposition as a store of value for the future, since it is likely to increase the value, not just preserve value.

Bitcoin's higher spatial salability makes it possible to have a high degree of cash reserves on hand. This is because individuals can withdraw their assets far more easily than in banks and physical currencies. They can also perform international settlement with it at a tiny fraction of the cost of physical gold, and so are far less reliant on monopolistic banks and payment rail operators. The lower the salability of a currency across space, the more reliant individuals are on physical infrastructure and government oversight to conduct their trades. Thus, it is harder for them to sever a banking relationship should the bank engage in behaviors that put clients at risk. While bitcoin cannot offer everyone the chance to make on-chain transactions every day, it can offer many millions, and maybe billions, an affordable credible threat of withdrawing their balances and taking full possession of their coins in a matter of minutes. With bitcoin's blocks acting as clear consensus checkpoints on ownership of coins, which are fully audited by all network members, there is a clear demarcation between present bitcoins and future bitcoins, allowing for an easily verifiable public test of liquidity and the ability to fulfill financial obligations.

Individuals might initially buy bitcoin for short-term price speculation, to conduct black market transactions, or as an experimental technology in payments. Some might be ruined by the volatility in the short term. Many will quit. But bitcoin's relentless upward trend will make the value proposition of holding bitcoin as cash clear to most holders. People who allocate a small percentage of their net worth to bitcoin will likely watch it become a progressively larger fraction of their portfolio over time. Others will notice and copy them. Financial analysts will notice the spectacular rise over time and start recommending allocations into it. This process has intensified over the last few years, with a growing number of people worldwide now saving a fraction of their paychecks in bitcoin via dollar-cost averaging, and a growing number of services dedicated to this.

Corporations are also likely to recognize this value proposition and consider replacing parts of their cash balances in bitcoin rather than in national currencies. In mid-2020, we saw the first example of a company using bitcoin as a cash reserve asset, when MicroStrategy, a billion-dollar publicly traded firm, announced that it bought 21,454 bitcoin, worth $250 million at the time, to hold as a cash asset on its balance sheet. This makes it the first publicly traded company to hold bitcoin in its cash balance and the first company to hold bitcoin as cash despite having no operational or business reason for holding bitcoin.

MicroStrategy is not a bitcoin exchange or mining company whose business revolves around bitcoin and for whom holding bitcoin is necessary. This is a strategy and consulting firm whose work does not have any connection to bitcoin. MicroStrategy is not buying bitcoin to use it as a payment network. Nor is it wasting resources on the futile quest to use "blockchain technology" applications that do not involve bitcoin, as corporations like Microsoft and IBM have done over the past few years, with exactly zero return. MicroStrategy is buying bitcoin to hold it on its balance sheet because it has recognized it as a superior cash reserve asset to the U.S. dollar.

In their announcement, MicroStrategy explains why they chose Bitcoin:

> This investment reflects our belief that Bitcoin, as the world's most widely-adopted cryptocurrency, is a dependable store of value and an attractive investment asset with more long-term appreciation potential than holding cash. Since its inception over a decade ago, Bitcoin has emerged as a significant addition to the global financial system, with characteristics that are useful to both individuals and institutions. MicroStrategy has recognized Bitcoin as a legitimate investment asset that can be superior to cash and accordingly has made Bitcoin the principal holding in its treasury reserve strategy.
>
> We find the global acceptance, brand recognition, ecosystem vitality, network dominance, architectural resilience, technical utility, and community ethos of Bitcoin to be persuasive evidence of its superiority as an asset class for those seeking a long-term store of value. Bitcoin is digital gold—harder, stronger, faster, and smarter than any money that has preceded it. We expect its value to accrete with advances in technology, expanding adoption, and the network effect that has fueled the rise of so many category killers in the modern era.
>
> We have a large amount of USD on our balance sheet and we have carried that for a while. Over time, the yield on our dollar values has decreased and at points, we had an expectation that we would get higher real yields,

and therefore, there was no real urgency to address this issue. But as of today, we're expecting negative real returns or a negative real yields on U.S. dollars, and that's an expectation that has materially changed over the course of the last three months.[102]

Demonetizing the World

The nonmonetary alternatives fiat man must use as cash cannot perform the role of money much more satisfactorily than a spoon can perform the role of a knife. Bonds and stocks can no longer offer yields that beat money supply inflation, and both carry heavy risks. Real estate is highly illiquid, indivisible, and requires high maintenance costs. Gold and silver have low spatial salability, as there are no precious-metal-based banks allowed in the fiat era. They also entail heavy transaction fees with each purchase and sale. Managing a savings portfolio is an endless task of weighing a multitude of risks against potential returns for an endless variety of markets.

The absence of a workable medium of saving also results in the distortion of markets for all other alternative monetary goods. Excess demand for bonds rewards undeserving borrowers, most notably governments, misallocating capital and causing periodic default crises. Excess demand for real estate leads to the rise of real estate valuations. This prices out younger generations and causes periodic housing market crashes. The increased demand for anything that offers scarcity causes a rise in valuation for art, resulting in the incredible inflation of valuation for products hardly differentiable from children's scribbles. Commodity and equity markets are heavily distorted by the excess demand looking to avoid inflation. Across the board, the quest to protect value from inflation has disconnected prices from reality.

If bitcoin's liquidity grows significantly, it would offer an increasingly compelling and efficient alternative to these technologies. Demand for these assets would become purely industrial and commercial rather than monetary.

---

102 "MicroStrategy Adopts Bitcoin as Primary Treasury Reserve Asset." *BusinessWire*. 11 Aug. 2020. Web.

Housing would return to being thought of as a consumer good rather than a savings account or capital good. House prices would reflect demand for houses only as places to live, not as savings accounts. Commodities' prices would reflect demand for the commodity itself. Equity would reflect the underlying fundamental values of the company rather than being a gauge for monetary policy as it is now. Artists might need to return to learning skills and putting effort into their work to sell it and not just rely on people's search for anything scarce to buy their products.

Unbonding the World

The monetization of bitcoin competes directly with the monetization of fiat debt, a hugely significant fact with far-reaching implications for traditional bond markets. The continued growth of bitcoin would likely result in a reduction of demand for debt instruments as a method of saving. As national currencies are expected to devalue significantly, they constitute a small part of what investors think of as their cash balances. These assets include gold, bonds, and debt instruments that are free from equity risk. As more individuals and corporations like MicroStrategy buy more bitcoin to hold as their high liquidity low-risk asset, they will demand fewer bonds and debt obligations.

Should this trend continue to grow until it reaches an appreciable volume of global financial assets, bitcoin will have a profoundly transformative effect on the shape of the world's capital markets, banking sector, and government spending. The enormous incentive to borrow in the fiat standard, discussed extensively in Part 1 of this book, is ultimately driven by the monetization of debt, which creates a huge incentive for lenders to create more loans, and also driven by savers' need to hold debt instruments with yield to compensate for inflation's erosion of purchasing power. But demand for holding these loans would decrease when investors choose instead to hold bitcoin, and so the demand for lending would decline too.

Chapters 3 and 11 outlined in some detail how the operation of the fiat standard revolves around the central bank monopoly for banking licenses and foreign transactions. This places all bank accounts and financial assets under the custody of the central bank, allowing it to lend to the government with the citizens' wealth as collateral. Whether through explicit default or subtle inflation, the value of the assets will decline as the bonds are issued and the money supply grows. The devaluation of the currency itself is what creates the demand for the bonds, which in turn allows for the devaluation of the currency, in the eternal perverse cycle of fiat monetary damnation of the last century. This cycle is what allowed government debt to grow to the extent it has over the past century, far beyond what governments' credit-worthiness would merit. Almost $100 trillion of bonds have been issued by government entities at the time of writing, making this arguably the largest malinvestment in human history. By turning government credit into money, the fiat standard has acted as a continuous drain of resources from productive members of society to governments that spend with very little accountability.

What happens if savers increasingly prefer to hold hard money over government debt? The impact may not necessarily be sudden, leading to a collapse of bond markets, but if combined with continued devaluation of national currencies, it could lead to the gradual decline in the economic value of the bond market in real terms even as nominal fiat numbers continue their unending rise.

Bitcoin offers superior salability across space and time to bonds, gold, and government cash. But its main drawback is still its relatively small liquidity. At the current market price of around $40,000, the total market value of all bitcoin in circulation is around $800 billion. This is a sizable number that positions bitcoin among the largest national currencies, but still a drop in the bucket of the total market value of bonds, which is around $140 trillion. Bond markets still offer significant depth and liquidity for the largest institutional investors. But bitcoin, as it grows, has the advantage of being a monetarily fungible good, so demand for bitcoin can be met by any bitcoin seller. In the bond market, on the other hand, while overall market liquidity is quite large, the liquidity available for individual bonds and maturities are fractions of the overall liquidity. The homogeneity of bitcoin and its lack of a yield give it a natural advantage over bonds in playing the role of money.

Gold was chosen as a money on the market precisely because it has no yield. The role of money optimizes liquidity at the expense of risk and return, while equity optimizes for return at the expense of liquidity. In a world where there is little incentive to monetize debt, it is doubtful that any demand would exist for bonds.

Robustness

A financial system built on a hard monetary asset at its base would be far more robust than one built on debt obligations at its base. It would also cause far fewer financial and liquidity crises. The monetization of debt, through the treatment of future promises of payment as being monetary assets like cash on hand, creates an inherent fragility to the fiat monetary system. During times when financing conditions are favorable, banks can meet their financial obligations, as can most of their customers. But market financing conditions can turn unfavorable for many reasons: monetary policy tightening, collapse of large borrowers or financial institutions, natural disasters, and wars are just some examples. When funding conditions become unfavorable, most, or all, debt obligations are valued at a discount by the market, which places financial institutions using them as their financial assets in a precarious position. This creates the liquidity crises that plagued the fiat standard in the twentieth century and which mainstream economists have come to agree can only be treated through the injection of liquidity into the monetary system.

A financial system built on full cash reserves would not experience such liquidity crises. Financial institutions would keep on-hand cash instruments equal to the face value of all their liabilities that are redeemable on demand. Whatever the state of the credit market, the bank would have on hand enough cash to satisfy all depositors and creditors to the full extent of their claim, as the claims are themselves denominated in that cash, and the quantities of cash are held on hand. The growing monetization of bitcoin allows more people to peacefully opt out of having to hold debt as their prime treasury reserve asset and allows them a hard cash asset whose value is not contingent on future cash flows and credit risks.

Full Reserve Banking

The processing of payments can be understood as a market good that becomes more valuable as the scale of an economy grows and the circle in which a person trades expands. The increasing value stems from the clear economies of scale banks have in clearing, netting, and settling large numbers of transactions as opposed to individuals carrying these out individually. Some examples are paper notes backed by gold, bills of exchange, modern credit cards, and PayPal accounts.

In any monetary system, such networks for banking and settlement will emerge, and they will benefit from economies of scale by holding many accounts for people and netting transactions, bypassing the need to physically transfer money (or in the case of bitcoin, the need to transfer assets on-chain). Under the gold standard, the physical movement of gold was expensive and insecure, and economies of scale accrued to those that physically amassed reserves and thus could provide a centralized clearing mechanism. As a result, only a few global central banks could cost-effectively trade gold internationally. The emergence of fractional reserve banking on top of this system can then be understood because of the banks' ability to expand credit. They are backed by their operational capital and aided by a trusted network of banks with which they can clear.

In a sense, fractional reserve banking could be sustainable when the alternative to dealing with banks is too expensive, and banks' reserves are high enough to make crisis-level mass withdrawals unlikely. If the physical settlement is expensive and the network of banks is indispensable for its customers, banks could conceivably get away with not keeping all deposits on hand without experiencing a bank run. It is possible for fractional reserve banking to continue in a bank that is the only one in a town, or where it enjoys some monopolistic privilege from the government because there are no easy alternatives for clients to process payments if they choose to withdraw their money from the bank. This becomes particularly easy if the money is easy for authorities to use to prop up insolvent banks.

The degree to which a bank can get away with fractional reserve banking is a positive function of the cost of the final settlement of the monetary asset and the ease of debasing the monetary asset. Under a gold standard, the cost and time required to move gold around are relatively high, so the economies of scale from centralization will provide existing banks a degree of leeway in extending unbacked credit without their depositors noticing or being able to do anything about it. Yet this system is not very sustainable, because the longer it lasts, the safer banks feel, the more risks they take, until it comes crashing down, as was the case during the nineteenth century. Since it is not easy to increase the supply of gold on demand, and no lender of last resort can print it to bail out banks engaged in fractionally lending gold-backed notes, fractional reserve banking was the bug that kept on derailing the gold standard. Eventually, the gold standard itself was sacrificed to keep fractional reserve banking alive when a dollar-based standard was used for settlement. This makes settlement entirely centralized with a government monopoly while leaving the currency elastic to the demands of the banking sector.

Here we see an advantage that bitcoin has over gold: it can provably perform hundreds of thousands of settlements a day. Compared to the physical movement of gold, the final settlement costs are much lower, which translates to fewer economies of scale for centralized bitcoin clearing, and thus even less incentive for a central banking ecosystem around bitcoin to emerge. Any system for bitcoin settlement would be far more distributed at its core than gold. The benefits from economies of scale are not as pronounced as with the case of gold. There is room for far more institutions to be able to perform settlements with one another. With higher spatial salability comes higher capacity for more transactions and less unbacked liabilities.

Equity Finance

Bitcoin-based financing will probably cause a shift toward more equity investment rather than credit instruments and interest-based lending. We can identify three drivers of this trend. First, if bitcoin continues to rise, the seigniorage benefit from monetizing debt will dissipate, as people monetize a hard asset instead. This on its own would reduce the incentive to issue debt.

Secondly, the lack of a lender of last resort further reduces the incentive for issuing interest-bearing debt. With a strictly fixed and perfectly auditable supply, there is little scope for any entity such as a central bank to pass off its liabilities as money and increase the money supply. Fiat allows banks and central banks to pass off their liabilities as money because they ultimately have monopoly control over the infrastructure that gives the money its spatial salability. Under the gold standard, too, gold's limited spatial salability and the difficulty and cost of physical redemption also gave banks, particularly larger ones, the ability to pass off their obligations as money and to act as lenders of last resort. Without a lender of last resort, offering a fixed-interest loan with a guaranteed return becomes exceedingly difficult for a bank, as there can never be a guarantee that the bank or its borrowers will not face insolvency. The risk of complete ruin is ever-present in any business enterprise, and any bank that backs its demand deposits with loans issued to businesses is taking on a large risk. There can never be a mechanism for guaranteeing the return of capital if it is to be involved in business activity. Even with insurance, there are acts of war and nature that cannot be insured against, or where the insurance companies go bankrupt themselves. Banks cannot always make good on a promise to return capital to the depositor with an interest. They are undertaking risky investments, and the depositors are always taking on the risk of being wiped out without a lender of last resort able to compensate them for their loss by distributing it over existing currency holders through inflation.

With bitcoin's high spatial salability and quick final settlement capabilities, the possibility for a bank to offer fixed interest returns for on-demand deposits is unlikely. With bitcoin able to perform so many global transactions, there is likely to be less advantage to access the payment rails of any one bank than there is to access fiat monopoly payment rails. Depositors who suspect their deposits are being lent out can very quickly withdraw and leave the bank insolvent. It is doubtful that the extra returns banks can generate from lending demand deposits, as they do in a fractional reserve banking system, are even possible in a hard money economy where no lender of last resort exists to protect the banks and their clients from the downside risk. With the clarity brought about by the fixed supply, and the efficiency brought about by the high spatial salability, banking likely bifurcates into its two essential and demarcated functions: deposit banking and equity investment. One could argue the gray area of investing in credit and fixed-interest rate lending is a function of the limitations of spatial salability and supply vagueness of fiat money.

With a highly salable money like bitcoin, depositors who want access to their money will only be able to get it safely by placing it as a deposit and paying a fee for its safekeeping. Investors who would like to earn a positive nominal return on their bitcoin would need to accept the high degrees of risk. With the downside unlimited, there is little reason to agree to an investment with a fixed upside, as is the case with fixed-interest loans. Since the money is all at risk, investors who accept fixed-interest loans in the long term will lose capital, as their upside is limited, but their downside is unlimited. With enough investments, the losses will accumulate. They will likely be outperformed by investors who take an equity stake and thus match their unbounded downside with unbounded upside, collecting better returns.

The third driver of equity finance is the growing accumulation of cash balances. As cash's zero nominal returns translate to positive real returns with hard money, cash becomes a more attractive financial instrument than debt on individual and corporate balance sheets, leading to a growing abundance of it. The availability of hard appreciating cash reduces the incentive to lend to secure a return, and the resulting abundance in cash reduces the return on lending. As human civilization progresses, and money improves as a technology, humans accumulate more cash balances, and that leads to lower interest rates on the price of capital.

The process of human civilization, as the lowering of time preference, is driven by, and in turn drives, more savings and lower interest rates. Austrian economist Eugen von Böhm-Bawerk said that the cultural level of a nation is mirrored by its rate of interest, as explained by Schumpeter:

[Interest] is, so to speak, the brake, or governor, which prevents individuals from exceeding the economically admissible lengthening of the period of production, and enforces provision for present wants—which, in effect, brings their pressure to the attention of entrepreneurs. And this is why it reflects the relative intensity with which in every economy future and present interests make themselves felt and thus also a people's intelligence and moral strength—the higher these are, the lower will be the rate of interest. This is why the rate of interest mirrors the cultural level of a nation; for the higher this level, the larger will be the available stock of consumers' goods, the longer will be the period of production, the smaller will be, according to the law of roundaboutness, the surplus return which further extension of the period of production would yield, and thus the lower will be the rate of interest. And here we have Böhm-Bawerk's law of the decreasing rate of interest, his solution to this ancient problem which had tried the best minds of our science and found them wanting.[103]

This lowering of interest rates is a process that has been taking place throughout human history, as discussed in detail in Homer and Sylla's *The History of Interest Rates*, which documents 5,000 years of data on interest rate history. The data show interest rates are in a long-term declining trend, interrupted by various catastrophes. By the end of the nineteenth century, after decades of the international gold standard and the ensuing capital accumulation, the lowest interest rates were around 2%. The move to fiat and the ensuing world wars reversed this trend in the twentieth century, but there is no reason to assume it would not continue with a return to hard money. And as it continues, it is hard to escape the conclusion that rates would head to zero. Lending would be done at a nominal rate of return of zero, but a positive real return, which is the result of both the appreciation of the monetary asset, as well as the lender saving on their storage cost and risk of loss or theft. Carrying a cash balance always involves a cost and risk, and by lending, the lender is able to offload that cost and risk to the borrower, so that even receiving a 0% interest would be an improvement.

103 Schumpeter, Joseph A. *Ten Great Economists: From Marx to Keynes*. London: Routledge, 1997, p. 182. Print.

I suspect that the end result of developing hard-to-confiscate, strictly scarce hard money with an extremely high capacity for decentralized fast global settlement is that interest rates would naturally go to zero. Interest-based lending would cease to exist. Given that money would be expected to constantly appreciate, a 0% rate of interest is a positive interest rate in real terms. And given that the holding of deposits would usually incur a cost, and carry a risk of loss of theft, there is an opportunity cost to holding on to money rather than lending it. By lending at a 0% interest rate, the lender is deferring the costs of custody and the risk of loss to the borrower, making the rate of return on a 0% loan positive. Combined with increased savings and lower time preference, all this is likely to lead to there being an approximately 0% nominal rate on credit. Creditworthiness will be what matters to securing loans, not willingness to pay an interest rate. But such lending is more likely to take place between family, friends, and people likely to interact with each other repeatedly. For lending between strangers and professional relations, it is hard to see lenders willing to forego capital and take on venture risk merely to save on storage costs. Rather than seek a fixed yield for lending, lenders would seek an equity stake and a share of the business's revenues.

Every business, including banks, can go to zero. In a fractional reserve banking system, central banks protect depositors against such an outcome by generating new easy money. In a hard money system, there is no amount of financial risk engineering that can protect savers from the loss of their capital in a venture. Banks can diversify but can never make a guarantee for a minimum return or maximum loss. Without the ability to protect the downside of the saver, there is no reason the saver should not prefer to be fully exposed on the upside as well. Why settle for a fixed return on their investment if it succeeds but unlimited downside if it fails? The more attractive model for savers will be one in which they make a real return from the businesses in which the bank invests their money, sharing in the profit and loss. The role of the bank will be in matching maturities and risk profiles between borrowers and lenders and identifying the correct projects in which to invest.

Chapter 16

Bitcoin and Energy Markets

Bitcoin Mining: Antifiat Technology

As discussed in the first section of this book, the fiat standard solves the problem of spatial salability of physical money by replacing the need to move the physical money with government-controlled fiat payment networks. By establishing a monopoly on the issuance and clearance of monetary tokens, fiat converts all underlying monetary assets into virtual tokens arbitrarily assigned or deleted by the central fiat node. Any transaction can be reversed, any balance can be confiscated, and large amounts of these tokens can be conjured out of thin air into any particular balance—all purely by fiat. All value and truth in the banking system can ultimately be decided politically, and as time goes by, this kind of assignment of value overtakes economic production as the source of wealth creation in a fiat society.

Supplanting free-market economic forces as the determinant of value with political connectedness degrades and destroys the institutions and economic arrangements of society. The longer fiat monetary systems operate, the more they come to resemble a loyalty rewards scheme for the government. When the path to power and wealth lies in political control of the financial system, economic actors will spend fortunes in order to influence politicians and agents of the central government. Domestic and international politics are more likely to degenerate into violent conflict when the winner gets control of the mechanisms for capriciously creating and destroying wealth.

Bitcoin offers an entirely different technology for operating a monetary and financial system, a system built entirely on verification, with no functional role for fiat authority. To transfer the control of a certain number of coins from one address to another, the network requires the command of the private keys associated with the sending address—nothing else. No economic, financial, political, or religious form of authority is capable of transferring coins without the associated private keys, neither can they reverse the transfer of coins by someone who controls their private keys. This technology is what makes bitcoin a neutral, apolitical technology for money and payments. Using bitcoin is more akin to the use of a knife or wheel than a credit card; it is a technology that just does its job if you use it properly, and it doesn't require the supervision of authorities to work. At some point in time, telephones required a manual operator made of flesh and blood to connect your call to the party you wanted to contact. The automation of telephones reduced the cost of calling to an infinitely small fraction of its manual cost. Bitcoin is the implementation of this concept to international transfers and monetary policy.

Proof of work is the remarkable engineering feat that allows for the automation of record keeping. This unique technology completely obviates the role of any supervisory authority. Thanks to proof of work, no central government or major financial conglomerate can tamper with or alter the transactions verified on the blockchain. The decentralized nature of bitcoin ensures that everyone, rich and poor alike, plays by the same set of rules. Bitcoin is a network of nodes that voluntarily choose to arrive at consensus on the record of transactions and ownership. Proof of work is the technology that allows automated consensus formulation within a predetermined set of rules, without deference to any particular authority. It's a system of rules without rulers.

In the bitcoin system, every node is free to use any record of transaction or monetary policy it desires, and no authority can stop it from, or punish it for, using fraudulent records. But in order for the node to be operating in consensus and synced with the network, it needs to only consider additions to the blockchain presented by miners who have solved the proof-of-work mathematical problems. Nodes can verify the validity of transactions miners want to add to blocks, as well as the validity of the proof-of-work solution, very cheaply and almost instantly. However, presenting transactions to the network is very expensive for miners, because doing so requires the solution of the proof-of-work problem, which requires running mining equipment and consuming electricity. Thanks to the difficulty adjustment, that cost is always close to the reward from mining the block. This asymmetry between the cost of solving the proof-of-work problem and the cost of verifying the solution is at the heart of bitcoin's security model. This asymmetry makes it expensive for miners to commit fraud—or even attempt fraud—and makes the problem of arriving at consensus between nodes very easy, as they only have to consider and audit a very small number of blocks, those presented by miners who solved the proof of work.

Agreement is easy when fraud is expensive to present but cheap to reject. By ensuring the cost for presenting each new block is always roughly in the range of the reward that comes from it, bitcoin nodes streamline and compress the computational and political burden of arriving at consensus, allowing them to achieve it peacefully, reliably, indisputably, and simply.

In any monetary system that does not employ proof of work, the cost of attempting fraud, fake transactions, or inflation is small. Fraud can be tried cheaply with huge potential upside in the absence of proof of work. Financial claims and disputes naturally multiply in large economies, and these conflicts require adjudication and punishment, which will ultimately lead to the development of some form of authority able to decree validity and overrule the decisions of others. A monetary system without proof of work is ultimately subjective, and given humans' self-interested nature, and given the historical track record, such systems don't remain neutral for long. Instead, they operate based on the outcomes of political and military conflict.

One can view proof of work as an efficient technological replacement for political and geostrategic conflict as a way of determining the validity of a record of transactions. When using fiat currencies and their attendant monetary infrastructure, one is reliant on the honesty and competence of the government authorities controlling them. When one uses bitcoin, no reliance on any particular individual or authority is required. The bitcoin network will clear the transactions and maintain the monetary policy because it is a mechanical process that only requires that some humans, anyone anywhere, desire to profit from the users and receive the block reward.

Bitcoin effectively puts the truth of the ledger up for sale to the highest bidder but attaches a very high cost to the bid, and it provides the other members of the network with a very cheap mechanism to detect fraud and rule-breaking. As a result, the bidders have an overwhelming incentive to be honest, and many thousands of network members arrive at peaceful, non-controversial consensus roughly every ten minutes. The key to making this system work is that the bidder has to expend resources to make their claim; the bitcoin network nodes do not consider blocks presented without the solution to the proof-of-work problem, and that has proven an effective mechanism for guaranteeing that bids are only made by people who have carried out activities with demonstrable "unforgeable costliness."[104]

The fiat system's payment rails do not require proof of work to function, but the fiat system effectively still does. While very little cost or energy is needed to update fiat ledgers, a lot of energy is spent to acquire the ability to control that ledger in the form of political conflict and war. Fiat is a technology that allows whoever is in power to expropriate all other users, so nation-states will fight for power and expend a lot of energy to secure it. The cost

---

104 Szabo, Nick. "Shelling Out: The Origins of Money." *Satoshi Nakamoto Institute*. 2002. Web. 3 Oct. 2021.

of proof of work in a fiat system—and the control of the ledger—ultimately comes down to raw power: war. The ledger will always be determined by groups with the ability to direct overwhelmingly large amounts of energy in short bursts at enemies to force them to accept a version of consensus.

Military conflict is ultimately a contest of power in its most primitive sense, as the winner is the one able to move more equipment and channel more kinetic energy into the destruction of its enemy. The first world war birthed fiat money in England, and the second world war placed the U.S. at the pinnacle of world power, giving it the ability to architect the postwar fiat system and export its inflation to the world. U.S. monetary supremacy is to this day propped up by military power through a network of military bases spread across the entire planet and a large fleet of aircraft carriers ready to deploy overwhelming military might and explosive power across the planet at very short notice. This expression of sovereign power allows the flow of the dollar worldwide, keeping it as the underlying base layer of the global monetary system. The power expenditure needed to maintain the U.S. military's imperialism abroad, and the constant churn of wars the U.S. carries out across the globe, represents the work and energy expenditure required to keep the dollar, and its supervisory authorities, in charge of a global financial system that facilitates the movement of capital worldwide.

The point of this analysis is not to rail against U.S. foreign policy, much as that would be deserved, but to illustrate that in a world in which billions of people are spread out over two hundred countries across the globe, there are no easy ways for them to all trade with one another using one monetary system if they do not all submit to the same political authority. If the U.S. had spent the entire twentieth century following an isolationist foreign policy, another government would likely have taken over the role of the world's central banker. A world of fiat money requires a central global authority to impose rules on all transacting parties, and the reward for being that authority is enormously attractive. With fiat as the pinnacle of monetary technology, the alternatives to U.S. global imperialism are likely to be imperialism by another country, or perpetual conflict combined with the Balkanization of monetary systems, and consequently, of trade areas, reducing the extent of trade and division of labor worldwide, with devastating humanitarian and economic consequences. Regardless of whichever political authority controls the system, fiat's proof-of-work mechanism is simply too costly and inefficient.

Bitcoin is an ingeniously efficient technological workaround for the political conflict that is the hallmark of fiat. Instead of having the work done on battlefields, bitcoin front-loads the work into highly efficient machines, bitcoin miners. Anyone can choose to be in charge of updating the global ledger of transactions; they just need to pay the going market rate for the honor. This is similar to the reality of the fiat system, where anybody can control the local payment system and the distribution of local fiat tokens if they take over their central government and central bank, and anyone can potentially take over the global monetary system if they are to defeat the U.S. in military conflict. Technological progress and global trade allowed fiat money to effectively destroy the honest model of money offered by gold and replace it with a model where might makes right.

Bitcoin formalizes the reality that power controls the ledger but brings the power expenditure forward and subjects it to infinitesimally cheap verification by all network members. By using the network, bitcoin members implicitly accept this security model and trade-off: no single authority can decide what is correct and fraudulent, and anyone can present any record of transactions they want, but they can only do so after expending costs roughly equivalent to the amount they stand to gain from the block of transactions they present. Bitcoin is based on a sober recognition of the reality of power and an ingenious engineering solution to tame this power with voluntary verification in the service of truth and peace.

Difficulty Adjustment: The Secret Sauce

In order for bitcoin to operate, its security model requires that miners expend resources before they are able to provide blocks to be added to the consensus chain of transactions. For this to work, the value of the proof of work needs to be high enough to discourage spam attacks, but it cannot be so high as to discourage even honest miners from mining. Bitcoin ensures this is the case by deploying an algorithm for adjusting the difficulty of mining, i.e., the expected time to solve a proof-of-work problem.

Bitcoin miners solve proof-of-work problems by repeatedly guessing and checking to discover the correct answer. This is a probabilistic process, and the more processing power dedicated to the guessing, the more guesses are made per unit of time, and the faster the correct answer will be found. The bitcoin mining difficulty is a measure of the difficulty of guessing the correct answer. The network adjusts difficulty every two weeks as a way to calibrate the time it takes the current computing power on the network to arrive at the correct solution to ten minutes.

At its inception, the bitcoin difficulty was set to 1, meaning that the computers on the network would be expected to solve the proof-of-work problems in ten minutes on average. As the computers on the network increase, the time it takes them to arrive at the solution will decline, and blocks will start arriving faster. If the processing power on the network were to decline, the time it takes to clear blocks would be longer than ten minutes. With every 2,016 blocks, or two weeks approximately, the time of block clearing is compared to the ten-minute optimum, and difficulty adjusts to attempt to calibrate the time to ten minutes with the average processing power that was present over the previous two weeks. Importantly, this is not a precise process but a calibration that takes place over two weeks. Block times are rarely at exactly ten minutes, but the average block time stays close to ten minutes in the long run.

Most elements of bitcoin's architecture are not original to bitcoin but had existed before Satoshi Nakamoto released the bitcoin white paper. Public key cryptography, peer-to-peer networks, proof of work, hashing, and Merkle trees had all been invented years before bitcoin. The genius of bitcoin was in combining them all together, and the magic ingredient that made this recipe possible was the mining difficulty adjustment algorithm.

The mining difficulty adjustment is the link between the bitcoin network and the world's economy. The difficulty adjustment keeps bitcoin functioning as planned regardless of new microchip technology or geopolitical shifts that shutter major mining operations. It allows bitcoin to operate at whatever scale it is demanded without needing to alter its structure. Adjusting the difficulty to calibrate around ten-minute block times means that the network will continue to maintain its monetary policy, with coin production not deviating from its set schedule, and that the security model discussed above remains intact: the cost of presenting a block for the network is always close to the cost of the reward for doing so. As the value of the network grows, the difficulty adjustment raises the cost of committing the transactions to the network, making it more expensive to attack the network with fraud, inflation, or disputes. The difficulty adjustment ensures the security of the network by ensuring the cost of mining a new block is roughly equal to the mining block reward. As the price of bitcoin rises, the energy resources dedicated to mining bitcoin increase, and the value of an attack on the bitcoin network, in the form of inflation or fraud, also goes up. The difficulty adjusting upward ensures that the cost of submitting a block for the network nodes rises commensurately as well.

The difficulty adjustment simply takes everything in the economic reality of the world and presents it to the bitcoin network in one metric: the block time. The protocol adjusts the difficulty to calibrate the block time around the desired ten minutes, so the network continues to function as expected, irrespective of demand. This property makes bitcoin the only liquid commodity with a perfectly inelastic supply. In other words, the supply of bitcoin is strictly limited and cannot respond to increased demand. Regardless of how many more computers join the network to mine bitcoin, there is no increase in the supply of bitcoin, only an increase in the difficulty of mining it through proof of work. This automatic adjustment is how bitcoin is uniquely different from all other monetary assets. If demand for any metal increases, the production of that metal will accelerate, and thus its supply will grow at a quicker rate than before. For every other market commodity or monetary asset, the increase in demand will generate more supply. For bitcoin, however, the increase in demand only results in increasing the security of the network.

Bitcoin mining is like a sports competition: only one trophy will be handed out, and if more people compete, more trophies aren't made; winning the trophy just becomes harder. This effectively ensures that the cost invested in producing a bitcoin is roughly equal to the value of a bitcoin, which is what ensures bitcoin is hard money. If a miner could produce bitcoin cheaply, it would be so profitable that other miners would join, and the difficulty would rise, increasing the cost of production until the profit is eliminated, or preserved for only the miners with the lowest electricity cost.

Difficulty adjustment is the crucial ingredient missing from previous digital currency attempts that allowed bitcoin to succeed. It ensures that the cost of producing a bitcoin always trends close to its price, thus ensuring that bitcoin remains hard money. Nobody is able to produce money at a cost significantly and persistently different from the market price. The difficulty adjustment also turns bitcoin into an indomitable, all-conquering positive feedback loop of economic incentives, as visualized in figure 18. Only by understanding the difficulty adjustment can one understand bitcoin's tremendously quick rise in value.

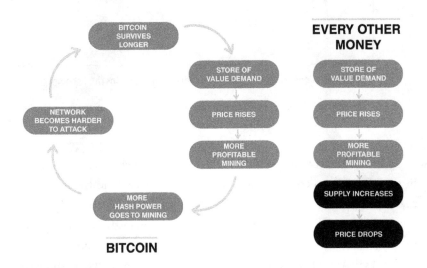

Figure 18. Bitcoin's monetary uniqueness.

As the bitcoin price has risen over time, bitcoin production has proceeded according to the original schedule, while the amount of processing power

dedicated to the network, in terms of hashrate, has continued to rise inexo-
rably. As the security has increased, so has the value stored on the network.
Difficulty adjustment converts demand for producing more bitcoin into
more security for the bitcoin network, while ensuring the supply continues
to only grow according to the predetermined schedule.

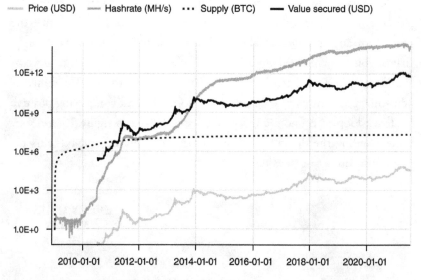

Figure 19. Bitcoin price, hashrate, supply, and value secured.
Source: Coinmetrics.io.

To be secure, bitcoin does not need a fixed sum of electricity or hashrate.
Instead, it needs to create a liquid market in electricity and hashing power
that constantly attracts a serious amount of capital infrastructure to produce
mining hardware. By simply providing a highly liquid instrument as a reward
for expending electricity and processing power, bitcoin continues to attract
the most efficient producers of electricity and processing power to monetize
their resources. As long as this unique market continues to exist and offers
valuable rewards, it will make any attack considerably expensive and unlikely
to succeed. In particular, bitcoin's impact on the electricity market means
that it is a voracious buyer of any cheap electricity that exists anywhere in the

world. Whereas any attacker would need to mobilize enormous amounts of expensive energy in centralized locations to try to attack the network, bitcoin can draw on the cheapest sources of energy in many locations worldwide by offering rewards for selling electricity that producers would not be able to sell elsewhere.

Ultimately, doomsday scenarios in which bitcoin fails due to a technical design glitch do not take into account the economic incentives it provides to keep the system running successfully. As long as demand for digital hard money exists, many millions of people around the world are motivated to find solutions to continue its existence. Bitcoin has a very straightforward technical requirement to operate, and it performs a very simple job that requires very little technical sophistication but enormous incentives.

Bitcoin Fuel

One of the most common misconceptions about energy is that it is scarce or limited. In the popular imagination, the earth has a limited supply of energy that humans consume whenever they heat or move anything. This scarcity perspective views energy consumption as a bad thing because anything that consumes energy depletes our planet's finite supplies of energy. Mainstream media and academia act as if energy is a zero-sum game, whereby any individual consuming energy in the world is taking it away from others. But energy is a product humans produce from nature, and so its consumption only incentivizes more production. The scarcity of energy lies not in its absolute quantities but in having it delivered, at high power, at the time and place where it is desired.

The total amount of energy resources available for humans to exploit is practically infinite, beyond our ability to even quantify, let alone consume. The solar energy that hits the earth every day is hundreds of times larger than global energy consumption. The rivers that run every hour of every day also contain more energy than global energy consumption, as do the winds that blow, and the hydrocarbon fuels that lie under the earth, not to mention the many nuclear fuels we have barely begun to utilize.

To begin with the most obvious of energy sources, the sun alone showers the earth with 3.85 million exajoules of energy every year; that is more than 7,000 times the amount of energy humans consume every year. In fact, the amount of solar energy that falls on earth in one *hour* is more energy than the entire human race consumes in one year. The amount of wind energy alone blowing around the world is around four times the total energy consumed worldwide. Some estimates put the potential hydroelectric yearly power capacity at around 52 PWh, or a third of all the energy consumed in the world. The earth's reserves of hydrocarbons continue increasing every year with increasing human consumption, because as consumption increases, so does oil prospecting and excavation and new technologies like hydraulic fracturing. Energy companies discover more and more reserves all the time.[105]

Humanity does not have an energy scarcity problem because energy cannot run out so long as the sun rises, the rivers run, and the wind blows, and because the hydrocarbon and nuclear fuels under the earth are far larger than our ability to even measure. Energy is constantly available for humans to use as we like. The only limit on energy availability is how much time humans dedicate toward channeling these energy sources from places where they're abundant to places where they're needed. All energy is ultimately free if you don't think of the cost of channeling it to the right place at the right time at the right intensity. Energy costs come from the need to pay the supply chain of individuals and firms to transport this energy to where it's needed and in a usable form, at specific quantities over specific periods of time. Therefore, discussing energy as a scarce resource, which implies a fixed, God-given quantity for humans to consume passively, makes no sense. In its usable form, energy is a product that humans create by channeling the forces of nature to where they are needed. As with every economic good other than bitcoin, there is no natural limit to the production of this good; the only limit is how much time humans dedicate to producing that good, which in turn is determined through the price mechanism sending signals to producers. When people

---

105 For a more detailed discussion of this point, see my *Principles of Economics*, https://www.saifedean.com/principles-of-economics.

want more energy, they're willing to pay more for it, which incentivizes more of its production at the expense of producing other things. The more people desire it, the more of it can be produced. The scarcity of energy, like all types of prebitcoin scarcity, is relative scarcity, whose cause lies in the opportunity cost in terms of other goods.

Bitcoin mining is unique in being an energy-extensive and highly profitable use of energy that can operate from anywhere and can sell its output digitally. Bitcoin requires an ever-growing expenditure of power in order to arrive at consensus without having to trust in a single authority. And to secure that power, the network's design initiates relentless competition between potential miners to find the cheapest sources of energy worldwide, and to deploy their equipment most efficiently. Bitcoin will buy cheap energy wherever it is located and however it is produced, and to do so, it requires no expensive pipelines, trucks, tankers, or trains—just an internet connection at the energy source's electric output. Bitcoin is an entirely new technology for buying electricity digitally, with a profound transformative impact on how electricity can be produced and sold, making it more fungible and liquid. Unlike all other uses of electricity, bitcoin does not require power to be transported to it; it can buy the power anywhere it is available and is insatiable in its demand of cheap, reliable electricity. The implications of this single point are only beginning to be understood.

1. Waste Energy

The inescapable conclusion one reaches after understanding the bitcoin difficulty adjustment and the geographic mobility of bitcoin mining is that bitcoin will inevitably consume cheap, wasted, and stranded electricity—energy with zero opportunity cost. Mining is consistently profitable only for the miners who mine using electricity secured at rates significantly cheaper than the majority of world electricity prices. The global average price of electricity is estimated around fourteen cents per kWh.[106] At any particular price of bit-

---

106 "Electricity Prices." *GlobalPetrolPrices.com*. Web. 3 Oct. 2021.

coin, there are billions worldwide who have access to electricity which they could use to mine bitcoin at a price of fourteen cents per kWh or less. As more of these people attempt to mine bitcoin, the difficulty of mining rises, thus reducing the expected return to bitcoin miners, eroding the profitability of miners mining at higher prices of electricity. As the difficultly adjusts upwards, miners who cannot find inexpensive electricity will start mining at a loss. As losses accumulate, these miners eventually go out of business, leaving behind only those with significantly lower cost of electricity. The entire bitcoin network collectively finds and rewards cheap, stable, efficient electricity.

Reliably profitable mining operations are those able to secure stable electricity at rates lower than five cents per kWh. At higher electricity rates, miners can be profitable during periods where the bitcoin price rises quickly, but they will lose profitability when the price goes down or when difficulty adjusts upward. The nature of bitcoin's difficulty adjustment is to create ruthless competition between miners. This competition means only those able to secure electricity at extremely cheap prices will thrive.

Wherever energy is in high demand by residential, commercial, or industrial facilities, using that energy to produce bitcoin will carry a significant opportunity cost, as there are people who would pay to use it in their daily life to meet their needs, whereas isolated and stranded energy sources have no alternative demand, and thus carry a zero opportunity cost. In many places, the energy has a negative value, as it is a nuisance or danger, which is expensive to dispose of safely. For example, excess gas at hydraulic fracturing sites is normally flared off and wasted. Hydroelectric dams can have overflows of water. Volcanoes can erupt, producing dangerous amounts of fumes and lava. This energy is difficult to utilize because transporting it to residential and industrial centers is expensive.

Given the high costs of transporting and storing energy, electricity production leads to very large quantities of power getting lost in the attempt to move from suppliers to consumers. In 2019, the world produced around 173,000 TWh. Around a third of that energy is wasted, leaving humanity to consume around 117,000 TWh. The entirety of the bitcoin network currently consumes around 120 TWh, or around 0.1% of the total energy

wasted in the world. But unlike all other uses of energy, bitcoin can consume—and in all likelihood, is consuming—the energy that would have
been otherwise wasted.

With the invention of bitcoin, the methane that would otherwise be
flared, the rivers that would otherwise overflow, the abandoned oil fields, and
the volcanoes that would otherwise erupt can be monetized, channeled, and
consumed. Difficulty adjustment ensures that bitcoin is only mined with the
electricity sources with the lowest opportunity cost, and that incentivizes
the mass of bitcoin miners to locate and use inexpensive energy.

Bitcoin could grow 1,000-fold and still not consume more energy than
humanity has wasted. Bitcoin will continue to grow by consuming this
energy, primarily, because this energy has a zero opportunity cost and very
few potential buyers other than bitcoin, if any. All other electricity that has
demand will find a higher bidder than the bitcoin network because the bitcoin network can buy the cheap electricity at prices unavailable to those who
need valuable electricity near large demand.

2. Bitcoin Incentivizes Energy Generation

The essential property of capital goods is to increase the marginal productivity of the producers who use them. The fisherman who catches fish with
a modern trawler has a much higher hourly productivity than the fisherman
using a little boat and net, whose productivity is in turn higher than that
of the fisherman on the coast holding a fishing rod, whose productivity is
higher than anyone trying to catch fish with his hands. As the stock of capital
increases, the marginal productivity of the worker increases, and that is why
countries that have higher capital stocks have higher income than poorer
countries. The march of human progress and civilization is the march of capital accumulation to produce more output per unit of effort expended by a
human being. The more capital is accumulated, the more productive humans
are, and the lower the marginal cost of the goods produced.

Applying this analysis to the question of bitcoin power consumption has
startling implications. Bitcoin isn't "consuming" the world's energy; bitcoin

is providing a powerful market incentive for energy producers worldwide to increase the production of cheap energy. By giving a large financial incentive to anyone able to mine at an electricity cost below that of the market, bitcoin makes the development of cheap, reliable sources of electricity, anywhere in the world, very rewarding. This financial reward in turn leads to growing investment in capital infrastructure for cheap energy sources, which leads to increased energy production and decreased cost. This is particularly interesting in light of the discussion of Chapter 10, where we saw how fiat hampers the development of low-cost and reliable sources of energy by mandating and promoting unreliable and intermittent energy sources. Bitcoin's growth is the antidote to the damage caused by the growth of these fiat fuels, as it continues to offer a large bounty to anyone who can produce cheap and reliable electricity. Governments may be taxing and regulating reliable energy and making it far more expensive, but bitcoin is reversing this with poetic justice: it is taking away seigniorage from governments and using it to finance cheap energy production worldwide.

The growth of bitcoin is the monetization of a digital commodity produced from electricity, and growth in demand for bitcoin will result in growth in demand for electricity. The full extent of the powerful upgrade that bitcoin represents becomes apparent when one realizes bitcoin's monetization will drive the production of electric power, one of the most important economic goods humans ever invented, while replacing the fiat monetary system which monetizes debt and government fiat, driving the growth of indebtedness and government power. Rather than direct the benefits of seigniorage to governments, bureaucracies, lenders and borrowers, and belligerent militaries, bitcoin directs them to the production of the miraculous commodity that has allowed humanity to prosper and conquer darkness, cold, disease, and the violence of nature.

3. Reliable Energy

Computer equipment is the other major cost of mining bitcoin, and production of computers capable of mining bitcoin effectively has now grown into a highly specialized and competitive multibillion-dollar industry. The cost of these machines is also bid up as bitcoin's price rises, and the miners who will be able to afford to pay their prices are the ones who will operate them the most profitably. To operate them most profitably at capacity, the miner must have them connected at all times to reliable and stable power. When the miner is not connected to electricity, the computers depreciate in value and fail to produce the expected return, putting the owners at a disadvantage compared to miners who can use their equipment twenty-four hours a day, 365 days a year. Miner uptime is an essential part of profiting as a bitcoin miner.

Given the nature of bitcoin's demand for electricity, it is possible to identify a few trends in the energy sources likely to power bitcoin mining. Solar and wind power are unlikely to play a major role in bitcoin mining, as these are intermittent sources of energy, unable to produce a reliable stream of energy around the clock. Machines that run on these sources will have significant downtime, which, given bitcoin's ruthless difficulty adjustment, means they will be unlikely to survive against miners with constant and reliable energy. As many of these sources are heavily subsidized, it is plausible that they could be used to mine bitcoin in the short term, but it is doubtful these operations can operate successfully for long. It is completely unrealistic to expect these sources to be supplemented with battery technology to store energy, as the cost of electricity coming from batteries increases by several multiples. Instead, currently available systems that are both cheap and reliable will likely grow in their share of the bitcoin network's hashrate.

4. Bitcoin's Energy Future

Oil, coal, and gas power plants are also unlikely to be major sources of bitcoin energy because of the high opportunity cost associated with power generation and the significant running cost of fuel supply. Hydrocarbon power plants are built in areas of high demand for reliable power, and that means their electricity prices are significantly higher than the five cents per kWh profitable bitcoin miners need. This high opportunity cost makes it unlikely for profitable mining to be performed at scale on grids connected to hydrocarbon plants. These plants could mine bitcoin with spare capacity if they have that. Bitcoin could help finance the building of large power plants accounting for future growth by allowing the operators to cover some of the costs by mining with spare capacity until demand grows. Bitcoin can also help finance the building of some margin of standby spare capacity, which would be needed for emergencies or failure of other power sources. As the world's grids are becoming more fragile thanks to the mandating of unreliable fuels, power generators could use bitcoin mining to finance building spare capacity to bring online at the times when wind and solar inevitably fail.

Hydrocarbons are much cheaper to transport than hydroelectric energy. They are thus in high demand everywhere humans settle. They can be used for cars, homes, cities, or all kinds of other uses. They will always have a high opportunity cost, relatively, because there is always someone who could use them for something highly productive. Hydroelectric energy, on the other hand, usually has a very low opportunity cost, or even a negative opportunity cost, when one considers the dangers posed by flooding. Unlike hydrocarbons, hydroelectric energy is frequently generated far away from areas of high demand and requires little running cost, as there is no fuel needed to operate it. Unlike solar and wind, hydroelectric power has the advantage of being reliable and predictable around the clock. The average cost of electricity from hydroelectric plants is usually in the range of three to five cents per kWh, which is ideal for bitcoin miners. Operating hydroelectric power facilities away from population centers appears to be a very successful long-term strategy for mining bitcoin profitably.

Nuclear power is also likely to be suitable for mining bitcoin, since it is usually very cheap and reliable, and since many nuclear plants have the ability to produce a lot of power that may exceed local demands. And as mentioned earlier, another very important potential source of mining is the flaring of methane gas from oil fields. The production of oil leads to the inevitable production of large amounts of methane gas which is unprofitable to transport from remote oil fields. Oil fields usually flare, i.e., burn, this energy, but bitcoin is able to buy it on-site by installing a generator and miners. Waste incineration plants are another potential source, as these are usually situated far from population centers.

The total amount of methane that is flared and burned away every year contains 1,500 TWh of energy,[107] which is around ten times larger than the consumption of the bitcoin network. Hydroelectric energy alone produced 4,306 TWh in 2019, or more than thirty times what bitcoin consumes. With bitcoin allowing for the building of hydropower plants in areas unconnected to major grids and population centers, the generation capacity of hydropower can increase much further. With spare nuclear capacity, as well as backup and spare capacity in hydrocarbon-powered plants, there is ample room for bitcoin to grow purely on spare capacity, wasted, and stranded energy sources at very low costs. The hysterical screeching by fiat media and academia about bitcoin consuming all the planet's energy is completely unfounded. Difficulty adjustment ensures bitcoin's energy consumption will predominantly draw on sources with very low opportunity cost.

---

107 "Flaring Emissions." *International Energy Agency.* Jun. 2020. Web. 3 Oct. 2021.

Chapter 17

Bitcoin Cost-Benefit Analysis

With the analysis of the previous three chapters, it is now possible to discuss the true costs and benefits of a bitcoin monetary system and how they compare with the fiat monetary system discussed in Chapter 12. As always in matters of human action, theoretical debate cannot substitute for, or overrule, the outcomes emerging from human action. Engineers, economists, and politicians may have strong opinions about what is a useful or wasteful monetary system, but the only actual answer that matters is the one that humans offer with their actions, in the goods they consume and produce in response to the market reality offered by these technologies. Intellectual arguments are very cheap, but actions are very costly.

Should people find no value in the bitcoin network, they would not be paying for its continued operation. The proper professional response of an economist, in this case, is to analyze where the value lies for the users. It is not to throw hissy fits declaring the network is worthless because they cannot see the usefulness, as has been the reaction of most fiat economists. Rather than take the well-worn path of dismissing the network's value based on fiat textbook theories, this chapter attempts to explain why a growing number of users find value in bitcoin by examining the costs and benefits associated with upgrading from fiat to bitcoin. From the perspective of fiat academics, reality is wrong by not agreeing with the government-sponsored theories in their textbook. But a simpler and more logical explanation is that bitcoin's fast rise is the return of a free market to money, and we are witnessing a superior-good rise at the expense of an inferior good.

Bitcoin Costs

Electricity Cost

The amount of energy that bitcoin consumes can theoretically be estimated from its hashrate. It is the direct output of the energy consumption of the machines that secure the network. The machines that mine bitcoin have known specifications in terms of how much electricity they consume and how many hashes they can produce. The bitcoin hashrate can be estimated from the difficulty and the block time. The hashrate and some reasonable assumptions of the composition of bitcoin mining equipment can give us a roughly accurate idea of how much electricity is used by the bitcoin network at any point in time. Current best estimates put bitcoin's energy consumption somewhere in the range of 100–150 TWh/year. This is an enormous amount of energy, and the fact that it is deployed voluntarily is a testament to the amount of value people place on the network and its assets.

As discussed in the last chapter, most of this energy would otherwise have been wasted. It is almost always electricity that is quite cheap by international standards, probably in the range of two to five cents per kWh. At that cost, and at its current hashrate, bitcoin is consuming around two to six billion U.S. dollars worth of electricity every year, most of which would be wasted otherwise. By being able to buy electricity anywhere, and by allowing only the most profitable miners to survive, bitcoin only buys the cheapest electricity and does not compete for the expensive sources of electricity in high demand.

Overall Security Cost

Bitcoin mining is a very competitive industry. The costs incurred by miners on hardware and electricity to secure bitcoin will be roughly in the range of the rewards they can collect from the network. The cost of securing bitcoin can be approximated to be equal to the aggregate miners' reward. It is the sum of bitcoin received by miners in bitcoin block rewards, including the block subsidy (new coins) as well as transaction fees.

The daily mining reward is precisely ascertainable from the bitcoin client. When combined with the daily average price, it can give us the dollar market value of daily rewards received by miners throughout bitcoin's existence. At the time of writing, bitcoin is trading at around $43,000 while the daily mining reward is running around 1,000 bitcoins per day, giving a security expenditure of $43 million daily. When examining bitcoin's entire lifetime until the end of July 2021, we find that it has consumed $29.42 billion in security expenditure. This can be considered a reasonable estimate of the total expenditure of miners for operating the bitcoin network.

Bitcoin Benefits

Secure Savings

We can understand bitcoin as an electricity-based technology for saving economic value. It takes electricity and hardware as inputs and produces savings protected from inflation and fraudulent manipulation. We can measure its efficiency as a savings mechanism by measuring the value stored in it compared to the value spent on securing it. The economic value stored in bitcoin can be approximated by the market value of the total supply of bitcoin, as a minimum bound. This is because anyone holding bitcoin at that price is signaling that they value it more than they value holding its value in other currencies or assets or consuming its value by buying the consumer goods. The cost of securing bitcoin is equal to the miners' rewards.

The mining reward consists of the transaction fees paid by users, as well as the block subsidy, which contains the new coins created with each block. So far, transaction fees have been lower than 5% of the total block reward for most of bitcoin's existence. This means that the total block reward has been closely similar to the block subsidy. If we consider the operational efficiency to be measured as market cap over mining reward, and reward approximates subsidy, then it is a number remarkably close to the percentage growth rate of the bitcoin supply, or the inverse of the stock-to-flow ratio. This brings us back full circle to the discussion of stock-to-flow at the beginning of *The Bitcoin Standard*, where I argue that the stock-to-flow ratio is an extremely important metric for quantifying monetary status. Goods with a low stock-to-flow ratio will see a significant increase in their liquid stockpiles as a result of any price increases. But goods with a high stock-to-flow ratio will only witness small increases to their existing liquid stockpiles. Calculating bitcoin's operational efficiency as a savings vehicle reveals that it is close to its stock-to-flow. That is an engineering explanation of the nature of the role of money. Money is only as efficient as its ability to resist debasement. The better it is at resisting debasement, the more it will be valuable. As bitcoin's supply growth rate has declined, its monetary operational efficiency has increased, and the amount of value it has attracted has increased.

Up until this point in bitcoin's existence, the mining reward has been tied closely in value to the block subsidy, but as the block subsidy declines, transaction fees will necessarily become a larger fraction of the total block reward, and the operational efficiency of bitcoin will diverge from the stock-to-flow ratio. It will converge toward the ratio of transaction fees to total market capitalization. It will be fascinating to watch what happens to the ratio of transaction fees to total market capitalization as the block subsidy goes to zero, and whether it stabilizes at a specific level.

Appreciating Savings

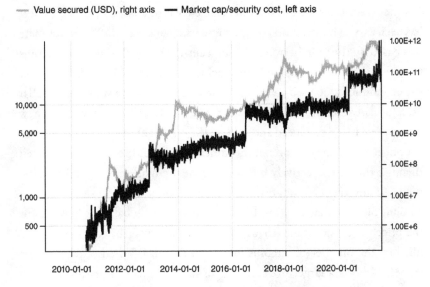

Figure 20. Bitcoin value secured and efficiency.

Source: Coinmetrics.io.

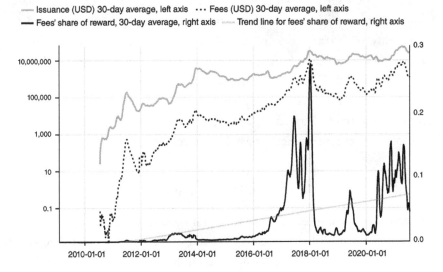

Figure 21. Issuance and transaction fees, in US dollars, and fees' share of reward.

Source: Coinmetrics.io.

Another way of thinking of bitcoin's efficiency is to consider how efficient it has been as a savings technology for those who have used it. We can estimate this based on the ratio between the total current market value of all bitcoins to the value that was invested in producing these coins. We can approximate the economic value used to produce bitcoin as being the sum of the dollar value of daily bitcoin production over its existence. On any given day, new bitcoins are being produced and sold on the market at the predominant market price. This is the case even if the miner who mines the coins does not sell them, as they are effectively buying them at the market price and holding them. At any given bitcoin price, the production of new coins increases the amount of value that needs to be held in bitcoin cash balances in order for the price to stay constant. That increase is equal to the bitcoin price multiplied by the number of bitcoins mined on that day. Whether through bitcoiners holding a larger market value of bitcoin balances or through new buyers buying new bitcoin, each day witnesses increased new expenditure that is approximately equal to the market value of new coins produced.

Summing the daily dollar value of market rewards results in a sum of $27.33 billion spent over the previous twelve and a half years, at a time when bitcoin's market capitalization is in the range of $0.62 trillion. This is roughly a 2,200% average return on investment. Effectively, the bitcoin network's native tokens have appreciated an average of twenty-three times their original value since their creation. As a mechanism for saving wealth into the future, bitcoin's efficiency is off the charts. As a superior technology for saving, bitcoin is attracting a growing amount of wealth, and bitcoin's reliable scarcity causes preexisting holders' bitcoins to appreciate.

Global Money Transfer

Bitcoin does not just secure savings; it can also move economic value around the world. Up until July 2021, bitcoin had carried out 660 million transactions. Estimating bitcoin's efficiency as a mechanism for transferring value can be done by measuring the ratio of transaction values to the fees paid to transfer them. For the period between October 2010 and July 2021, the average daily transaction fees came up to around 0.02% of the value of the transactions. For the vast majority of bitcoin's life, the transaction fees paid were less than 0.05% of the value of transactions. There is a clear uptrend in transaction fees as a percentage of transaction values coinciding with the decline in the daily mining subsidy of new bitcoins.

This trend is likely to continue as bitcoin's new supply subsidy increases. That people subjectively value bitcoin creates demand for holding it and

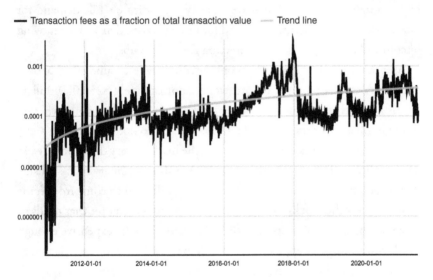

Figure 22. Daily transaction fees as a percentage of transaction value.
Source: Coinmetrics.io.

transacting with it. The bitcoin asset cannot be owned outside of transactions confirmed in bitcoin blocks, which inevitably creates a market for this scarce block space. Bitcoin's difficulty adjustment algorithm ensures the scarcity of this block space (and thus the bitcoin token itself) by raising the hash power, and thus the cost, required to produce these blocks. The cost to produce bitcoin blocks is merely a reflection of the market's valuation of bitcoin, which is ultimately the subjective value people place on it when transacting with it on the market for other monies or goods and services.

A market value for bitcoin block space creates an economic incentive for miners to provide this block space securely. In all markets, demand incentivizes entrepreneurs to find the most effective ways to provide the goods that people want. The costs and the methods of payment can differ widely, but if the demand exists, the goods will be supplied. Consequently, if there is demand for holding bitcoin, then demand will also exist for transacting in it, and people will pay the necessary transaction fees to get their transactions into blocks. There is no conceivable scenario in which demand for bitcoin is high enough to necessitate massive security expenditure while demand for block space is nonexistent. If demand for bitcoin exists, demand for moving bitcoin will have to exist, and transaction fees will go up.

As it stands, each bitcoin block contains, on average, around 1 MB of data, but it carries an economic reward worth approximately $250,000 dollars. This is a cost that is ultimately borne by the users of the network, whether through inflation or transaction fees. Even if they do not recognize this, the roughly 900 new coins currently entering the market every day devalue existing bitcoins in order to subsidize miners. As this inflationary block subsidy diminishes, the payment incentivizing miners will need to come from transaction fees for the blocks to clear. There is no fixed security fee that needs to be paid to make bitcoin operate; the mining needs to be expensive enough to allow spending to happen securely without double-spends and long reorg attacks. Should such attacks become a problem for bitcoin users, this will incentivize them to pay transaction fees so their transactions get confirmed, and fees will rise. The incentive structure around bitcoin ensures that miners and users can easily find a transaction fee that finances the network's security. The economic incentives of bitcoin have proven resilient enough to motivate people to spend the resources needed to keep the network secure. If bitcoin dies, it will not have died because of misaligned economic incentives (high transaction fees). It will have died because the demand for it declined.

We already have evidence that strongly suggests bitcoin users will be happy to pay higher transaction fees. In December 2017, fees rose to around fifty dollars per transaction. This suggests that if people want to hold hard money, the transaction fee has a lot of room to grow. If we look at the exchange fees people usually pay to buy bitcoin, we find that they are usually much larger than on-chain transaction fees. Bitcoiners still have no problem paying these extra fees, so it is hard to imagine them giving up on bitcoin because on-chain fees have increased. Premiums for buying bitcoin in places where exchanges do not operate are even higher, and it is not uncommon for buyers on LocalBitcoins, a peer-to-peer bitcoin purchasing service, to demand and get a 10% markup.

If demand for bitcoin declines or disappears, then the price will likely crash and bitcoin will collapse and/or be attacked, regardless of whether the miners are being paid in inflation or transaction fees. But if bitcoin continues to appreciate for the next twenty years, even at a rate no more than one-tenth of its historical growth over the past ten years, it will become a global settlement network valued at tens of trillions in today's dollars. Would people not be willing to pay for the daily settlement of the equivalent of trillions of modern dollars of transactions globally?

The best way to gauge the willingness to pay for these fees is to look at international settlement costs today. As bitcoin's value, salability, and

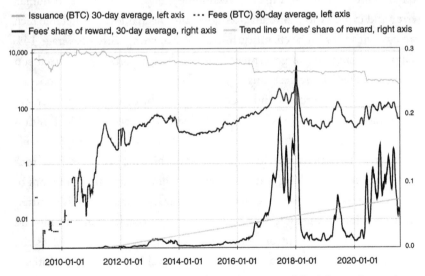

Figure 23. Issuance and transaction fees, in bitcoin, and fees' share of reward.
Source: Coinmetrics.io.

liquidity increase, more valuable transactions can be done on the network. The only real alternative to a bitcoin payment, as a form of hard cash whose value is not a government's liability, is the settlement of gold cash reserves, which is a hugely expensive process. When compared with international gold transaction fees, which come up to around 1% of transaction value, bitcoin transaction fees at around 0.02% of transaction face value are still a rounding error. Given the unique service bitcoin provides, there is enormous scope for growth in transaction fees on top of the bitcoin network. Should the network and liquidity continue to grow, transaction fees will likely rise as a percentage of transaction value and in absolute market value.

Is Bitcoin Worth It?

Functionally speaking, bitcoin replaces existing technologies for saving and international money transfer. It is useful to think of the improvements bitcoin brings to the functions of central banking as technological upgrades. A clear picture emerges from the comparison of the full costs and benefits of bitcoin and fiat. Fiat is a manual technology, highly vulnerable to human error and exploitation. Bitcoin is a digital and mechanical, predictable technology with very high reliability. Instead of struggling with an average 14% supply inflation rate of government monies, bitcoin offers you a fixed supply with a predictable declining supply inflation rate. Instead of a monetary policy run by politicians and special interests, bitcoin offers perfect predictability and transparency. Instead of financing unaccountable, limitless government spending, bitcoin finances the development of cheap reliable energy resources all over the planet. Instead of shipping heavy lumps of rock across oceans and melting and recasting them, bitcoin uses proof of work to ensure far less human labor is involved, and far less security risk is incurred. Instead of fomenting violent and vicious power struggles domestically and internationally over control of the monetary system, bitcoin resolves the validity of its ledger voluntarily with electric power and no violence. Bitcoin cannot end war, but it can significantly dent the state's ability to use inflation to finance war, and, perhaps more importantly, it massively reduces the spoils of war by taking the monetary system out of it. Rather than conflict and dominance, bitcoin allows the redirection of monetary energy to the development of cheap and plentiful energy for humanity.

The washing machine saves humans time on hand-washing and delivers us a superior washing experience by consuming electric energy, which people willingly pay for, because they value the output more than the cost. The car similarly consumes a lot of energy, but people willingly pay that price to travel faster and safer, and to not deal with horse manure. Steel-reinforced houses require power-hungry coal-fired furnaces to produce their steel, but people willingly pay the cost to live in sturdy houses that protect them from the environment. A computer requires far more energy to operate than an abacus, yet computers continue to be purchased in increasing quantities worldwide. Virtually everyone on earth who has a choice between manual washing and washing machines, between walking long distances and driving, between an abacus and a computer chooses the more energy-intensive option.

The millions of people who have chosen to hold more than $800 billion of economic value in the bitcoin network are clearly making a similar judgment to these users of modern energy-intensive technology. Generating energy and using it to operate faster, better, safer, more precise, and more reliable machinery is the essence of human technological progress and human civilization itself. Electrification has massively improved countless human products, and bitcoin is just another electric product humans are adopting rapidly. No matter how large its energy consumption, that quantity is only growing because of real-world demand for its service. Objecting to bitcoin's energy consumption is Luddism, no different from demanding others forsake any useful modern technological product for sentimental, nonsensical reasons. Fortunately for bitcoin users, the luddites are powerless to stop bitcoin from operating.

Chapter 18

Can Bitcoin Fix This

F iat economists' most commonly held misconception about bitcoin is that the network requires official, credentialed approval to continue to function. Government control of the monetary system and scientific funding has convinced generations of economists that reality is the product of fiat edict and given them a thoroughly top-down approach to understanding the world. In the fiat economists' world, bureaucrats, scientists, politicians, journalists, and other fiat authorities are society's enlightened vanguards who decide how the plebs should live their lives. To this day, economists continue to engage in belabored theoretical discussions on whether bitcoin fits their preferred definition of money, whether it is worth the energy it consumes, and whether it should be permitted to operate. The longer bitcoin continues to operate, the more these concerns begin to resemble the quaint superstitions of primitive tribes during their first contact with modern machinery.

Bitcoin's continued successful operation, its ability to perform final settlement internationally without requiring any government oversight, and its credibility in maintaining its monetary policy over twelve years delivers a shattering blow to the worldview of those who think reality comes out of fiat. Bitcoin does not need to convince any fiat authority of its worth; it just needs to keep surviving in the free market by offering value to its users.

Bitcoin is the world's first digitally scarce asset and the first liquid asset with strict verifiable scarcity. It offers no yield and is therefore not held for its returns, like stocks. It is instead held for its own value, like cash. Austrian economists explain that cash is held because of uncertainty. In a world of no uncertainty, where all your future income and expenditures are perfectly predictable, there is no need to ever hold cash, as you can always place your money in capital markets to earn a return, which can be liquidated at the exact time you need to spend it. But in the real world, with uncertainty pervading life, people do need to hold cash balances to meet their uncertain future obligations. Investment in assets that offer a yield always involves risk.

As discussed in Chapter 5, fiat's inflationary nature has eroded its ability to function as cash, and as a result, people have sought several cash substitutes. People primarily hold government bonds, as well as physical gold, real estate, and equity as a way to recreate the ability of cash to save value for the future. Bitcoin is just another asset that can be added to this list. However, it differs from the other assets listed in that it can be accessed entirely outside the traditional fiat banking system and does not require legal, political, and regulatory oversight to function internationally. Bitcoin is also different from these other assets because its supply cannot be increased in response to demand. The supply of fiat credit, bonds, stocks, real estate, art, commodities, and all other kinds of cash substitutes can increase in response to increases in demand. This means that their roles as monetary media are inherently limited. Rises in their prices will inevitably cause oversupply and big crashes. Bitcoin's scarcity means that its price crashes to continually and significantly higher levels than past prices. In its twelve years of existence, bitcoin has never been down over a four-year period. Except for one day, it has always been valued at more than fivefold its price four years earlier. Bitcoin's four-year performance averages a 365-fold increase. Examining only the past five years of data, bitcoin has averaged a 26.05-fold increase over its price four years earlier.

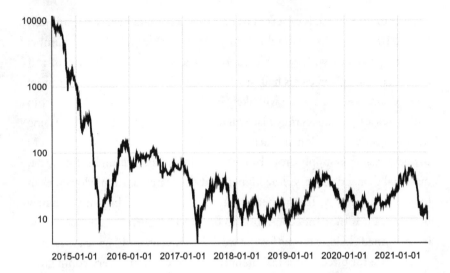

Figure 24. Multiple of bitcoin's price over its price four years earlier.

Source: Coinmetrics.io.

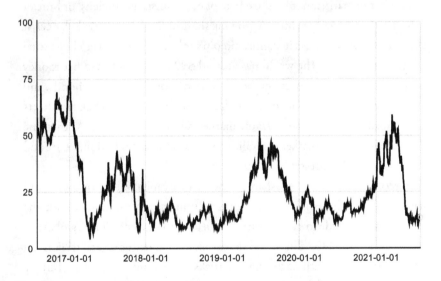

Figure 25. Multiple of bitcoin's price over its price
four years earlier. Aug. 2017–Aug. 2021.

Source: Coinmetrics.io.

One bitcoin block is expected to be produced around every ten minutes. Every 210,000 blocks, or roughly four years, the protocol halves the number of coins produced with each block. This means that the daily bitcoin production on any given day is half of what it was four years earlier. Four more years of successful operation will likely increase people's awareness of bitcoin and increase the chances they place on its continued survival, thus increasing their subjective valuation and demand for it. So as long as bitcoin continues to operate, and its supply drops by half every four years, it is highly likely that marginal demand for it will be higher, and the marginal supply lower, than four years previously. This monetary time bomb keeps clicking with each new block, and it is time for economists to begin to seriously contemplate what its continued clicking means for the world's monetary and financial system.

The case for bitcoin as a cash item on a balance sheet is very compelling for anyone with a time horizon extending beyond four years. Whether or not fiat authorities like it, bitcoin is now in free-market competition with many other assets for the world's cash balances. It is a competition bitcoin will win or lose in the market, not by the edicts of economists, politicians, or bureaucrats. If it continues to capture a growing share of the world's cash balances, it continues to succeed. As it stands, bitcoin's role as cash has a very large total addressable market. The world has around $90 trillion of broad fiat money supply, $90 trillion of sovereign bonds, $40 trillion of corporate bonds, and $10 trillion of gold. Bitcoin could replace all of these assets on balance sheets, which would be a total addressable market cap of $230 trillion. At the time of writing, bitcoin's market capitalization is around $700 billion, or around 0.3% of its total addressable market.

Bitcoin could also take a share of the market capitalization of other semi-hard assets which people have resorted to using as a form of saving for the future. These include stocks, which are valued at around $90 trillion; global real estate, valued at $280 trillion; and the art market, valued at several trillion dollars. Investors will continue to demand stocks, houses, and works of art, but the current valuations of these assets are likely highly inflated by the need of their holders to use them as stores of value on top of their value as capital or consumer goods. In other words, the flight from inflationary fiat has distorted the

U.S. dollar valuations of these assets beyond any sane level. As more and more investors in search of a store of value discover bitcoin's superior intertemporal salability, it will continue to acquire an increasing share of global cash balances.

Monetary status is an emergent outcome of market choice for monetary assets and not the result of economists' theoretical appraisals of monetary properties. Modern economists have never contemplated the possibility that free-market competition could apply to money, the holiest of prerogatives for modern fiat governments that pay their salaries. With every passing day in which bitcoin operates to the satisfaction of its millions of users, the full-time detractors and government-paid economists who constantly attack bitcoin begin to sound like deranged conspiracy theorists obsessed with stopping happy customers from wearing a shoe brand they like.

Bitcoin has grown from nothing to having nearly a trillion dollars of market value on global balance sheets in the space of twelve years. It has done so without a leader, without corruption, and without governments being able to stop it. In the past ten years, it has achieved an average compound annual growth rate of 215%. If it were to experience a similar growth rate in the future, it would overtake the $230 trillion benchmark by 2026. If it were to experience annual appreciation of *only* 20% per year, a tenth of what it experienced in the last ten years, it would arrive at the $230 trillion nominal valuation by around 2050. Rather than argue with ancient textbook definitions from the prebitcoin *jahiliyya*, economists would do far better trying to think in practical terms: How much can bitcoin continue to grow? What are the implications of its continued growth? This chapter examines some of the most common ways bitcoin could be derailed and then discusses how it would evolve if it were not derailed.

Government Attacks

The most commonly discussed scenario for bitcoin's death is a government attack. Anyone who lived in the twentieth century has been conditioned to assume that anything governments do not like will be banned, and initially there is little reason to suspect bitcoin will be different. Government attacks can come in many varied forms, some of which were discussed in *The Bitcoin Standard*. Rather than discuss the technical feasibility of individual attacks, I will focus on what I view as the deeper underlying economic incentives that give bitcoin a chance to survive such attacks.

On a functional level, bitcoin is an extremely basic technological implementation that performs a very simple and easy task: the propagation of a block of transaction data usually of 1 MB in size (though it can be as much as 3.7 MB) roughly every ten minutes to thousands of network members worldwide. To be a peer on this peer-to-peer network, which allows you to validate your own transactions in accordance with the protocol's consensus rules, all one needs is a device capable of receiving up to 3.7 MB of data every ten minutes. To merely send or receive a transaction without a node only requires a device that can send a few hundred bytes of data for each transaction.

Bitcoin is a far simpler and lighter program than Amazon, Twitter, Facebook, Netflix, or many of the popular online services that involve more extensive interactions and operations. The technical requirements for sending a few megabytes of data around the world continue to get cheaper and simpler as technology develops and the accumulation of capital in the computer and communication industries increases. There are currently tens of billions of devices worldwide capable of sending and receiving data, including almost all the world's personal computers, smartphones, and tablets.

The common misconception many nocoiners have about how the internet works is that all these computers need to connect to some central server in order to access the internet, but that is simply not the case. The internet does not have a central hub that distributes content; it is simply a protocol that any computer can use to connect to other computers. As long as two devices can be connected to one another physically or through various mechanisms to transmit data, then the internet survives, and so can bitcoin. Were the internet a centralized institution, then shutting it down would be straightforward. Because bitcoin's computing requirements are as low as they are, and the value held in it is large enough to motivate people to try their best to maintain the network, it is likely that bitcoin transactions and blocks would continue to be generated through any kind of ban.

As bitcoin continues to grow, attracting more attention from the technical community, developers will continue to innovate ways to transmit bitcoin data quicker and cheaper. Mesh networks and radio waves are two of the most interesting examples because they allow the use of the network even without a connection to the internet. Even the absence of internet-capable devices is now not much of an impediment, as it is becoming easier to join the network with any device that can send and receive data.

Bitcoin has found a way to make access to a hard form of money globally available at a much lower cost than the previous alternative, gold. Since hard money is a hugely important and beneficial technology, people also have a strong incentive to meet the costs of using this hard money. As time goes on, the liquidity and utility of bitcoin only increases, strengthening the incentive for people to use it.

Ultimately, if bitcoin provides value to its users, they will make sure they can access it. That motivation, more than any technical detail, is the real impediment to government attacks on bitcoin. History provides many illustrations of the power of economic incentives and their ability to repeatedly overcome government regulations. A good introduction to this can be found in the great book *Forty Centuries of Wage and Price Controls: How Not to Fight Inflation*.[108] Bans and controls generally fail because government edicts cannot overturn economic reality; all they can do is change the economic cost/benefit of specific actions and cause people to adjust their behavior accordingly to still get the benefits while trying to avoid the costs. This is why price controls lead to shortages, black markets, queuing costs, violent conflict, and all manner of perverse and unintended consequences, but very rarely lead to achieving their intended goal.

A government clampdown would be far from a guaranteed way to destroy bitcoin. It would likely strengthen the network by advertising its real potential and value proposition to the world. Government attacks on bitcoin can only happen by restricting individual and financial freedom, the pursuit of

---

108 Schuettinger, Robert L., and Eamonn F. Butler. *Forty Centuries of Wage and Price Controls: How Not to Fight Inflation*. Washington, DC: Heritage Foundation, 1978. Print.

which is the best reason to buy bitcoin. The simple statist mind assumes that reality is subject to government orders: "If government bans X, then X ceases to exist." In reality, such government intervention just makes the provision of X much more profitable and increases the levels of risk people are willing to undertake in order to provide it.

For example, a government order to stop banks from allowing their clients to use their balances to buy bitcoin might hurt demand for bitcoin in the short run, but it would signal to people everywhere that the financial sovereignty and censorship resistance bitcoin provides is extraordinarily valuable. Attempted bans would clearly communicate to people that the money in their bank accounts is not theirs to spend as they please; it is the government's money, and it is limited to only government-approved uses. As this reality begins to sink in, more and more people will want to hold on to a monetary asset whose value is independent of government preferences and whims, and so the demand for bitcoin will likely rise (along with the profitability of supplying it).

The American war on drugs offers an instructive example. For almost fifty years, the U.S. government has killed and incarcerated millions of people in the U.S., Mexico, Colombia, Afghanistan, and many other places in the world in a feeble attempt to stop drugs that can still be bought on the streets of every U.S. city. Drugs come from plants that usually need to be grown in sunlight, then processed and shipped around the world through a long network of suppliers before reaching the end consumers. Drug distribution is a far more complicated and demanding task than distributing bitcoin blocks, which do not need physical supply lines and can be transmitted using the simplest data transfer technologies. While drugs give their users a large incentive to consume and pay for them, it is still not as strong as the monetary and economic incentive to use bitcoin, which can be a matter of life and death for many people. With a stronger incentive than drugs, and an infinitely easier distribution mechanism, any government that tries to ban bitcoin has a tricky task ahead of it.

Another nontrivial obstacle for a government attack to overcome is that bitcoin has become ingrained in political and financial systems.

Senator Cynthia Lummis of Wyoming is an open advocate of bitcoin, as is Congressman Warren Davidson of Ohio. Many other members of Congress have disclosed their ownership of bitcoin. Over the past five years, bitcoin has broadened its base in the U.S. and abroad. Its detractors may bemoan it, but its satisfied users continue to grow. It seems highly unlikely that members of Congress are going to pass laws against their own colleagues, families, and friends. Even bankers that viscerally and rabidly hate bitcoin are watching helplessly as their children's interest in it grows. JP Morgan CEO Jamie Dimon spent many years derisively dismissing bitcoin, but his own daughter bought bitcoin and outperformed his bank stock, and now his bank is offering it to their clients. Large public companies have started accumulating bitcoin reserves with the approval of regulatory authorities. Gary Gensler, the new commissioner of the U.S. Securities and Exchange Commission (SEC) has studied bitcoin extensively and has even taught a course on it at MIT.

Bitcoin now has a motivated and very vocal minority of the population interested in it. A motivated and organized minority is likely to get its way in U.S. politics for the simple reason that it cares more than other groups about its own issue. While people think of democracy as the rule of the majority, it is more accurate to think of it as the rule of the organized minorities. Corn farmers, for example, are a tiny fraction of the total population of the U.S. but still manage to get enormous subsidies. Although these subsidies are a cost to everyone else in the U.S., they are a small cost per head of the population; conversely, the benefit to corn farmers is massive, and they have every incentive to make it their prime voting and lobbying issue. From a politician's perspective, supporting the corn lobbyists will get you votes and money, but going against them get you neither. Bitcoin's motivated minority is growing into this kind of force in political systems worldwide. Any politician who attempts to clamp down on bitcoin will be faced with indifference by the vast majority of the population but strong opposition from bitcoiners. All of these developments suggest it is highly unlikely that the government could crack down on bitcoin in a similar way to its crackdown on drugs.

The Chinese government's ban on bitcoin mining operations on its soil in 2021 provided a fascinating test of bitcoin's resilience to government attacks. Most bitcoin miners operated in China at the time, and this was always viewed as a particular vulnerability of bitcoin. The ban had a discernible effect on the bitcoin network, as the estimated hashrate fell by some 50%, from around 180 exahash/second on May 14, 2021, to around 85 exahash/second on July 3, 2021. The price also fell by more than 50% from its all-time high of $64,000 in mid-April to a low of under $30,000 in late July. This was likely the result of Chinese miners needing to liquidate their bitcoin holdings to relocate. The drop in hashrate resulted in the slowest average block time for any difficulty period in bitcoin's history, thirteen minutes fifty-three seconds per block instead of the protocol's target of ten minutes. As a result, the difficulty adjustment on July 3 of −27.94% was the largest downward adjustment in bitcoin's history. This process powerfully illustrated bitcoin's adaptability and robustness. As the number of miners attempting to solve the proof of work declined, the network slowed down, but the downward difficulty adjustment allowed block production intervals to return closer to the ten-minute mark. Around a half of the industrial capacity of the bitcoin network had to relocate internationally, and three months later, the result seems to be a slowdown in blocks, and a crash to levels that were at an all-time high only six months earlier. The price crash likely hurt many bitcoin investors, yet bitcoin was still roughly threefold its price year-on-year, hardly devastating for long-term holders.

So even a Chinese ban on bitcoin mining only caused a short-term crash in prices and a few weeks of slower blocks, after which time bitcoin resumed its normal service. Further, banning mining in China, the one country where miners were the most concentrated, led to the dispersion of mining capacity among nation-states, making the network less vulnerable to such an attack in the future.

Bitcoin might well be a genie that has grown beyond the ability of governments to put it back in its bottle. The secret is out. Millions of people worldwide have discovered this internet-native hard money and are interested in using it. The number of satisfied users continues to grow by the day. They are willing to invest time and effort into ensuring it continues to be available to them. Government clampdowns may inflict suffering on individual bitcoiners and perhaps cause short-term price falls, but it is doubtful they can derail the entire project.

Software Bugs

Back in September 2018, a bug was found in the code of Bitcoin Core versions 0.14 to 0.16.2 which could have allowed the total supply of bitcoins to be increased above 21 million. Had the bug been discovered by a malicious actor, they may have been able to use it to attack the network. Jimmy Song has provided a great analysis of this incident, and he suggests that, although the likely ramifications of exploiting this bug would have created problems for the network, it was unlikely to have been fatal.[109] Nonetheless, the episode made vivid one more type of threat hanging over bitcoin: malfunctioning code or software bugs. Whether through an innocent mistake in its coding or through the malevolent design of an attacker, it is not inconceivable that there could be problems with the bitcoin code that could cause it to malfunction.

The threat of bugs and malfunction is far more serious for bitcoin than for most other computer programs because bitcoin's value proposition depends on its immutability, reliability, and complete predictability. If it is evolving to fulfill the role of digital gold, then the most important characteristic it needs to copy from gold is its constant reliability and predictable supply. A bug that hinders the operation of the software or allows some users to create more coins would severely compromise the network and the likelihood of it continuing to succeed as digital gold. Rather than focus on the technical details of this bug and how it was fixed (which Jimmy's article discusses), I would like to focus on how bitcoin's open-source development counters this threat.

Linus Torvalds, the original creator of the Linux operating system, said that "with enough eyeballs, all bugs are rendered shallow." That is a great explanation of the prime value proposition of open-source software. While

---

109 Song, Jimmy. "Bitcoin Core Bug CVE-2018–17144: An Analysis." *Hackernoon.*
       21 Sep. 2018. Web.

open-source software usually relies on the efforts of volunteers who are not paid to be fully focused on the software, its collaborative nature can attract many people to review the code and improve it, which helps prevent critical bugs from emerging. This has proven to be a surprisingly successful and robust model. Whereas proprietary software development employs a few full-time, highly focused individuals, open-source development allows anyone to contribute and gives all users of the software the choice to adopt anyone's contributions. The process of constant innovation, variation, and user selection creates a strong evolutionary pressure that drives the code's improvement.

Open-source development is also a good example of Friedrich Hayek's concept of spontaneous order, or order that emerges not through any preconceived individual design but through human action. Most market and societal institutions were not designed top-down by one individual. Instead, they emerged over many years through the actions and interactions of multitudes of individuals. Hayek argues that most of the human institutions that shape our lives, from language to customs to economics, ethics, and manners, are all emergent products of human action and not the conscious effort of human design.

This simple but powerful concept is helpful in understanding how bitcoin has continued to evolve after Satoshi left the project with nobody in charge. In the ten years since he has disappeared, the bitcoin software has improved significantly, and yet no single individual can possibly be viewed as responsible for these changes. While each change to the software can be viewed as a product of rational design by one or a few programmers, the choice of which changes get adopted by users, how the changes build on one another, and the general direction of open-source development are the complex and emergent result of the interaction of variations and individual choices.

There is no single person in charge of bitcoin or responsible for it. Bitcoin has voluntary users who choose to run open-source software at their own discretion; it is not the responsibility of the person who volunteered their time to build it. Bitcoin's lack of central control, and the absence of a rational constructivist approach to its programming, is far from a disadvantage; decentralization is the most effective way for it to remain predictably neutral.

This lack of central control also gives it a huge edge in dealing with software bugs, with a wide variety of users from all over the world examining the code and trying to find mistakes in it. This is the process that keeps all manner of open-source software running, as mentioned by Linus. In the case of bitcoin, the process has a powerful economic incentive for thousands of technically competent people who have a vested interest in it succeeding. Some of the best minds in software development are motivated to hunt for bugs merely to protect the wealth they hold in bitcoin.

In other words, what ultimately protects bitcoin from software bugs is the economic incentive for its users to remove and deal with bugs as quickly as they emerge. And the 2018 bug is a good example of that. While it might have been theoretically possible for a well-funded attacker to exploit the bug, it was highly unlikely in practice due to the economic incentive for all bitcoin users to detect these bugs before they can be exploited. Attacking bitcoin offers very little economic reward, and so it is unlikely to attract the same number of users motivated to this end. An attack on bitcoin is destined to be a top-down design with a few focused and highly skilled individuals trying to execute it. Bitcoin's defense consists of many thousands of users and coders who are constantly vigilant and defending the network against anything bad happening to it.

As Song concludes:

> Bugs will always exist, but the important thing is to have a robust process for dealing with them. Open source software development has shown itself to be more reliable in the long run. Bitcoin adds to it strong economic incentives for many economic parties from developers to businesses to invest heavily in this process as well.[110]

Beyond that, bitcoin's extremely conservative and meticulous design ensures there is another layer of safety for dealing with any critical software

---

110 Song, Jimmy. "Bitcoin Core Bug CVE-2018–17144: An Analysis." *Hackernoon*, 21 Sept. 2018, hackernoon.com/bitcoin-core-bug-cve-2018-17144-an-analysis-f80d9d373362.

failures: the ability to roll back the chain and return to the historical state before the bug struck. This would likely mean that any critical bug would be temporary rather than permanent. If one were to compare this to aircraft maintenance, it would be akin to having a function that allows you to return a crashing flight to its precrash state and perform maintenance on it, inconveniencing the passengers rather than killing them.

Provided bitcoin continues to operate successfully, its growth becomes likelier with each passing day. Any technology takes time to spread; most users will never become technically competent enough to understand all the nuances of its functioning. People need to see technology operating successfully, safely, reliably, and consistently for a significant period of time before they consider using it. Most people eventually got on airplanes, not because they studied jet aviation but because they had seen and heard of airplanes operating reliably, likely for years. Similarly, people will start to trust a digital form of storage, not due to an extensive study of bitcoin and cryptography, but rather after seeing it work reliably for years for others.

The Gold Standard

As discussed briefly in *The Bitcoin Standard*, the government policy that would likely be the most destructive to bitcoin would be the implementation of a gold standard similar to that at the end of the nineteenth century. All government restrictions on bitcoin are restrictions on financial freedom, and the desire to be free from government restrictions is exactly what creates demand for bitcoin. Given that the technical requirements for operating bitcoin are becoming increasingly simpler, government activities that aim to restrict bitcoin will inevitably result in greater incentives for people to overcome these restrictions.

Contrary to the statist instinct to want to ban anything that sounds objectionable, the more effective path for governments to undermine bitcoin would be to undermine the economic incentive for people to use it. However, this would mean increasing the financial and monetary freedoms that individuals have. The monetary system that would allow governments to maintain some form of monetary control while allowing the largest margin for a free market in money would be the adoption of the gold standard. In theory, a government could introduce a hard money standard with its own currency, and commit to not increasing the supply beyond a specific percentage. However, such a commitment would never be as credible as making government money redeemable into physical gold, offering everyone the ability to verify the gold backing, and tying the government's hands.

A move to a gold standard would undermine all the drivers of bitcoin adoption, and it remains an open question whether, in such a world, demand for bitcoin would be enough to prevent attacks and secure the network. Gold currently has a far larger liquidity pool than bitcoin. The value of all aboveground gold is around $10 trillion, more than ten times the value currently stored in the bitcoin network. This very large pool of liquidity means that gold currently has more salability than bitcoin. In other words, for someone looking to buy or sell something, the probability that they will find a counterparty for that trade willing to pay or accept gold is larger than the chance of finding someone willing to pay or accept bitcoin. A move to gold would be far more palatable for the majority of the world's population since they either own gold or currencies backed by gold.

Moving to a gold standard would curtail the ability of governments to intervene in the banking system and protect incumbents from outsiders. This would likely unleash innovation and experimentation in financial systems, as it has done throughout human history, and it is not difficult to imagine the development of highly convenient payment technologies backed by gold. There is no reason why any of the modern payment innovations developed for fiat money and digital currencies could not be implemented on top of gold with 100% reserve backing. The cost of gold final settlement would be far higher for governments than settling fiat liabilities, and the effect on government budgets would be too devastating politically for any politicians to attempt. Were modern fiat governments endowed with a low time preference, they might conclude that the pain of voluntarily adopting a gold standard today would be less severe than a future where they lose monetary status to bitcoin completely. But that seems fanciful to any observer of modern governments.

Politically, culturally, and intellectually, there seems to be little chance of a gold standard adoption. Modern political institutions, academia, media, and public opinion are largely shaped by Keynesians and statists. The monetary role of gold is viewed with scorn and disdain among most educated and influential members of society. The influence of corporate interests that benefit from easy money is far too strong to imagine any kind of constructive monetary reform emerging from the political process.

Bitcoin, however, is a hard monetary system that can gain adoption whether or not the entrenched easy-money interests approve of it. And even a readoption of the gold standard would likely only delay the inevitable move to an internet-native money with higher spatial and intertemporal salability. Gold will soon have a lower stock-to-flow ratio than bitcoin, and it will continue to have a much higher cost of transfer. Even if the adoption of bitcoin slows considerably and there are significant crashes in its price, the slow increase in its supply will still make it likely to recover and appreciate in the long run and hold its value better than gold.

The above analysis does not constitute an ironclad prediction of bitcoin's inevitable success, but it should at least suggest that its continued long-term survival is a distinct and realistic possibility. So how would bitcoin grow in a fiat world?

Central Bank Adoption

Could central banks adopt bitcoin as a reserve asset? Nothing inherent to bitcoin would make such adoption impossible. The case for it is clear: if bitcoin increases in price, any country that uses it as a reserve asset will witness its international cash reserve account rise in value, which would make it less likely for their government or central bank to run into balance of payment problems. The more the reserves appreciate, the more leeway the government has with its own spending and international payments. Further, adopting bitcoin allows central banks to engage in international payment settlements with other central banks, financial institutions, and foreign exporters without needing to resort to the U.S. Federal Reserve's global payment settlement infrastructure, avoiding the risk of sanctions and confiscations. This is likely most appealing to countries at odds with U.S. foreign policy. The threat of other nation-states holding bitcoin reserves first could in itself encourage governments to make the first move. Geopolitical rivals accumulating a harder currency would likely increase their spending power.

In 2021, El Salvador was the first country to adopt bitcoin as legal tender. As a dollarized economy, El Salvador had no seigniorage revenue to lose by adopting bitcoin. El Salvador also stands to gain from the large number of its citizens who work in the U.S. using bitcoin Lightning apps for remittances. It remains to be seen how successful this move is for the people of El Salvador and their government, and whether that encourages others to follow suit.

There are several reasons to suspect this is a move that will not be quickly imitated by major central banks. The first reason is that if we understand bitcoin as an alternative to central banking, then central banks are clearly the last institutions that need it. Central banks are the institutions that provide the services that bitcoin most closely approximates, and so they will likely remain the last to see the value of an alternative to their services.

The second reason is that while countries like China, Russia, Iran, North Korea, and others may hate the U.S. dollar-based global financial system, they love having their own fiat currencies far more than they hate the dollar. The dearness with which central banks treasure their ability to inflate their respective country's money supply could act as a strong constraint against moving to a bitcoin standard. China, Russia, and Iran may like to make a lot of noise about the unfairness of the U.S. dollar monetary system and how it privileges the U.S. internationally, but these governments are not run by sound money economists who would like to see a return to the nineteenth-century gold standard. Decades of Western cultural imperialism mean that even these countries are ruled by the kind of leftist, socialist, Keynesian, and similarly inclined economists who idolize inflation as the key to solving all of life's problems. These governments do not oppose fiat money; they just hate other governments' fiat money. They recognize that their extremely elaborate states and bureaucracies, with far-reaching control of their citizens' lives and large monopoly industries to benefit them and their cronies, are utterly dependent on their ability to continue creating their own money.

We know this because while these countries have long talked about shifting to gold for international payment settlement and as a reserve asset, they have never done it. While they have accumulated gold as a hedge against their dollar reserves, they refuse to settle their own trade using gold and continue to rely on fiat networks. It is doubtful that it is merely the cost of gold settlement that is preventing these governments from moving to a gold standard. It remains to be seen whether bitcoin's superior salability across space and value appreciation will tempt governments where gold failed.

Aside from the self-interest of the ruling elites in these countries, U.S. power is another important factor that may stop them from adopting gold. The IMF has long banned its members from tying their currency to gold. The U.S. still has the world's strongest military and the strongest currency, and any global financial crisis that happens, while having its root causes in the dollar, is likely to only make the dollar stronger, not weaker, as happened in 2008. For all its flaws, the dollar is still the most liquid of all national currencies, and the one bearing the lowest default risk. All other central banks have liabilities in the dollar.

Another reason you might not expect central bank adoption of bitcoin is that modern central bankers have only managed to obtain their jobs by being so completely and thoroughly inculcated with Keynesian and statist propaganda economics that they will be the last in the world to understand the viability and significance of bitcoin as an alternative to what they do. The fiat mental baggage makes the central banker the last person capable of understanding that money does not need the state, and the last person to get the significance of bitcoin.

Finally, understanding bitcoin's value proposition as a long-term store of value despite its short-term fluctuations requires a certain degree of low time preference, which you cannot expect to find in abundance in modern government bureaucracies. The uncertainty and short-term nature of democratic rule instills a short-term orientation in these bureaucrats, and all but guarantees that politics is a short-term power and money grab. Politicians or bureaucrats can be expected to rationally prioritize their self-interest in short periods in office over their constituents' long-term future. Chapter 1 of Hans-Hermann Hoppe's masterpiece *Democracy: The God That Failed* contains an excellent discussion of this point.[111]

This book's analysis of the debt mechanisms of fiat suggests one more reason why bitcoin might prove attractive to central banks: the monetization of a present good allows individuals and firms to hold on their balance sheet a liquid asset independent from the risks of the credit market, reducing their dependence on central bank monetary policy. The conundrum of today's central bankers is that they are at once asked to provide the accommodative monetary policy for government spending and private sector expansion, while also having to ensure savings and investments do not devalue too much. Will some central banks choose to outsource some of the demand for savings to the neutral apolitical bitcoin network, which is unaffected by credit market dynamics? Or will they try to maintain as much wealth as possible in their own network to finance government spending through devaluation?

While El Salvador provides a compelling counterargument, several reasons suggest it is likely bitcoin will continue to develop as described in the subtitle of *The Bitcoin Standard: A Decentralized Alternative to Central Banks*.

Monetary Upgrade and Debt Jubilee

The most widely held prediction about how a bitcoin economy develops usually involves the entirety of the world economy collapsing into a heap of hyperinflationary misery, similar to the one you see in Venezuela today. The dollar, euro, sterling, and all other global currencies would collapse in value as their holders drop them and choose to move their capital to the superior store of value that is bitcoin. Governments would collapse, banks would be destroyed, global trade supply lines would come crumbling down. But there are several reasons to be optimistic that this may not be the case.

---

111 Hoppe, Hans-Hermann. *Democracy: The God That Failed*. Rutgers, NJ: Transaction Publishers, 2001, pp. 1–43. Print.

The first reason is that the hyperinflationary scenario assumes the collapse in demand for national currencies would lead to their values collapsing. But historically, hyperinflation has always been the result of a large increase in the money supply and not a sudden decline in money demand. The demand for rai stones, glass beads, seashells, salt, cattle, silver, many national currencies, and various other monetary media did drop over time as market participants introduced harder alternatives. However, that decline would likely be gradual unless there was a quick increase in the money supply. Hyperinflation can only happen as a result of governments and central banks increasing the money supply, as a close study of any and every modern case of hyperinflation would show.

In Venezuela today, the local currency has dropped to less than a millionth of its value just a few years ago. Venezuela the country is still there, and the size of its population is the same as before the currency collapse. Venezuelans still need money and are demanding more of it. Demand for holding the bolivar has dropped significantly, but demand for local currency units could not possibly have dropped to a millionth of where it was. Venezuelans still need the currency to settle all their government-related business, an ever-growing occurrence thanks to the socialization of the economy. The only way to understand the bolivar's collapse in value is as a result of the rapid increase in supply; any reduction in demand was rather an effect, not a cause, of that currency's value dropping. Venezuelan money supply statistics show the supply of the bolivar increased by a multiple of one hundred between 2007 and 2017, at which point the Venezuelan government stopped publishing money supply figures, suggesting an even more significant increase. Similarly, in Lebanon, the central bank has increased the supply of physical bills and coins by around 650% in the last two years, while the currency has plummeted by more than 90% against the U.S. dollar.

To understand the likelihood of a hyperinflationary collapse, we need to focus on the nature of fiat money creation. Should fiat money continue to function as discussed in Part 1, with lending as the equivalent of mining, the likelihood of hyperinflation is reduced by two forces. First, it is not easy to quickly expand credit to a hyperinflationary degree, and second, credit expansion is self-correcting because it brings about financial bubbles that liquidate large amounts of the money supply. The business cycle is the brutal and highly inefficient fiat equivalent of bitcoin's difficulty adjustment: if credit expands too quickly, it causes speculative bubbles in particular sectors of the economy, like the stock market, housing, or high-tech sector. As investments in these sectors increase, assets become overpriced, beyond what the fundamentals of their balance sheets imply. This incentivizes the production of more financial assets, causing the price of the assets to eventually fall, liquidating a lot of loans and contracting the money supply. Should this dynamic continue, bitcoin's rise alone is unlikely to cause hyperinflationary collapses. If hyperinflation were to happen, as it is happening in Venezuela and Lebanon today, it would be the result of governments overriding the credit creation process and resorting to increases in the base money, most likely through physical money printing, or its modern digital equivalent, through central bank digital currencies. If the credit nature of fiat money is preserved, it could avoid hyperinflationary collapse even if bitcoin continues to consume more of its share of money demand.

Secondly, it is instructive to think about the impact of the rise of bitcoin on the process of fiat money creation. Bitcoin does not just compete with fiat currency for cash asset demand, it also competes with fiat debt. The devaluation of fiat money drives demand for debt instruments that are not exposed to equity risk and which offer returns that compensate for inflation. The demand for a store of value is what leads to the enormous issuance of debt. If more individuals and companies start to hold bitcoin instead of debt instruments on their balance sheets, that would reduce the demand for credit creation, reducing fiat money creation, making hyperinflation less likely. By undermining the incentive to hold debt instruments, bitcoin actively combats the inflation of the fiat money supply.

Thirdly, bitcoin has a similar effect on the incentive to borrow. In a world of artificially low interest rates and easy fiat money that is expected to constantly devalue, individuals are likely to borrow rather than save. The discovery of bitcoin gives individuals and corporations the chance to save in a hard asset that appreciates over time, making them less likely to need to borrow to meet their major expenses.

The fourth reason we can expect there to be no hyperinflationary collapse as a result of the rise of bitcoin is that hyperinflation happens when the entire monetary system of a society collapses, thus destroying the complex web of calculations and interactions that coordinate the activities of individuals across a large modern society. A modern society relies on money as the medium in which prices are expressed, and these prices are what coordinate economic activity and allow individuals to calculate what to produce and consume. No modern society, with its sophisticated infrastructure, is possible without a highly complex division of labor, dependent on the price mechanism and economic monetary calculation, to coordinate economic activity. The collapse of money destroys this division of labor and makes economic coordination impossible, unraveling modern life into a primitive disaster. But all of this happens when the only monetary system of a society collapses, and in a fiat standard, local government fiat is the only monetary system available to people in any given country. Historically, as national currencies have collapsed, citizens have usually not had an available monetary alternative with salability across space and time. Governments experiencing hyperinflation do not just allow their banks to offer banking services with foreign currencies. When they do, such as in the case of the dollarization of Ecuador, hyperinflation ends, and economic production, growth, and normalcy resume on a harder money.

Due to its superior salability across space, bitcoin is much harder to ban than foreign national currencies. It also offers a refuge from hyperinflation rather than being the cause of it. As a national currency collapses, any citizen can shift their wealth to a growing pool of liquidity with which they can trade, allowing economic production and calculation to proceed and averting a humanitarian catastrophe. Should bitcoin become widespread enough to destroy demand for government currencies, then the network will be large enough to support an increasing amount of coordination, trade, and investment. Unlike in a hyperinflationary scenario, a move to bitcoin without a large increase in the supply of government money would not lead to a catastrophe; it would be a global upgrade—a peaceful technological upgrade of society's monetary infrastructure. Anyone who wants to keep using government money can continue doing so, but as bitcoin undercuts both its demand and supply, the government money bubble shrinks and withers away, while the bitcoin economy grows.

Rather than a threat that can destroy fiat money, bitcoin may turn out to be the neat technological solution that allows fiat to unwind peacefully. Bitcoin simultaneously reduces fiat demand and the incentive to create more fiat supply. It is like someone skillfully and neatly dismantling the fiat house of cards into a deck of cards by removing each set of two cards leaning on each other at the same time: the card of fiat demand and the card of fiat supply.

If governments of advanced economies, which have done a semi-respectable job in managing their currencies over the past few decades, manage this process wisely, they would allow the credit and money contraction to happen naturally. The fiat-denominated economy would continue to shrink in relation to the bitcoin economy as more people upgrade to the superior, harder, and faster monetary asset. The fiat monetary system could operate for the next fifty years in the same way it has operated for the last fifty. But by the end of the next fifty years, it may well be a tiny fraction of the size of the bitcoin monetary system. Rather than go out with a bang, the current global monetary system would just slowly and naturally get downsized into irrelevance as its currencies lose their value, and market share, to bitcoin.

Rather than an attack on the fiat system, bitcoin might allow the fiat economy an exit from its spiral into ever-more debt slavery, as it devalues the fiat debt that saddles everyone in the fiat system. If more people move to bitcoin, and fiat-denominated debt devalues in real terms, the vast majority of the world's economy benefits enormously from the devaluation of its obligations. The sooner one upgrades to the bitcoin economy, the sooner their fiat debts become insignificant.

In a world where the possibility of saving were available again, you would expect a growing portion of the population to be free of debt and to have enough savings to finance their expenses, as well as to finance their businesses. Fewer people would resort to loans in order to buy cars, houses, or consumer goods because they could save up for them in hard money. More interestingly, perhaps, would be the shift in business financing, as more people become wealthy enough to finance their own businesses with their own savings rather than from bank credit. Bitcoin truly has the potential to transform the current mass of debtors into entrepreneurs, and the consequences of this for human flourishing and prosperity are scarcely imaginable.

Under sound money regimes, a free market in capital emerges in place of central monetary planning. Productive individuals are able to accumulate capital and watch it appreciate in value, and so they can finance themselves and their businesses. Productivity is rewarded with compounding growth in value over time, giving the holders of capital more of it, and thus placing increasingly more capital in the hands of the productive.

In large, centrally planned, credit markets, such as those that exist under government money, capital is centrally allocated by government bureaucracies that determine who gets new capital, devaluing the capital accumulated by the productive members of society. In such a world, being productive is punished over time, and credit financing is more likely to go to those who can afford to brace the bureaucratic hoops of government credit boards. Firms grow larger to afford lawyers and PR firms to communicate their stability to creditor banks, and smaller businesses become less viable. This is why firms tended to be smaller under the gold standard, and far more smaller businesses thrived. It is said that when Britain was the prime industrial global force, its average factory had twenty workers. A free market in capital would similarly encourage the development of a diverse array of smaller firms, as opposed to rent-seeking megacorporations, and these smaller firms would serve as laboratories for a multitude of inventions and innovations. It is no wonder that the golden era of innovation in the nineteenth century, la Belle Époque, ran on a hard money. That hard money is what allowed many inventors and tinkerers the capital and freedom to experiment with outlandish ideas. The Wright brothers were two bicycle shop owners whose savings allowed them to experiment with flight and change the world.

The rosy transition scenario for bitcoin is that it leads to a growing parallel monetary and financial system which offers its adopters significant benefits for upgrading to it. Individuals, businesses, and local governments are likely to gradually migrate to this monetary system. Eventually, the only part of the economy that would remain wedded to government money would be government itself, and the parts of the economy dependent on government money, both of whose contribution to valuable economic production is approximately zero. But this is not a foregone conclusion.

Speculative Attacks

A counterpoint to consider to the preceding section's analysis is the impact of the strategy of borrowing dollars to buy bitcoin. While many people would be tempted to exit fiat debt entirely and shift to holding hard bitcoin savings, the continued existence and wide availability of fiat debt will offer a strong incentive to borrow fiat and use it to accumulate bitcoin. One of the smartest and most farseeing analysts of bitcoin, Pierre Rochard,[112] had identified this scenario as early as 2014. He outlined how bitcoin allows investors world-wide to carry out a speculative attack on all national currencies, similar to what George Soros and beneficiaries of low interest rate lending have been doing to weak national currencies for decades with spectacular success.

The speculative attack is, then, the natural evolution of what inevitably results when easy money meets hard money, amplified by the force of fiat credit. The speculative attack strategy is to borrow the weak currency and use it to buy the stronger currency. Borrowing the weak currency causes an increase in its supply, and selling it for strong currency causes a decrease in demand for it, which results in the decline of the value of the weak currency next to the stronger currency. This reduces the value of the weak money loan the attacker owes, while increasing the value of the hard currency he holds—a highly lucrative combination. Because bitcoin is a harder currency than all national currencies, it could be the perfect vehicle for attacks against national currencies.

As large corporations and financial institutions are now accumulating bitcoin while also borrowing large amounts of fiat, a speculative attack is arguably brewing, even if its participants may be unaware of what they are

---

112 Rochard, Pierre. "Speculative Attack." *Satoshi Nakamoto Institute.* 4 Jul. 2014. Web.

doing. As these public companies with significant treasuries watch their bitcoin balance grow in nominal value, their balance sheets become stronger, allowing them to take on more fiat debt, increasing the supply of fiat, and providing them more fiat with which to buy more bitcoin. The profitability of this move can be understood as the market rewarding the move to the better monetary asset. How far can these speculative attacks go?

A couple of restraining forces can be identified. Corporations are now finding it easy to borrow on capital markets as they accumulate bitcoin, but only because of the very large amount of capital looking for debt obligations without equity risk. As bitcoin investment becomes more accessible to institutional investors, many of these lenders will choose to just purchase bitcoin instead of lending to financial firms that purchase bitcoin, limiting the credit available for launching speculative attacks.

Should private lending decline because of the rise of bitcoin, credit is likely to become even more centralized and government-controlled. As lending becomes more politicized, it would not be a surprise to see fiat governments restrict lending to any entities with bitcoin on their balance sheets. The centralization and politicization of credit in the hands of governments undermines the possibility of speculative attacks, but it also undermines the credit nature of fiat, rendering it more of a digital version of ubiquitous government papers that have been the hallmark of hyperinflation.

Central Bank Digital Currencies

Between starting to write this book and its completion, the tone of central banks toward bitcoin has changed completely. In 2018, the average central banker would have summarily dismissed bitcoin by muttering irrelevant references to apocryphal tales and folk songs about the prices of tulip bubbles rising in seventeenth-century Amsterdam.[113] In 2021, central bankers

---

113 Boissoneault, Lorraine. "There Never Was a Real Tulip Fever." *Smithsonian Magazine*. 18 Sept. 2017. Web. See also: French, Doug. "The Truth About Tulipmania." *Mises Daily Articles*, Mises Institute. 26 May 2007. Web.

are racing to implement what might be the most important upgrade to the fiat network in five decades: bitcoin-inspired central bank digital currencies (CBDCs).

Central bankers present CBDCs as a technologically progressive step that allows for faster and more secure digital payments. However, their transformative potential for surveillance, political patronage, and economic central planning is underadvertised. CBDCs would give central banks full real-time surveillance capabilities of all citizens' wallets and spending. CBDCs would also allow governments to tax and pay their citizens more directly and effectively, increasing the efficiency by which governments disrupt the workings of the market economy. As the popularity of government handouts surges in the postpandemic world, CBDCs offer a great product-market fit for governments looking to distribute large amounts of money to their citizens.

Whereas the current fiat system allows all lenders to mine fiat into existence by issuing loans, CBDCs will likely centralize this process in the hands of the central bank. With all balances held at the central bank, and credit increasingly politicized and centralized, the fiat system would take a very decisive turn toward an authoritarian and socialist society. CBDCs might herald the end of fiat as credit money generated through loans, and transform it into a pure digital commodity money issued by the central bank, with important implications for the rise of bitcoin. As the corrective mechanism of fiat credit bubbles collapsing is sidestepped by the move toward fiat noncredit CBDCs, the brakes on fiat inflation would be severed. CBDCs would continue to increase in supply as governments indulge in fiat-century spending habits, but there would be no credit collapses to reverse the increase. The orderly monetary upgrade scenario becomes less likely.

Since the 2008 financial crisis and the increased intervention of fiat central banks into financial, credit, housing, and many other markets, fiat central banks have been overriding the correcting mechanism of money supply collapse. An increasing share of the world's bond and stock markets is now held by central banks, and their valuation is increasingly determined by central bank fiat, with the normal workings of the credit cycle overruled through infinite quantitative easing.

The 2020 global pandemic crisis resulted in most governments engaging in increased payments to their citizens under various guises, and clamor is growing for turning these into regular Universal Basic Income payments. CBDCs would allow for the implementation of such inflationist schemes with high efficiency, allowing for increased central planning of market activity. Government spending would proceed unabated by whatever little discipline credit markets currently exert. Real-world prices are likely to rise, which would lead to more control over economic production to mandate prices.

CBDCs are perhaps most devastating for the banking sector, which would increasingly get disintermediated in the pervasive relationship between government and serf. The closest analog to the operation of the CBDC is the Gosbank, the State Bank of the USSR, which was the only bank in the Soviet Union from the 1930s until 1987. All citizens who had bank access had access to only one bank, and it decided on all economic decisions. Limiting the role of private banks, or eliminating them in favor of money generated by pure government fiat, is likely to lead to a highly centrally planned economic system with tight government control over all aspects of economic life.

If inflation is a vector, as explained in Chapter 4, CBDCs will likely lead to a fast rise in the price of highly desirable and scarce goods, while industrial goods will likely witness small declines in price, and digital goods will continue to get cheaper. The same tricks of the 1970s can serve to maintain inflation in a politically desirable range: skewing the composition of the basket of goods used to measure CPI to favor goods with low price inflation, and directing consumers toward these choices through the use of fiat incentives. As we have seen since the 1970s, price inflation will drive political pressure on citizens to reduce consumption of nutritious food and high-power sources of energy. The growing popularity of these narratives in fiat academia and media in recent years suggests they are very likely to become the subject of government and monetary policy.

Government CBDC fiat is likely to finance more fiat science to find fault with meat and hydrocarbons, our most reliable technologies for nutrition and power, and thus the most price-sensitive products. We can already see how the old religious narratives about energy and food, discussed in Part 2, are becoming increasingly popular as inflation causes the prices of food and energy to rise. As access to money and banking becomes centralized, this power can be very conveniently wielded to prevent official CPI numbers from looking bad through heavy taxation, rationing, or an outright ban of the purchase of certain goods. The push to promote fiat foods and fuels will likely take a far more coercive turn with the implementation of CBDCs. The past year has also shown how public health concerns can contribute to this totalitarian monetary control: lockdowns are increasingly looking like a permanent feature of the modern fiat economy, small businesses are being destroyed, savings are devaluing, and citizens and businesses are increasingly dependent on government spending to make ends meet.

The Soviet Union continued to produce very impressive numbers for economic growth into the late 1980s, even as Soviet citizens were going hungry thanks to shortages. In the same way, modern government-run central banks can project an illusion of wealth despite a contrary reality. Paul Samuelson and William Nordhaus, two of the most important postwar economists in the U.S., both of whom have won the Bank of Sweden Prize (commonly misidentified as a Nobel Prize), wrote in their 1989 *Economics* textbook, which is standard issue for most undergraduate students around the world, "The Soviet economy is proof that, contrary to what many skeptics had earlier believed, a socialist command economy can function and even thrive."[114] Modern macroeconomics shares Soviet macroeconomics' faith in the ability of high priests with PhDs to divine and optimize the working of an economy through models, metrics, and statistical analysis.

Central banks' increasingly monopolistic control over economic affairs and statistics allows them to produce numbers that can mask and embellish the economic reality for the majority of the population. The likely outcome for the sclerotic, propagandized economies surrounding governments is a slow terminal decline into irrelevance, similar to what happened to

114 Samuelson, Paul A., and William D. Nordhaus. *Economics*. 13th ed. New York: McGraw-Hill, 1989. Print.

the Soviet economy. Ultimately, the structures for these shambolic organizations can remain, but they will become hollow and less attractive to the people who follow their own self-interest to a new economy. While government-connected firms may continue, they will lose their relevance and value.

In this kind of scenario, the bitcoin-based hard money economy would grow, and more holders of that hard money would witness an appreciation of their wealth. At the same time, government-based economies would shrink, both in size and in relative wealth, as the widespread emigration of society's productive class punishes centrally planned economies. The fiat economy will continue to provide people with lucrative careers and alluringly large fiat-denominated salaries, but increasingly fewer quality, scarce, and desirable goods. As the producers of economically valuable goods move to a harder monetary standard, these fiat-denominated monetary units will buy less, as people trade the valuable fruits of their labor for the harder currency. Fiat-denominated monetary units will continue to maintain a semblance of value only when used to purchase mass-produced economic goods.

You can imagine two new global economies emerging across the world. On the one hand, there is the easy money, centrally planned economy of which government, media, and academia insist you must be a part. It provides comfortable jobs secured from competition and controlled prices to ensure everyone gets their government-recommended soy, bug, and high fructose corn syrup rations, stays in a tiny home, consumes little energy, and has few or no kids to avoid burdening the planet with inconvenient inflationary pressure. And on the other hand is a growing, innovative, and apolitical economy which draws in the most ambitious, creative, and productive people in the world to work hard on providing goods of value to others.

As the fiat mining process becomes increasingly centralized and monopolized by central governments, economic and political power will also follow. Those who are well-connected to the digital printer will likely be the only ones who can afford the highly desirable goods whose prices are increasing most rapidly, while the vast majority witness their purchasing power, wages, and investments failing to keep up with inflation. Centralized inflation will create a monetary caste system similar to that which exists in socialist societies: a ruling class with an abundance of desirable goods, and a majority surviving thanks to a black market.

In this dystopian world, the black market is bitcoin, and it affords the serfs a superior monetary asset to what their government offers. It is common to hear CBDCs discussed as an alternative to bitcoin, but a clear examination of the nature of the two shows that CBDCs are the best advertisement for bitcoin. They are superficially similar in that they are both digital, but importantly, their fundamental characteristics are stark opposites. Bitcoin makes payment clearance a mathematical and mechanical process that cannot be controlled by intermediaries, whereas CBDCs make every transaction subject to approval and reversal by the central bank. Further, bitcoin makes monetary policy mathematically certain and free from any human tinkering, whereas the raison d'être of central banks is to dictate monetary policy. As essential goods like fuel and meat become increasingly difficult to acquire using centralized currencies, and as operating businesses will entail heavy compliance costs to access banking services, the appeal of bitcoin will only grow. As inflationary monetary policy causes the value of CBDCs to decline, bitcoin's contrasting ability to appreciate in value will shine.

The growth of purely fiat CBDCs will make an orderly upgrade to a harder money less likely and instead will probably result in economic apartheid between two hostile monetary systems: bitcoin and fiat. The fiat economy will be fully regulated and surveilled, constantly subject to inflationary pressure, and financing increasingly violent and totalitarian governments that control their serfs' purchasing decisions. The bitcoin economy would be a free market based on hard money, allowing its sovereign members to save, trade, and plan for the future freely while financing the growth of cheap energy production worldwide.

Acknowledgments

This book was published independently thanks to the support and patronage of my readers and members of my online learning platform, Saifedean.com. My heartfelt gratitude goes to everyone who preordered copies of this book before its publication, subscribed to receive chapters as they were written, enrolled in my online courses, or attended my weekly seminars. Having a platform where I can interact with sharp thinkers while remaining financially independent of fiat academia is an honor I will never underestimate or take for granted. Your interest in my work and constant constructive feedback are the building blocks from which this book was built.

I am also very thankful to the sponsors of Saifedean.com and *The Bitcoin Standard Podcast* for supporting my work. They are: NYDIG, OKCOIN, Cyphersafe, CoinBits App, Nodl, and Coldcard.

This considerable task of editing this book was completed thanks to the heroic efforts of Steve Robinson, Alex McShane, and Chay Allen, as well as some help from Principia @grokology, Oscar Webb, and Michael Dewa. Tamara Mikler produced the graphics, Peter Young provided research assistance, and the rest of the team at Saifedean.com worked heroically to produce and self-publish this book, so my thanks go out to the dream team of

Pavao Pahljina, Marko Pahljina, and Dorian Antešić. Publishing this book with Scribe Media has been a highly enjoyable and efficient experience. I am very thankful to my publishing manager Vi La Bianca, and to editors Tara Taylor and Areil Sutton.

My sincere thanks also go to the following individuals who had an instrumental role in the writing of this book. Ross Stevens provided extensive feedback on the early drafts of this book, which helped me organize my ideas and improve the language extensively. The inspiration of this book came from watching a talk by Giacomo Zucco on steelmanning altcoin apologia. Pierre Rochard's analysis of saving and investment, and his understanding of bitcoin as a saving technology were instrumental in the development of the ideas of the book. Michael Saylor's indispensable and original analysis of fiat inflation, and his feedback on earlier drafts of this book helped me understand the problem at hand much better, improving this book immensely. Michael Goldstein always provided me with valuable knowledge on bitcoin, economics, and nutrition. Max Guimaraes's thoughtful and thorough questions in our weekly Saifedean.com seminars clarified for me the importance of spatial salability as a framework for understanding fiat. Greg Foss and Shaun Cumby provided me very valuable insights on the workings of the bond market. Adam Tzagournis provided editing and helpful feedback on earlier papers that were to develop into this book. Dimitriy Molla provided me with valuable background knowledge to understand modern and classical architecture.

I am grateful to Manuel, Maria, and Stepan for their work on data and graphics for this book, and to Ioni Appelberg for producing a very nice video trailer of this book. I am also thankful to all the developers who have worked on Linux Ubuntu and Libre Office and made them good enough for me to write this entire book without having to use the broken windows of the world's most fiat software company and its founder, the world's most fiat man.

The long hours of writing this book were mostly spent listening to classical Arab music, and I would be remiss to not thank the great Um Kulthum, Riad Sunbaty, Mohammad Abdelwahhab, Baleegh Hamdy, and Sabah Fakhry, as well as the National Arab Orchestra, who have done an amazing job reviving the treasures of Arab classical music in the U.S.

Finally, I must thank my wife and children for providing me the inspiration to write and for putting up with the many days over the past three years when I drowned in writing at their expense.

Bibliography

"A (Not Quite) Complete List of Things Supposedly Caused by Global Warming."
What Really Happened. Web. 3 Oct. 2021.

Ammous, Saifedean, host. "Michael Saylor & Microstrategy Adopt *The Bitcoin Standard.*" *The Bitcoin Standard Podcast*, episode 5, Saifedean Ammous, 24 Sep. 2020, https://saifedean.com/podcast/the-bitcoin-standard-podcast-seminar-5-september-24-2020.

Ammous, Saifedean. "Principles of Economics." *Saifedean Ammous.* Web. 3 Oct. 2021.

Ammous, Saifedean. "Slowdown: Aviation and Modernity's Lost Dynamism." *SSRN Electronic Journal*, Elsevier BV. 25 May 2017. Web. Crossref, doi:10.2139/ssrn.3036275.

Ammous, Saifedean. *The Bitcoin Standard.* Hoboken, NJ: John Wiley & Sons, Inc., 2018. Print.

Anson, Michael, et al. "Your Country Needs Funds: The Extraordinary Story of Britain's Early Efforts to Finance the First World War." *Bank Underground.* 8 Aug. 2017. Web.

Auer, Raphael. "Beyond the Doomsday Economics of 'Proof-of-Work' in Cryptocurrencies." *Bank for International Settlements.* 21 Jan. 2019. Web.

Bailey, Ronald. "Renewable Energy Mandates Are Making Poor People Poorer." *Reason.* Jun. 2018. Web. 3 Oct. 2021.

Ball, Ben, Richard Tabor, and Thomas Lee. *Energy Aftermath: How We Can Learn from the Blunders of the Past to Create a Hopeful Energy Future.* Boston: Harvard Business School Press, 1990.

Barnichon, Regis, Christian Matthes, and Alexander Ziegenbein. "The Financial Crisis at 10: Will We Ever Recover?" *Federal Reserve Bank of San Francisco*. 13 Aug. 2018. Web.

Bartholomew, James. "Degrees in Disaster." *The Spectator*. 25 July 2015. Web.

Barzun, Jacques. *From Dawn to Decadence: 500 Years of Cultural Life, 1500 to the Present*. New York: HarperCollins, 2000. Print.

Bentley, Jeanine. "U.S. Trends in Food Availability and a Dietary Assessment of Loss-Adjusted Food Availability: 1970–2014." *Economic Research Service*, U.S. Department of Agriculture. Jan. 2017. Web. 3 Oct. 2021.

Bier, Jonathan. *The Blocksize War: The Battle Over Who Controls Bitcoin's Protocol Rules*. Self-published, 2021. Print.

Boden, T. A., G. Marland, and R. J. Andres, "Global, Regional, and National Fossil-Fuel CO_2 Emissions." *Carbon Dioxide Information Analysis Center (CDIAC)*, Oak Ridge National Laboratory, U.S. Department of Energy. 2008. Web. 3 Oct. 2021.

Boissoneault, Lorraine. "There Never Was a Real Tulip Fever." *Smithsonian Magazine*. 18 Sept. 2017. Web.

"Breaking Land: The Loss of Organic Matter." *Soil Quality for Environmental Health*. 19 Sep. 2011. Web.

"California." *Environmental Progress*. 30 Aug. 2021. Web.

Chesterton, G.K. *The Thing: Why I Am a Catholic*. New York: Dodd, Mead, & Co., 1929. Print.

Constable, John. "The Brink of Darkness: Britain's Fragile Power Grid." *The Global Warming Policy Foundation*. 10 Jun. 2020. Web.

"Currency Composition of Official Foreign Exchange Reserves (COFER)." *International Monetary Fund*. 30 Sep. 2021. Web.

Damant, G C. "Notes on the "Laurentic" Salvage Operations and the Prevention of Compressed Air Illness." *Journal of Hygiene*, vol. 25, no. 1, Feb. 1926, pp. 26–49. Print. Crossref, doi:10.1017/s0022172400017198.

"District of Columbia Private Schools by Tuition Cost." *Private School Review*. Web. 3 Oct. 2020.

Domar, Evsey D. "Capital Expansion, Rate of Growth, and Employment." *Econometrica*, vol. 14, no. 2, Apr. 1946, pp. 137–47. Print. Crossref, doi:10.2307/1905364.

Easterly, William. "The Cartel of Good Intentions: The Problem of Bureaucracy in Foreign Aid." *The Journal of Policy Reform*, vol. 5, no. 2, Dec. 2002, pp. 223–50. Crossref, doi:10.1080/1384128032000096823.

Easterly, William. *The Elusive Quest for Growth: Economists' Adventures and Misadventures in the Tropics*. Cambridge, MA: MIT Press, 2001. Print.

Easterly, William. *The Tyranny of Experts: Economists, Dictators, and the Forgotten Rights of the Poor.* New York: Basic Books, 2014. Print.

Easterly, William. *The White Man's Burden: Why the West's Efforts to Aid the Rest Have Done So Much Ill and So Little Good.* New York: Penguin, 2006. eBook.

Eisenhower, Dwight. "Farewell Address." *Dwight D. Eisenhower Presidential Library, Museum & Boyhood Home.* 17 Jan. 1961. Web. 3 Oct. 2021.

"Electricity Prices." *GlobalPetrolPrices.com.* Web. 3 Oct. 2021.

Enig, Mary. "Fats and Oils and Their Impact on Health." *The Weston A. Price Foundation.* 14 Jan. 2004. Web.

Enserink, Martin. "Sea of Doubts: Dozens of Papers Linking High Carbon Dioxide to Unsettling Changes in Fish Behavior Fall Under Suspicion." *Science.* 6 May 2021. Web.

Epstein, Alex. *The Moral Case for Fossil Fuels.* New York: Portfolio / Penguin, 2014. eBook.

Etheridge, David, et al. "Natural and Anthropogenic Changes in Atmospheric CO_2 over the Last 1,000 Years from Air in Antarctic Ice and Firn." *Journal of Geophysical Research* 101.D2 (20 Feb. 1996): 4115–28. Print. Crossref, doi:10.1029/95JD03410.

Fallon, Sally, and Mary G. Enig. "The Skinny on Fats." *The Weston A. Price Foundation.* 1 Jan. 2000. Web.

"Farm Runoff in Mississippi River Floodwater Fuels Dead Zone in Gulf." *PBS News Hour.* 18 May 2011. Web.

Fergusson, Adam. *When Money Dies: The Nightmare of Deficit Spending, Devaluation, and Hyperinflation in Weimar Germany.* New York: Perseus Books, 2010. eBook.

"Flaring Emissions." *International Energy Agency.* Jun. 2020. Web. 3 Oct. 2021.

"Flour." *Goldkeim*, Systains. Web. 3 Oct. 2021.

"Food and Nutrition through the 20th Century: Government Guidelines." *University of North Carolina, Health Sciences Library.* 20 Aug. 2021. Web.

French, Doug. "The Truth About Tulipmania." *Mises Daily Articles*, Mises Institute. 26 May 2007. Web.

Friedman, Milton, and Anna Schwartz. *A Monetary History of the United States, 1867–1960.* Princeton, NJ: Princeton University Press, 1963. Print.

Fryar, Cheryl D., Margaret D. Carroll, and Cynthia L. Ogden. "Prevalence of Overweight, Obesity, and Extreme Obesity Among Adults Aged 20 and Over: United States, 1960–1962 Through 2013–2014." *National Center for Health Statistics, Center for Disease Control and Prevention.* 5 Sep. 2018. Web.

"Germany." *Environmental Progress.* 22 Sep. 2011. Web.

"Gold, Banknotes and Money Supply in the First World War." *NatWest Group Remembers*. Web. 3 Oct. 2021.

Goldstein, Michael. "Just Eat Meat." Web. 3 Oct. 2021. justmeat.co.

Hall, J. Storrs. *Where Is My Flying Car? A Memoir of Future Past*. Self-published, 2018. eBook.

Hanke, Steve H. and Charles Bushnell. "Venezuela Enters the Record Book: The 57th Entry in the Hanke-Krus World Hyperinflation Table." *Studies in Applied Economics* 69 (Dec. 2016), Johns Hopkins Institute for Applied Economics, Global Health, and the Study of Business Enterprise. Web.

Hanke, Steve. "Lebanon Hyperinflates." *Cato Institute*. 23 Jul. 2020. Web.

Harrod, R. F. "An Essay in Dynamic Theory." *The Economic Journal*, vol. 49, no. 193, Mar. 1939, pp. 14–33. Print. Crossref, doi:10.2307/2225181.

Hayek, Friedrich. *Denationalisation of Money—The Argument Refined: An Analysis of the Theory and Practice of Concurrent Currencies*. London: Institute of Economic Affairs, 1976: 35. Print.

Hayek, Friedrich. *Monetary Nationalism and International Stability*. London: Longmans, Green, and Company, 1937: 4+. Print.

Hess, John. "Harvard's Sugar-Pushing Nutritionist." *The Saturday Review* (Aug. 1978): 10–14. Print.

"Holistic Management." *Savory Institute*. Web. 3 Oct. 2021.

Homer, Sidney, and Richard Sylla. *A History of Interest Rates*. Hoboken, NJ: John Wiley & Sons, 2005. Print.

Hoppe, Hans-Hermann. "'The Yield from Money Held' Reconsidered." *Mises Daily Articles*, Mises Institute. 14 May 2009. Web.

Hoppe, Hans-Hermann. *Democracy: The God That Failed*. Rutgers, NJ: Transaction Publishers, 2001. Print.

Hoppe, Hans-Hermann. *The Great Fiction: Property, Economy, Society, and the Politics of Decline*. 2nd ed. Auburn, AL: Ludwig von Mises Institute, 2021, p. 174. Print.

Hülsmann, Jörg Guido. "Banks Cannot Create Money." *The Independent Review*, vol. 5, no. 1, Summer 2000, pp. 101–10. Web.

"Ice-Core Merged Products." *Scripps CO_2 Program*. Scripps Institution of Oceanography, UC San Diego. Web. 3 Oct. 2021.

Ioannidis, John P. A. "Why Most Published Research Findings Are False." *PLoS Medicine*, vol. 2, no. 8, 30 Aug. 2005, p. e124. Print. Crossref, doi:10.1371/journal.pmed.0020124.

Jones, C., J. Hickman, S. Rumbold, J. Walton, R. Lamboll, R. Skeie, et al. "The Climate Response to Emissions Reductions Due To COVID-19: Initial

Results from Covid MIP." *Geophysical Research Letters*, vol. 48, no. 8, 10 Mar. 2021, doi.org/10.1029/2020GL091883.

Jones, Claire. "How Germany Got Its Gold Back." *Financial Times*. 10 Nov. 2017. Web.

Kealey, Terence. *The Economic Laws of Scientific Research*. London: Macmillan Press, 1996. Print.

Keeling, Charles D., et al., "Exchanges of Atmospheric CO_2 and $13CO_2$ with the Terrestrial Biosphere and Oceans from 1978 to 2000." *Scripps Institution of Oceanography Reference Series* 1–6 (2001). Web.

Kemmerer, Edwin Walter. *Gold and the Gold Standard: The Story of Gold Money, Past, Present and Future*. New York: McGraw-Hill, 1944. Print.

Kinsella, Stephan. "Against Intellectual Property." *Journal of Libertarian Studies*, vol. 15, no. 2, 2001, pp. 1–53. Web.

Koonin, Steven. *Unsettled: What Climate Science Tells Us, What It Doesn't, and Why It Matters*. Dallas: BenBella Books, Inc., 2021. Print.

Levine, Matt. "The Fed Versus the Narrow Bank: Also Martin Shkreli, Elon Musk, LaCroix, Stock Buybacks and Private Jets." *Bloomberg Opinion*. 8 Mar. 2019. Web.

Livera, Stephan, host. "SLP213 Michael Saylor—Bitcoin Dematerializes Money." *Stephan Livera Podcast*, episode 213, Stephan Livera, 21 Sep. 2020, https://stephanlivera.com/episode/213.

Long, Caitlin. "Is Financialization a Double-Edged Sword for Bitcoin and Cryptocurrencies?" *Forbes*. 31 Jul. 2018. Web.

"Long-term Trends in Diabetes." *United States Diabetes Surveillance System*, Center for Disease Control and Prevention. Apr. 2017, p. 3. Web.

MacFarling Meure, C., et al. "Law Dome CO_2, CH_4 and N_2O Ice Core Records Extended to 2000 Years BP." *Geophysical Research Letters*, vol. 33, no. 14, 2006. Crossref, doi:10.1029/2006GL026152.

McClean, Paul. "A Correction 103 Years Late: How the BoE Covered Up Failed War Bond Sale." *Financial Times*. 8 Aug. 2017. Web.

McIntyre, Stephen. "Climate Audit by Steve McIntyre." Web. 3 Oct. 2021. https://climateaudit.org.

Menger, Karl. "On the Origins of Money." *The Economic Journal*, vol. 2, no. 6, Jun. 1892, p. 239. Print. Crossref, doi:10.2307/2956146.

"MicroStrategy Adopts Bitcoin as Primary Treasury Reserve Asset." *BusinessWire*. 11 Aug. 2020. Web.

Munson, Kenneth. *Jane's Pocket Book of Record Breaking Aircraft*. Edited by John Taylor. New York: Collier Macmillan, 1981. Print.

Nakamoto, Satoshi. "Bitcoin P2P E-Cash Paper." *The Cryptography Mailing List.* 31 Oct. 2008. Web. https://archive.is/20121228025845/http://article.gmane.org/gmane.comp.encryption.general/12588.

Nixon, Richard. "Address to the Nation Outlining a New Economic Policy: 'The Challenge of Peace'." *The American Presidency Project.* 15 Aug. 1971. Web.

Nosek, Brian. "Unreliable Research: Trouble at the Lab." *The Economist.* 18 Oct. 2013. Web.

O'Connor, Anahad. "How the Sugar Industry Shifted Blame to Fat." *New York Times.* 12 Sep. 2016. Web.

Officer, Lawrence. "Gold Standard." *EH.Net Encyclopedia.* 26 Mar. 2008, Web.

Osborne, John. "Gold and Silver." *The Bank of England 1914–21 (Unpublished War History).* Vol. 2. Bank of England Archive, 1926. Web. https://www.bankofengland.co.uk/-/media/boe/files/archive/ww/boe-1914-1921-vol2-chapter5a.pdf.

Perkins, John. *Confessions of An Economic Hitman.* New York: Plume, 2004. Print.

Price, Weston. "Studies of Relationships Between Nutritional Deficiencies and (a) Facial and Dental Arch Deformities and (b) Loss of Immunity to Dental Caries Among South Sea Islanders and Florida Indians." *The Dental Cosmos: A Monthly Record of Dental Science,* vol. 77, no. 11, Nov. 1935, p. 1038. Print.

Price, Weston. *Nutrition and Physical Degeneration: A Comparison of Primitive and Modern Diets and Their Effects.* Great Barrington, MA: Keats, 1939. Print.

Roach, Stephen. "The Ghost of Arthur Burns." *Project Syndicate.* 25 May 2021. Web.

Rosenstein-Rodan, P. N. "Problems of Industrialisation of Eastern and South-Eastern Europe." *The Economic Journal,* vol. 53, no. 210/211, 1943, pp. 202–11. Print. Crossref, doi:10.2307/2226317.

Rothbard, Murray. *America's Great Depression.* 5th ed. Auburn, AL: Ludwig von Mises Institute, 2000, pp. 143+.

Rummel, R.J. *Death by Government.* New Brunswick, NJ: Transaction Publishers, 1994. Print.

Samuelson, Paul A., and William D. Nordhaus. *Economics.* 13th ed. New York: McGraw-Hill, 1989. Print.

Samuelson, Robert. *The Great Inflation and Its Aftermath: The Past and Future of American Affluence.* New York: Random House, 2010. Print.

Sanda, Bill. "The Double Danger of High Fructose Corn Syrup." *The Weston A. Price Foundation.* 19 Feb. 2004. Web.

Saylor, Michael [michael_saylor]. "In theory, the cash flows of a risk-free equity asset would need to grow faster..." Twitter, 24 Oct. 2020, http://www.twitter.com/michael_saylor/status/1319987529358200833.

Schuettinger, Robert L., and Eamonn F. Butler. *Forty Centuries of Wage and Price Controls: How Not to Fight Inflation*. Washington, DC: Heritage Foundation, 1978. Print.

Schumpeter, Joseph A. *Ten Great Economists: From Marx to Keynes*. London: Routledge, 1997, p. 182. Print.

Shellenberger, Michael. *Apocalypse Never: Why Environmental Alarmism Hurts Us All*. New York: HarperCollins, 2020. Print.

Shurtleff, William and Akiko Aoyagi. "The Seventh-Day Adventists and Ellen G. White: Diet, Health & Vegetarianism." *History of Soybeans and Soyfoods, 1100 B.C. to the 1980s*. Lafayette, CA: Soyinfo Center, 2004. Web. 3 Oct. 2021.

Smith, Adam and Bruce Yandle. *Bootleggers and Baptists: How Economic Forces and Moral Persuasion Interact to Shape Regulatory Politics*. Washington, DC: Cato Institute, 2014. Print.

Smith, Vernon L. "Constructivist and Ecological Rationality in Economics." *The American Economic Review*, vol. 93, no. 3, Jun. 2003, pp. 465–508. Print.

Sokal, Alan D. "Transgressing the Boundaries: Toward a Transformative Hermeneutics of Quantum Gravity," *Social Text*, no. 46/47, 1996, p. 217. Print. Crossref, doi: 10.2307/466856.

Song, Jimmy. "Bitcoin Core Bug CVE-2018–17144: An Analysis." *Hackernoon*. 21 Sep. 2018. Web.

"Soy Alert!" *The Weston A. Price Foundation*. Web. 3 Oct. 2021.

"The Surprising Reason Why Dr. John Harvey Kellogg Invented Corn Flakes." *Forbes*, 17 May 2016. Web.

Stare, Fredrick. *Adventures in Nutrition*. Hanover, MA: Christopher Publishing House, 1991. Print.

Stern, Gary, and Ron Feldman. *Too Big to Fail: The Hazards of Bank Bailouts*. Washington, DC: Brookings Institution Press, 2004. Print.

Szabo, Nick. "Shelling Out: The Origins of Money." *Satoshi Nakamoto Institute*. 2002. Web. 3 Oct. 2021.

Teicholz, Nina. "Dietary Guidelines & Scientific Evidence." Low Carb Denver 2019 Conference, Denver, CO. 9 Mar. 2019. Presentation. https://www.youtube.com/watch?v=qXtdp4BNyOg.

Teicholz, Nina. *The Big Fat Surprise: Why Butter, Meat, and Cheese Belong in a Healthy Diet*. New York: Simon & Schuster, 2014. Print.

Thompson, Susan. *Bright Line Eating: The Science of Living Happy, Thin, and Free*. Carlsbad, CA: Hay House, 2017. Print.

Todaro, Michael, and Stephen Smith. *Economic Development*. London: Pearson, 2014. Print.

Torpey, Kyle. "The Failure of SegWit2x Shows Bitcoin is Digital Gold, Not Just a Better PayPal." *Forbes*. 9 Nov. 2017. Web.

"Trends in Atmospheric Carbon Dioxide." *Global Monitoring Laboratory*, National Oceanic and Atmospheric Administration. Web. 3 Oct. 2021.

"Triennial Central Bank Survey: Foreign Exchange Turnover in April 2019." *Bank for International Settlements*. 16 Sep. 2019, p. 10. Web.

Twigger, Robert. "Inflation: The Value of the Pound 1750–1998." *House of Commons Library Research Paper 99/20*. U.K. Parliament (23 Feb. 1999), pp. 9–22. Web.

United States Department of State. *Proceedings and Documents of the United Nations Monetary and Financial Conference: Bretton Woods, New Hampshire, July 1–22, 1944*. Vol. 1. Washington, DC: United States Government Printing Office, 1948. Print. https://fraser.stlouisfed.org/title/proceedings-documents-united-nations-monetary-financial-conference-bretton-woods-new-hampshire-july-1-22-1944-430/volume-i-7570.

"V. Cryptocurrencies: Looking Beyond the Hype." *Bank for International Settlements*. 17 Jun. 2018. Web.

von Mises, Ludwig. *Human Action: The Scholar's Edition*. Auburn, AL: Ludwig von Mises Institute, 1998, p. 250. Print.

von Mises, Ludwig. *The Theory of Money and Credit*. 2nd ed. Irvington-on-Hudson, NY: Foundation for Economic Education, 1971, p. 22. Print.

"Welcome to the EM-DAT Website." *EM-DAT: The International Disaster Database, Center for Research on the Epidemiology of Disasters—CRED*, Université Catholique de Louvain. Web. 3 Oct. 2021.

Whipps, Heather. "How Sugar Changed the World." *Live Science*. 2 Jun. 2008. Web.

Willis, Catherine. *Images of America: Boston Public Library*. Mount Pleasant, SC: Arcadia Publishing, 2011, pp. 8–10. Print.

Wong, Joon Ian. "The US Senate Just Learned What Bitcoiners Mean By 'Hodl.'" *Quartz*. 6 Feb. 2018. Web.

World Gold Council, gold.org. Web. 3 Oct. 2021.

"World Payments Report 2020." *Capgemini*. Web. 3 Oct. 2021.

"Wright Brothers Aeroplane Company." *Wright Brothers Aeroplane Company*. Web. 3 Oct. 2021.

List of Figures

Index

CPSIA information can be obtained
at www.ICGtesting.com
Printed in the USA
BVHW081349231221
624747BV00015B/538/J

9 781544 526478